JOHN WILLIAM DRAPER

AND THE RELIGION OF SCIENCE

THE ALBERT J. BEVERIDGE MEMORIAL FELLOWSHIP OF
THE AMERICAN HISTORICAL ASSOCIATION FOR 1948 WAS
AWARDED TO THE AUTHOR FOR THE REVISION AND
COMPLETION OF THIS WORK

FOR THEIR ZEAL AND BENEFICENCE IN CREATING THIS
FUND THE ASSOCIATION IS INDEBTED TO MANY CITIZENS
OF INDIANA WHO DESIRED TO HONOR IN THIS WAY THE
MEMORY OF A STATESMAN AND A HISTORIAN

JOHN WILLIAM DRAPER
1811–1882

THE AMERICAN HISTORICAL ASSOCIATION

JOHN WILLIAM DRAPER
and the Religion of Science

By

DONALD FLEMING

OCTAGON BOOKS

A DIVISION OF FARRAR, STRAUS AND GIROUX

New York   1972

Reprinted 1972
by special arrangement with the University of Pennsylvania Press

OCTAGON BOOKS
A DIVISION OF FARRAR, STRAUS & GIROUX, INC.
19 Union Square West
New York, N. Y. 10003

LIBRARY OF CONGRESS CATALOG CARD NUMBER: 74-120254

ISBN 0-374-92750-2

Printed in U.S.A. by
NOBLE OFFSET PRINTERS, INC.
New York, N.Y. 10003

To my mother

PREFACE

ONE of the most vigorous enterprises of the nineteenth and twentieth centuries has been the creation of a mythology of science—not in the invidious sense of a collection of lies but of a compression of experience and dogma into symbols. The imaginary debasement of men by Copernicus; the alleged dependence of the mechanic James Watt on the theorist Joseph Black; the supposed tragedy of Jean Rey, stuck fast in the wrong century with the right theory of calcination; the verified taste of Dr. Einstein for ice cream cones—all are part of this great myth which we may expect to play an increasing role from year to year. Its significance for patent law has recently been pointed out, and its significance for the iconography of advertising need not be pointed out. John William Draper was one of the chief contributors to this mythologizing process in the nineteenth century. On the other hand, his own career, with his remarkable record in physical and chemical research, supplies a control for testing the dogmas about science and validating the symbols for the history of science which he and others helped to spread.

This book began as a doctor's dissertation at Harvard University. I am indebted to Professor Arthur M. Schlesinger for suggesting the subject, and to him and Professor I. Bernard Cohen for their comments as readers of the original manuscript on behalf of the university. Professor Cohen later read certain portions of the book in their revised form. I have also had the benefit of comments by the members of the Committee on the Albert J. Beveridge Memorial Fund of the American Historical Association: Professors Arthur P. Whitaker, chairman, Philip Davidson, Dorothy Burne Goebel, and Henrietta Larson; by the anonymous readers chosen by them from outside the committee; and by Professor Richard H. Shryock, who was engaged by them to advise me on the process of revision. The responsibility for the book as it appears ought not, of course, to be visited on anyone other than myself.

I also owe to the members of the Beveridge committee the honor of being awarded the Beveridge Memorial Fellowship for 1948, which carried with it the publication of this book. I am more grateful for this than I can well say.

One of the chief satisfactions which I got from my research was the chance to meet several members of the Draper family, who answered questions, fed me, answered questions, put me up for the night, lent me rare books and unique manuscripts—and answered

questions. Aside from letting me interview her at length on two occasions, Mrs. Dorothy Draper Nye gave me access to the letters in
her possession, by far the largest surviving collection, and made it
possible for me to use them to best advantage in a short time; her
brother and sister-in-law, Professor and Mrs. John William Draper,
let me draw out their recollections and gave me some sense of the
physical objects with which his grandfather lived; and their cousin,
Miss Antonia C. Maury, who made the important discovery of the
c-characteristic in stellar spectra, not only supplied me with a great
deal of information, critically assessed, but also brought home to me
in the most immediate fashion the vigorous scientific tradition of
the Drapers, who have now made distinguished contributions to
science in three successive generations. Without the friendly co-
operation of these, Draper's surviving grandchildren, I could not
have written this book; but they have not passed upon the manuscript and ought not to be blamed for any of its faults. I am also
indebted to Draper's grandnephews, Mr. Charles Lennox Wright
and Dr. Daniel Gardner, with whom I engaged in correspondence.

In the collection of my materials, I made use of the library of the
Boston Athenaeum, the Boston Public Library, the Congressional
Library, the library of the Historical Society of Pennsylvania, the
Huntington Library, the New York Public Library, the New York
University library, the University of Pennsylvania library, the
Widener Library, and the Yale University library. I am glad to ex-
press my thanks to their staffs, and in particular to those persons
charged with the keeping of manuscripts who gave me permission to
quote from their holdings. The librarian of New York University,
Dr. T. F. Jones, by his previous work in its archives made my own
task much simpler.

My greatest single debt is to my father and mother for their steady
encouragement in every way.

DONALD FLEMING

Providence, Rhode Island
January 1950

CONTENTS

Chapter I

EUROPE

THERE is a whole chapter of nineteenth-century history pressed together in the phrase "the conflict between religion and science." Like the teacake in *Remembrance of Things Past,* it sets off a train of associations: the raking fire of miters, the counterfire of microscopes as the two armies drew up their lines; interdiction by will of the Pope, registered in the *Index Prohibitorum,* beatification by grace óf E. L. Youmans, registered in the *Popular Science Monthly;* proof by Asa Gray of Harvard that evolution was right but not so very *big* as made out, counterproof by Agassiz of Harvard that it was big enough to swallow all contentment but dead wrong; and Our Mother Eve and the proto-Ape jostling for places at the head of the family tree.

The rubric under which this troop of disputants, with their cloud of issues, has gone down in history was composed by John William Draper (1811–82)—*The Conflict between Religion and Science.* He tried to make exact sciences of physiology, history, and politics; and in this cause he made as quick work as he could of dogmatic theology. Yet he had his failures of nerve in this undertaking: he slammed the door on other people's "metaphysics," and flung it wide for his own. By and large, however, he believed that there was no limit to understanding the world in natural rather than supernatural terms. In his rough, flagging way, he helped break new ground for an age of science, and brought to the level of laymen some of the issues with which they must grapple henceforth. But though he looked to the future, he had the gift of the great popularizer for seeming to leaven the loaf of tradition instead of throwing it away. The son of a Methodist minister, he was always transposing the formulas of Christianity into the key of materialism. He succeeded, however, in lending to new ideas the appearance of old ones. His work is therefore an excellent case-history of the way in which innovations are knit up into continuity with tradition, and revolutions in thought made palatable. But beneath the semantic crust he was setting off charges of dynamite.

There are at least two distinct accounts of the origin of the Draper family, and several cloudy variations on these.[1] The family seems to have disowned the father of John William Draper, so that the matter

1

is of less interest than if the son had come to know his relatives. In any event the line is clear enough from John Draper, who is connected with Liverpool, and his wife, Elizabeth Johnson, of London. Their son John Christopher, born in London on November 8, 1777, was the father of John William, the subject of this biography.[2]

Nothing much seems to be known about John Christopher Draper till as a man of "about twenty-one,"—say, in 1798—he and two friends went to have some fun at the expense of the Methodists.[3] Instead he got pulled up sharp by "converting grace." [4] His conversion is a kind of symbol of the sober, chastened spirit, the high seriousness and long praying, that fell over English society in the shadow of the French Revolution.[5] To see if he was up to the much higher standards of gravity among the Wesleyan ministers, Draper, who seems to have been read out of the family for changing his religion, served an apprenticeship as a "local preacher" till 1802.[6] Then he struck out as an itinerant, sent by the Conference to a new circuit of local societies every year or two.

About 1805 Draper married Sarah Ripley, some of whose people had emigrated to America before the Revolution to found a Wesleyan community.[7] When the couple set up housekeeping, housekeeping on the move, he was dark-haired and clean-shaven with a large broad nose and a thin mouth, of "good natural abilities . . . improved by reading and study," and she had (it is about all we know) a heart-shaped face.[8] They had tight budgets ahead of them. The standard salary for an itinerant was £12 a year for himself, £12 for the support of his wife, £4 for each child, and £6 for the board and wages of a servant; but the schedule was reasonably flexible and at one point when he was teaching his children at home Draper got £8 for each girl and £12 for his son.[9]

The upshot was to bring the main events in the history of a family—illness, the birth of a child—to the attention of the Conference, often for the purpose of getting a special grant from its fund. This close surveillance and mutual help by the Methodist preachers, with the endless shuffling of them all so as to put down every sort of local independence among the societies, hedged in the life of the Drapers. But into the bargain it looks like a life as high as heaven and as wide as earth. Any sermon might bring off the incalculable descent of grace, "the wonders of redeeming grace"; and perhaps there had never been so exhilarating a sense of the body of the philanthropic at work all around the world.[10] It was the age of Hannah More and Zachary Macaulay—also, we are told, the age of Lady Southdown, distributor in quantity of "The Sailor's True Binnacle" and "Fleshpots Broken; or, the Converted Cannibal," and Mrs. Jellyby, the "telescopic" philanthropist who believed in taking the broom to

Africa ahead of her front parlor,—the age of tracts and missions described in Draper's elegy:

> Christian philanthropy his soul possess'd,
> And bigotry was banish'd from his breast;
> With saints of different names he could agree,
> Who held the faith in bonds of charity.
> Forth as the zealous advocate he stood,
> Of every institution great and good;
> View'd Christian Missions as the cause of God,
> And helped to send his light and truth abroad;
> Bible, and Tract Societies he lov'd,
> And Sabbath Schools his firm attachment proved;
> The "Bethel Seaman's Union" held a part
> In the most warm affections of his heart.[11]

It was an atmosphere where grace was solicited, but not to the neglect of the Bethel Seaman's Union; where the benevolent joined hands across sectarian lines, in the tradition which had dried up the gin mill and founded the charity school but in the tradition also of nervous concern for fear of doing the poor so much good they would no longer want to be poor.[12] By the standards, say, of the great "Broad" prelates of the eighteenth century, it was an atmosphere of meager aesthetic drives, where the novel, to the indignation of Jane Austen and the younger Macaulay, was in almost as bad repute with godly people as card-playing, and Methodist opinion stood nearly balanced for and against organs to "guide" the singing. But by the standards of the enemies of evolution among the evangelical party in 1860, it was an atmosphere of surprising respect for natural studies, where John Christopher Draper's "Gregorian telescope" represented the honorable scientific traditions of Nonconformity.[13] In fact, in the elder Draper's prime one of the quiet times in the history of the tension between science and religion was drawing to a close, after both Newton and Locke had been digested without much trouble. The line, therefore, in which the Drapers took their place was, like every tradition, mixed. But along with this went an unmixed sharpening of the points of everyday existence, so that even small issues and minor data could start up into urgent life, if only one looked for and found what they had to do with God's purpose. And there was an awe-inspiring facility in narrowing down the scope of this purpose to the ethics of holding amateur theatricals, the explanation of crop failures, and the necessity of driving hard bargains.

In this setting John and Sarah Draper brought up four children. The oldest, Dorothy Catharine, was born in 1807 at Newcastle-on-Tyne, and another girl, Elizabeth Johnson, in 1809 at Penrith in

Cumberland.[14] A succession of small allowances for "domestic sickness" and traveling mark the growth of the family and its almost yearly transfer from station to station.[15] Among these accounts the large sum of £50 for "Brother Draper's expenses at St. Helens," on the outskirts of Liverpool, where he was never regularly placed, seems to represent a special assignment. It was probably the organization of a building fund for the first Wesleyan chapel there. On this mission of beating down social anarchy in the darkest days of the Industrial Revolution in Lancashire, his only son was born on May 5, 1811.[16] The great Jabez Bunting, heavy-jowled and portly, one of the Methodist popes, baptized the boy John William on June 23.[17]

After the special work at St. Helens the Drapers continued their tour of England. They appear next at the old cathedral city of Lincoln, where a final child, Sarah Ripley, was born in 1813, and from 1817 to 1819 they were at Namptwich.[18] It must have been here that a private tutor started the boy John on Latin at the age of six "and, to add to the absurdity, . . . out of a grammar written in the Latin tongue." [19] At eight he went on to Greek, also from a text in Latin, which "as yet I did not altogether know." By this age Macaulay (born in 1800) had produced a Universal History, a religious tract designed for translation into Malabar, and an epic "after the manner of Virgil"; and John Stuart Mill (born in 1806), the great Benthamite engineering project, had read in the original "the whole of Herodotus, and of Xenophon's Cyropaedia and Memorials of Socrates; some of the lives of the philosophers by Diogenes Laertius; part of Lucian, and Isocrates' ad Demonicum and ad Nicoclem" plus a batch of the more unsuitable dialogues of Plato.[20] Macaulay seems never to have had much self-searching about his education, and Mill thought that it was all to the good to learn so much so fast if only time were left for other things. But Draper, who got by no means as stiff a dose as Mill, later took a poor view of Greek in the nursery. "Many of us look back on the days of our earlier tuition with amusement and amazement." [21] But alongside his studies he learned on his own to like science. As a baby he was taken with his father to look for the first peas in the garden, and for his first experiment planted a Sunday's collection to see if the silver would sprout.[22] By the time he was six he was looking through the father's telescope and trying to build one of his own.[23]

In 1822 the boy entered a Methodist "public school" at Woodhouse Grove.[24] He studied the classics and mathematics under an American headmaster "of literary celebrity," who had written for Rees's encyclopedia.[25] Here Draper was coming in range of the reverberations from Ephraim Chambers' idea of an encyclopedia, which swelled into the *Encyclopédie* itself and then dwindled away into Rees's—a chapter of its own in the resolve to synthesize knowledge. It was probably this headmaster of whom Draper spoke fifty years later:

The shortcomings and sins of the day were not expiated on the spot, but an account was carefully kept during the week, and the balance struck on Saturday morning— . . . in double sense, not only by figures of delinquency added up, but also by the aid of a cane rattan which adjusted the whole account. I believe that this postponement of punishment was considered to be of excellent use as familiarizing the mind of youth with the doctrine of future rewards and punishments. I saw little of the rewards and enjoyed less, but of the punishment I obtained a singularly critical and comprehensive knowledge. The schoolmaster of those days thought it to be his business to drive the nail of knowledge through his pupils [*sic*] head and clinch it with repeated blows of his rattan at the other end.[26]

Draper's teacher also dealt out as punishment English and Latin poetry to be learned by heart.[27] As a reward for progress the boy made a speech before the Conference held at Leeds in 1824, when committees of the great Methodist legislature still examined youngsters in parsing.[28]

In the same year Draper went back to home instruction at Otley in the West Riding of Yorkshire.[29] From there the family went in 1826 to Sheerness, a royal dockyard at the junction of the Medway with the Thames, on the Isle of Sheppey.[30] Word of the change of address was sent up to London, where the elder Draper had bought two shares in the new model "London University." [31] The proprietors were trying to make a university on the recipe of Jefferson and Bentham, and provide higher education for scientists, workingmen, Dissenters, and Utilitarians, of whose existence official Cambridge and Oxford had got only distant reports. As a shareholder in this experiment J. C. Draper asked the Warden on June 28, 1828, to enter his son John William as a student.

Is it incompatible with the rule of the University for a regular Student to be at the same time a Private Tutor? If this be allowed, then my son would wish to enter his name as Private Tutor for the Mathematics and Natural Philosophy and Astronomy. He is turned 17 years of age, has followed no employment, but given himself up wholly to learning. As to his moral character I can vouch for that being good. As to his learning that had better, [*sic*] be decided by Professors [Augustus de] Morgan [a founder of mathematical logic] and [Dionysius] Lardner [in natural philosophy and astronomy].[32]

In February of the next year the father died, "enabled to rely with implicit confidence in the blood of atonement." [33] He worked nearly to the end, and the charge for pulpit "supply" in his sickness was gratifyingly low. There is no evidence that the son ever served as a tutor, but he must have begun his premedical studies at University College (as it became) in 1829 in even greater need of money than expected.[34] There is a tradition that his mother and possibly his oldest sister, Dorothy, taught to keep him in school.[35]

University College on Carmarthen Square, just past the British Museum, had a long, low façade with a slice off a Greek temple in the center, surmounted by a dome.[36] Here Draper, stocky, black-haired, with full face and large nose, may have rubbed shoulders with Frederick Denison Maurice, who went on to found Christian Socialism, and J. J. Sylvester, later the great mathematician, in the "refectory." [37] (But Sylvester was expelled at the age of fourteen "for taking a table-knife from the refectory with the intention of sticking it into a fellow student," and all of this may have happened just before Draper began his attendance.) The students got breakfast and dinner at 10s. 6d. a week, but they complained that the professors could overhear what they were saying.

Draper seems to have spent the most time in the Lower North Theatre, a horseshoe lecture room for chemistry and materia medica, to the far left of the central entrance hall on the ground floor.[38] There he studied under Edward Turner, the professor of chemistry. Just thirty, he was a young man on a faculty of young men, an early English admirer of Berzelius (whose revolutionary system of chemical notation he apparently introduced to the English-speaking world), the author of "the first tolerably complete account of organic chemistry in the English language," and an opponent of Prout's "whole number" theory of atomic weights.[39] Of all his teachers, Turner stuck the longest in Draper's memory.[40] Turner gave his career a decisive turn by showing the class a large glass vessel in which a piece of camphor had condensed in crystals on the side toward the light.[41] The beauty of these crystals fascinated Draper, and in the end he studied the chemical effects of light for nearly thirty years.

Turner also gave lectures in geology, and it may have been under his direction that Draper wrote with W. M. Higgins his first three scientific memoirs: "On Volcanoes," with its plea that geology "like chemistry, watch over its accumulating facts, jealous of hypothesis"; on the Dead Sea, with a geological account of the destruction of Sodom and Gomorrah and an attempted link between life in an "igneous" region and the genesis of fire-worship; and on electrical decompositions.[42]

University College had a system of electives—after the model of the University of Virginia—which could hardly be pulled together into a coherent program till Parliament broke the monopoly of

Oxford and Cambridge for granting degrees. In the meantime students might try for certificates in individual courses. After "diligently" attending Turner's lectures for the session 1830–31, Draper passed the written examination for a "certificate of honours" in chemistry.[43] The only other course he is known to have taken is jurisprudence. With John Stuart Mill, J. A. Roebuck, Edwin Chadwick, the three Romilly brothers, and Charles Buller—a galaxy of young Utilitarians who helped to change the face of the world—he enrolled under John Austin, whose classes, disproportionately brilliant and disproportionately small, were falling off from term to term.[44] Here, nearly at the source of Benthamism, Draper may have learned to test institutions by their utility in promoting the greatest happiness of the greatest number. Whether he studied under a lesser man, the professor of anatomy Granville Sharp Pattison, later his own colleague in the New York University Medical School, is unknown. If Draper never saw him stride into class in pink coat and riding boots, he certainly heard of the uproar when Pattison was fired for incompetence.[45]

When the Dissenters coöperated to found University College, they agreed that as sectarian theology could not be taught, the college should be nonresident. As many of the students as possible were to get religious instruction by living at home—and the tide of family prayers was rising fast at this point in English history. Perhaps the raw newness of the place wore off more slowly for not being lived in. It seems clear, however, that Draper, at least, got the idea of a modern university at the center of urban life, in daily touch with its needs—in the service of living wants instead of lost causes. The dreaming spires suspended over Oxford bred Matthew Arnold and John Henry Newman, and one ideal of the university; the heavy new masonry of University College, grounded on London earth, bred Draper and another ideal.

He must have got a good working knowledge of city life by walking through the heart of London from his boarding place in the Hyde Park district to the College. He lived with a friend of his father's, a Mrs. Barker, and so met her niece Antonia Gardner, a dark sensitive girl in her early teens, still at school.[46] She had been born in Brazil, the daughter of Dr. Daniel Gardner. The mother's identity is disputed; according to one account she was the Infanta Dona Isabel Maria, daughter of King John VI of Portugal and Brazil.[47] However this may be, Dr. Gardner had sent Antonia and her brother Daniel from Brazil to live with his sister in London.

The death of the father in July 1831 left the girl, then not older than seventeen, utterly crushed and bewildered. And this seems to have been partly the cause of Draper's proposing to her; if so, he grew to love her.[48] They were married at Sheerness on September 13, 1831.[49] If not before the wedding, then shortly afterward, the elder Mrs. Draper came to live with her three daughters, her son, and her daughter-in-law at Camberwell in South London. It was then an open place of isolated terraces, where Draper remembered his wife at the window "with her long black ringlets looking for me coming home." [50]

The relatives of the mother who had gone to America, before the Revolution and later, now urged her to bring her children to Virginia; and in 1832 with the promise of a teaching job for Draper, they crossed the Atlantic.[51] He was then twenty-one.

Draper took with him some experience in piling up and weighing scientific data, together with a long exposure to the counterurge to rush ahead and unify knowledge ahead of science. He also kept to the end of his life the sense of belonging to the European intellectual community, the sense, it would almost seem at times, of being in exile.

Chapter II

VIRGINIA

Draper, his wife Antonia, his mother, and his three sisters Dorothy Catharine, Elizabeth, and Sarah, had a slow passage to America. Antonia's brother Daniel, who was already Sarah's husband or soon to be, probably came along. The delay cost Draper the job he had been promised as teacher of natural history at a "local Methodist college," presumably in Mecklenburg County, Virginia.[1] Here, in the center of the state, just above the Carolina border, he found one of the strongholds of Methodism, where "the most awful sense of God's presence" swept through revivals and camp meetings time and again.[2] At University College Draper had already started, insensibly perhaps, to break with religious enthusiasm. And perhaps he got a push in the new direction by failing to arrive in time for the job.

With his family he settled about six miles from Christiansville (now Chase City) in Mecklenburg County.[3] They soon bought a farm from Benjamin Whitehead Coleman, a prominent Methodist of the neighborhood.[4] There they built a two-story white clapboard house on a knoll in a grove of oaks.[5] It is hard to say for sure where they got the money for this new start. But Dorothy Catharine, the oldest sister, probably contributed her savings from the teaching of art in London. This tireless woman, with straight black hair combed over her cheeks, had begun to set the pattern of Draper's family life: all of his people, weak and strong, fell to revolving about himself. With Dorothy there is the sense of strong will and quick spirits deliberately handed over for her brother to use as he liked.

On the new farm the three sisters promptly opened, or perhaps reopened, "The Misses Draper Seminary for Girls," with Coleman's daughters for students.[6] Draper himself set up his first laboratory, and practiced medicine (prematurely, for he had no degree) at least to the extent of helping to put down a smallpox epidemic.[7] The school was almost certainly the major source of income. To allow for more space, a local contractor threw up a one-story building ten feet away.[8] The main house was still crowded, and sometimes the family quarreled among themselves.[9] Antonia Draper, always cheerful and conciliatory, often made the peace.[10]

Despite the close quarters Draper stuck to his research, which he

9

took up again during his slow recovery from an "autumnal fever" in 1833.[11] "Resolved to be led astray by no vain or crude notion, but making experiment the means, to regard truth as the *end*," he seems to have used his work also as a way of beating down loneliness and nostalgia for London.[12]

. . . these experiments [with capillary attraction] . . . were begun in sickness, and in a land of strangers,—they were pursued in all the calamity of family bereavement [his mother's death in 1834?], and in the depths of forests, alike unused to music, to poetry, or to philosophy. Solitude . . . is . . . attended with many evils. . . . counsel and assistance . . . are wanting, and, indeed, those advantages which are supposed to result from tranquillity, are, for the most part, only fictitious appearances, which, like certain other apparitions, every one can discourse of, but no one can say he has seen.[13]

An Englishman's sense of rattling about in a vast, loose, empty sort of country made him speak elsewhere of standing by "the nightly watch fires in the wildernesses of the New World"—otherwise the Virginia tidewater in its decline.[14]

Between July 1834 and January 1836 Draper published eight research papers from his Christiansville laboratory.[15] In them he dealt with a variety of scientific issues: the nature of capillarity, the force of attraction "insensible at sensible distances" and the use of this force in Dutrochet's attempt to round out the economy of plant and animal life; the effort under Faraday's leadership to discover the full resources of electrical theory; and the current reëxamination of Newton's theory of light.

By 1835 Dorothy Catharine Draper had saved enough money from the lessons which she gave in drawing and painting to see her brother through his medical studies at the University of Pennsylvania in the winters of 1835 and 1836.[16] At the first American medical school, then heavily attended by Southerners, Draper heard lectures in the new building, with its $2,000 worth of French apparatus, on the Chestnut Street side of the old quadrangle.[17] "Our class repaired to the lecture-room, the professor made his appearance, read from his manuscript for an hour, the bell rang, the book was closed, and we were dismissed to another room to go through another—a similar performance." [18] In later years Draper spoke of the course of instruction as borne along by stolid disregard for half the subject matter and all printing presses.

[The lecture-system] . . . was perfectly adapted to . . . [medieval] times. This reading from a manuscript was admirably adapted to an age prior to the introduction of paper and printing. . . . But what answers perfectly in a non-reading community will not answer for one in which every person can read.[19]

Besides attending lectures, Draper worked in the laboratories of two restless men, Robert Hare of the University and J. K. Mitchell of the Franklin Institute. He made friends with both of them. Hare's oxy-hydrogen blowpipe led to the founding of the platinum industry.[20] He was already freely advising the public on currency and banking questions, but had not yet written *Standish the Puritan. A Tale of the American Revolution,* or brought back via his "spirito-scope" the blessing of Benjamin Franklin for his electrical researches —to the scandal of the elder Silliman. Portly, with dark lively eyes, aquiline nose, and mutton-chop whiskers, Hare in his prime was a decidedly favorable specimen of the investigator "more addicted to practical than to theoretical science" whom Tocqueville considered an American type. J. K. Mitchell, a dark, handsome, sociable Scot, shipped to Canton and Calcutta in youth; and on his way to the private practice of medicine he taught chemistry and wrote on osmosis.[21] During Draper's stay in Philadelphia, Mitchell may have been meditating the poem *Indecision, A Tale of the Far West* ("Hurrah for the Prairie! no blight on *its* breeze"). Perhaps both Draper and Mitchell's boy Weir first learned from this book of "the existence of literary opportunity amidst the most urgent and perplexing professional pursuits." [22]

When Mitchell made the first use in the United States of Thilorier's apparatus for liquefying carbon dioxide, Draper assisted him.[23] Moreover, to meet the requirements for the medical degree awarded by the University in March 1836, the younger man wrote a thesis which fell in with Mitchell's interest in osmosis. (They were both of them in the line of descent from Dutrochet.) If the faculty "specially commended" this thesis on "Glandular Action" and had it printed, no copy has ever been found.[24] An idea of its contents can probably be formed from two articles published shortly afterward.[25]

Draper represents gases as passing instantaneously through barriers that are not visibly porous, like soap bubbles, till a balance exists between the gas on one side and the gas on the other. He puts this forward as the rationale of the exchange of oxygen and carbon dioxide by the air cells of the lungs as we breathe. He argues besides for treating all bodily processes as chemically and physically identical with those in inorganic matter—in no way transformed by "vital force" or other mysterious intangibles. This exorcising of vitalism, in which Draper took his part, cleared the ground for more useful distinctions between life and nonlife, like Claude Bernard's "internal environment" with its wonderfully complex interadjustment of bodily processes to the end of continued existence together. Of this fruitful line of investigation Draper had at least a vision—hardly more

—when he called in the liver to set right the constitution of the blood stream.[26]

Armed with his doctor's degree—intended to get him a job teaching when the M.D. in America filled something of the place of the Ph.D. in the twentieth century as a license for professors of science—Draper went back to Virginia. There he found people sifting plans to revive the economic life of the state. Exhausted soil and the same crop relentlessly sown in the same field year after year chased each other about in a downward spiral. The thoroughly unstable adjustment effected by white emigration and by the domestic slave-trade, at its height just before the panic of 1837, did nothing much to check the decline. But Edmund Ruffin of Prince George County advocated smashing the circle by reforms in farming.[27] As in his famous essay on calcareous manures (1832), he told farmers and planters to save themselves by making an intelligent survey of existing resources and allying themselves with practical men of science. He was for his generation in America what John Taylor of Caroline had been for the preceding, and what Sir Humphry Davy (from whom he took fire) and Justus Liebig were for successive generations throughout the world: an advocate of the scientific temper among country people, a friend of change in the steadiest of social climates.[28]

Acting broadly in Ruffin's spirit—but there is a streak of gold fever about the whole business, that goes back not to Ruffin but to the more shiftless first settlers of Virginia—sixteen men, half of them trustees of Hampden-Sidney College, met at Prince Edward Court House in July 1836. Their object was "to consider, what measures are most likely to develop an intimate and extensive knowledge of the mineral wealth of the State of Virginia, and to put into operation such means as may tend to render those resources available to the purposes of public good." [29] They therefore projected a school of mineralogy with special attention to chemical analysis. "Gentlemen residing at a distance, and finding specimens on their estates, might have authentic information of their composition, furnished from the labors of the pupils of this school." [30] To this end a "Mineralogical Society of Virginia" was formed and Draper chosen as chemist and mineralogist, "an appointment deriving advantage from his knowledge of the geology and mining operations of South America." Such information he must have got second-hand from his late father-in-law, who had mining interests in Brazil, or from his brother-in-law Daniel. A letter from Edward Turner testified to his studies in University College as well.[31] Though Draper was instructed to lay plans for the proposed school, if anything came of this it was swallowed up by Hampden-Sidney. He taught there in the summer of 1836, and in the fall, at least partly owing to his medical thesis, the trustees appointed him professor of chemistry and natural philosophy.[32]

A small country college, Hampden-Sidney had sprung from the famous Presbytery of Hanover in the period of the Revolution—a late installment on the cultural dividends of the Great Awakening.[33] The school kept up an undenominational "church" spirit through the nineteenth century. The hold of the college on life was wretchedly feeble in the first half of the century, and never more than in Draper's time. Like many other Southern colleges (and too many Northern) Hampden-Sidney felt and yielded before the pressure to give simple instruction so as to take up the slack left by elementary schools. Since the college on this last account bore marked resemblance to an academy, with younger students than now, the time of the faculty was eaten into by disciplinary problems of the sort which sent J. J. Sylvester back to England in a huff from the University of Virginia in the early 1840's.

Unless this setting is borne in mind, Draper's stubborn determination to keep his hand in with European scientists loses its meaning. He stuck to his chosen work despite an unfavorable atmosphere for "pure" science, the frequent necessity for buying and designing his own equipment, the nagging daily task of teaching elementary students, and a pervasive climate of belief in the supernatural.

The account which he took of this climate left its mark on his career. If he sometimes seemed to be battering down open doors, he found them closed at Hampden-Sidney. A case in point is the first in his long series of annual "introductory lectures," where the trick was to get up wind quickly for a plausible flight very high above the subject-matter of the course to follow. Draper mastered this art-form early. But there is a want of ease, and almost a want of candor, about his lecture of June 1836. Instead of challenging the "active and mysterious agent" invoked by some "naturalists" to regulate organic processes, Draper came close to implying that he himself believed in this agent.[34] He also took great pains to make the natural world tell on the side of the supernatural: "That adaptation which we see in all the parts of this mysterious frame [the world], should teach us that if it require not [God's] . . . constant interference to keep up such complicated changes, it is a proof of the surpassing skill with which the plan was first laid. . . ."[35] There is no reason to regard this as hypocritical trimming with an eye to the main chance. It shows instead an uneasy fear of offending against orthodoxy—perhaps as much the orthodoxy of his own upbringing as of Hampden-Sidney.

After the summer's lecture course begun on this discreet note, Draper settled down with a full-time appointment at $1,000 a year ("if . . . not made up from tuition fees, Treasurer to pay the deficiency").[36] By the spring of 1837, if not before, his family apparently occupied four rooms "in the Steward's house." [37] Here in March 1837, when Draper's first child John Christopher was just two, another son, called Henry, must have been born.[38] Their father taught chemistry Mondays, Wednesdays, and Fridays from nine to ten—almost the middle of the long college day which began with morning chapel "30 minutes after sunrise" and circled on itself with afternoon chapel at four.[39] He also took his turn in handing out prizes for scholarship with remarks "on the occasion," and left his imprint on a memorial of the trustees asking the General Assembly of Virginia for "but a moderate appropriation" to keep up the college buildings and "an unusually large, and excellent Chemical and Philosophical apparatus." [40]

Outside of the classroom Draper's contributions to American and British learned journals show that he was keeping up with current science. The note of personal urgency that speaks from underneath the text of these experiments and theses is his need to cut a figure in European circles, and somehow to mediate between American and British research. He dealt with three questions: the creation of a scientific-minded community in America, the chemical effects of light, and the application of chemistry and physics to physiology.

In an article on "microscopic" chemistry Draper told people who thought they might like to try chemistry not to let themselves be frightened by "those large retorts, and bells, and complicated stopcocks, and furnaces, the innumerable company of vials, and tests, and electrical machines, and galvanic batteries, . . . not [to] be purchased in the country."

Operations on the large scale, are never performed, except by those who are public teachers, and here the necessity of rendering effect visible at a distance, calls for a degree of magnitude in experimenting, that unfortunately leads the pupil to conclude, that such pursuits can only be followed by the possessors of large fortunes and even that they would meet with "almost impossibilities," except they were residents of large cities.[41]

He recommended small-scale experiments—"microscopic" chemistry —for which ordinary people in the country could find the money and the apparatus.

If nothing more, educated men should learn to make meteorological observations. Draper put members of the junior and senior classes at Hampden-Sidney to recording the weather three times daily— except Sunday. In the *Journal of the Franklin Institute,* already an advocate of systematic records of this kind, Draper proposed in 1838 that all colleges train men to do the same work on a common plan.[42]

When the graduates scattered to their homes, the personnel would be at hand for a federal weather bureau "in case anything should be done by Congress to provide the means for making this kind of observations. . . ." [43]

Apart from trying to raise up a new generation of scientists, Draper began at Hampden-Sidney his experiments with light.[44] From the start he tried to untie the bundle of "imponderables," weightless substances then thought to be present in the sun's rays, and to find in these rays an imponderable agent working chemical effects. Thus he distinguished "calorific," "colorific," and chemical rays—not as occupying mutually exclusive regions of the spectrum, for in his thought at this time the colorific and the chemical share at least part of the visible region, but as producing heat, light, and chemical change respectively. Draper concluded also that there was interference of chemical rays.[45] One way of putting the matter is to say, as he did, that this is analogous to the interference of what he called the calorific and the colorific rays. But the real bearing of his conclusion is that interference phenomena are associated with all radiant energy; and if this energy is broken down in functional terms, of temperatures raised, or colors produced, or chemical changes effected, the phenomena of interference persist. But this is not at all what Draper made of the situation. Instead, he did at this early point what he continued to do till near the close of his career: he piled up evidence that radiant energy ought not to be split up into a set of discrete imponderables—and resisted the conclusion to which his own investigations were tending. In this sense, most of his work with radiant energy is a monument to the virtues of the experimental method, which wrings useful observations from doubtful hypotheses.

Within this broad area of studies, Draper's special interests were the effect of solar rays on the "breathing" of plants, the action of the spectrum on silver salts, and the motion of camphor toward the "illuminated" side of a glass vessel. (The last was a stubborn recollection from his student days in University College.) [46]

As Boussingault, Dutrochet, and Liebig in Europe were studying "the economy of life" by which plants and animals live, and live together, Draper attacked part of the same problem.[47] When he exposed plants to light through a variety of intervening media, "the young plants after reaching a certain size, were always green,—but those which grew in the dark had yellow leaves and white stalks." [48] But Draper considered the green pigment to be the result of feeding on the atmosphere instead of the necessary condition for the process. In the same year Dutrochet published his finding that the assimilation of carbon dioxide by plants (occurring only in sunlight) takes place exclusively in those cells containing chlorophyll.

Both Draper and Dutrochet therefore associated the crucial point in the life cycle with the conjunction of the green pigment and sunlight; and neither explained the correlation.[49] But in splitting up the question of this relationship into finer issues, Dutrochet showed the place of chlorophyll in the decisive synthesis; and in the same work of discrimination Draper went quite wrong. Perhaps the most interesting of his other suggestions in this field was the need for taking greater account of the nitrogen in plants.[50] Here he was on firmer ground, though not for adequate reasons, than Liebig himself, who systematically underestimated the importance of nitrogen (and muffed the question of its source).

The interest of Draper's which proved to be of the most immediate importance for his scientific reputation was the effect of the solar spectrum on the silver salts—bromide, chloride, and nitrate.[51]

These researches bore on the problem of fixing camera images. A small army of investigators were then trying to solve this problem. Though not in the front rank with Nicéphore Niepce, Louis Daguerre, William Fox Talbot, and Sir John F. W. Herschel, Draper made a shrewd survey of the difficulties involved. Before Talbot and Daguerre announced their successes in 1839—in 1837, if not earlier —Draper had followed the example of Wedgwood and Davy in making temporary copies of objects. Moreover, he took early note of Herschel's observation that "hyposulphite of soda" dissolved seemingly insoluble silver salts. This was the "fixing" agent later used by Daguerre and by Herschel himself to clear the recording surface of sensitive material unaffected by the light source.

I had long known what had been done . . . by Wedgwood and Davy, had amused myself with repeating some of their experiments, and had even unsuccessfully tried the use of hyposulphite of soda, having learnt its properties in relation to the chloride of silver from Herschel's experiments, but abandoned it because I found it removed the black as well as the white parts. This want of success was probably owing to my having used too strong a solution, and kept the paper in it too long.[52]

When Talbot's announcement that he had fixed (what would now be called) "negative" images on sensitive paper reached America in the spring of 1839, Draper repeated the experiments.[53] He tackled on his own initiative three related difficulties: how to reduce the time of exposure, how to sharpen the image, and how to make portraits. By using lenses of large aperture and short focus, he brought more light to bear on the "bromine sensitive paper." [54] In shortening the camera he took account of the distinction between the chemical and visual foci of lenses, on the ground that the rays most active in producing the image came to a focus nearer the lens than the rays perceived by the eye.[55] But if he could get "images of any brightly illuminated object, though too large and too faint," the nearest he came to a portrait was the silhouette of a person standing against a window.[56]

It was from considering the difficulty of getting an impression from colored surfaces as red or green, that I saw the necessity of enlarging the aperture of the lens, and diminishing its focus, so as to have the image as bright as possible; for it was plain that in no other way landscapes could be taken or silhouettes replaced by portraits. And when I had failed altogether in these particulars, I knew it was owing to insufficient sensitiveness in the bromine paper, and waited anxiously for the divulging of Daguerre's process, respecting which statements were beginning to be made in the papers.[57]

As he waited, therefore, to learn the details of Daguerre's process, Draper already had a well-reasoned plan for solving the problem of portraiture.[58]

Another line of research which he pursued at Hampden-Sidney was the chemistry of the human body. He called repeatedly for clearer views of physiological processes. As a first step he wanted to hear no more of "vitality, the recuperative forces, sympathy, antipathy, trains of morbid associations, and a thousand other obscure expressions which darken counsel with words without meaning." [59] If doctors would give up empirical dosing, they could learn instead "the normal condition of an organ . . . and the true mode of restoring it when in disease." [60] Here Draper spoke for the "therapeutic nihilism" which said (to turn inside out the slogan of the counter-revolutionaries in the next generation), *"Wir wollen klassifizieren, und nicht heilen."* But his object in mocking at the "practical" cures of today was to make and keep rational promises of health to morrow:

A watch, or other delicate machine that has stopped, might perhaps be made to move again by the rude jolting and shaking of a most ignorant man; but to find out the cause of its derangement, and to reinstate it fairly and without damage in its former integrity, requires one who knows its springs and wheels, their reciprocal action on each other, and the end they are to accomplish. We might perhaps smile at the rough attempts of such a pretending mechanic; but . . . we reflect that all the operations of our own science as physicians are carried on upon principles that are empirical, and directed to act upon organs whose offices and modes of action are for the most part unknown. . . .[61]

Once again Draper brushed aside "umbrage at any attempt to bring physiology under the dominion of physical science." [62] His is the tone and the matter of the young practitioner who spread such rankling discontent among the apothecaries of George Eliot's *Mid-*

dlemarch (which is said to begin in 1829): the voice of all the young men who had been to Paris or heard from afar the gospel of the French clinicians and were now commanding the old school to stand aside.[63] In the small towns of the Western world this kind of talk made for a revolution in local society, as patients chose their physician and plumped for his doctrines; and it had something to do with the alienation of public opinion from the medical profession in that old remedies were discredited and nothing much was supplied in the way of new ones.[64] But it was exactly the kind of shaking up needed in the medical schools.

Draper's writings on this subject seem in fact to have caught the attention of Dr. Martyn Paine, one of the men projecting a medical school nominally attached to the University of the City of New York.[65] As a result Draper got his original appointment to the medical faculty in 1837, but the depression of that year dealt the University a crippling blow.[66] The next year, however, the Council renewed its effort to bring Draper to New York. On the way to take passage for a trip back to Europe, his brother-in-law Daniel Gardner looked over the job prospects in the North.[67]

Gardner spoke of talking in Philadelphia with Robley Dunglison, professor of medicine in Jefferson Medical College.

—Called on Dunglisson [sic] advises me to call upon Mathews [chancellor of the] U. of N. York—and for you to write to him also to ascertain the prospects of the institution—Dr. D had an interview with Dallas Bache [president of the new Girard College, endowed by the Philadelphia banker] who states that there will not be any Professors appointed for 5 or 6 years at Girhard [sic]—but only Tutors—he thinks that your prospects would be better if you applied, holding the Situation at N.Y., than from H. Sydney [.] [68]

Another Philadelphian "acquainted with the noise at N. York—would not advise you to go there." This noise was the outcry by some of the members of the University Council at the desperate financial straits to which Chancellor James M. Mathews, the "very plausible man" of another of Gardner's tête-à-têtes in Philadelphia, had allegedly brought the school in the six years since its foundation.[69]

In the fall of 1838, at the very lowest ebb in the fortunes of New York University, Draper was elected professor of chemistry and botany in the college.[70] Eighteen students enrolled for that year.[71] For some reason, possibly the hope that by waiting he might find the medical school ready to function, Draper refused to go to New York the same winter. His appointment was revoked by the Council when it failed to find a temporary substitute. At the request of the medical faculty, however, the Council reversed itself and renewed the invitation on Draper's terms.[72] After he had got the wind up by reading in the newspapers that the medical school was facing further delays, Draper finally accepted the chair of chemistry on May 20, 1839, with the pledge to be in attendance on the session beginning in October.[73] In September the Council fixed his salary at $750 a year plus $7.00 for every paying student.[74] Daniel Gardner, piecing together a career in Draper's shadow, succeeded to his position at Hampden-Sidney.[75]

Chapter III

"THE BRIGHT SPECK IN EACH EYE"

WHEN John W. Draper went there from the quiet village of Hampden-Sidney at the age of twenty-eight, New York had about 325,000 people.[1] Their chief thoroughfare, the famous Broadway, stretched four miles from the Battery Gardens till it dwindled away in a country road. Omnibuses, hackney cabs, gigs, phaetons, and tilburies fought for the right-of-way with pigs on the loose and engines off for the latest fire. Politicians had already discovered that if a famous man rode down Broadway in the middle of the day he would divide people's attention with the busy shops, outdoor displays from pineapples to watermelons, and big blocks of ice on the way to barrooms. On the less fashionable Bowery, horses dragged wooden arks for passengers over a "railroad." Here carriages gave way to carts and wagons, clothes were ready-made (and trousers had a crease in them, which marked a decisive social boundary), and oyster-cellars, grog-shops, and bowling alleys flourished. Still lower in the social scale, the Five Points drew in the sailors from the busy harbor, with their coattails cut off to show they cared for no one's opinion. They stepped ashore in the shadow of "long forests of masts"—whalers just in from the "South Arctic" Circle after doubling "the spur of Cape Horn," and tea ships from China by way of the Cape of Good Hope. After dark, landlubbers or sailors could have their oysters and liquor or join a light-fingered, brawling gang and chase the fire engines. On a different social plane there were lecture halls like the Tabernacle, Clinton Hall, and the Stuyvesant Institute, which did a brisk trade in uplift for mixed audiences, including a fine tandem performance in the shape of a general on national defense and his wife on the horrors of war. Other people followed the arts, from blackface minstrels "jumping Jim Crow" to the ballerina Fanny Ellsler, at the Park and Bowery Theatres and Niblo's Gardens. Night and day, the new penny press kept tab on this exuberant city life, from a revolutionary costume ball for the best people to the murder of a poor cigar-girl in Hoboken.

With the arrival of the fast steam packet *British Queen* from Portsmouth on September 20, 1839, these and other papers hawked the details of Daguerre's process for fixing camera images, as reported in the London *Globe*.[2] Within a week D. W. Seager made the first American daguerreotype—of St. Paul's Church and the Astor House hotel—put it on display at Dr. Chilton's, chemist, of Broadway, and took to the platform of the Stuyvesant Institute to demonstrate the method.[3] But the real challenge was taking a portrait; and Daguerre himself doubted if it could be done. At least three men set to work to show that he was wrong: Alexander S. Wolcott, mechanic of First Street, S. F. B. Morse, professor of fine arts in the University of the City of New York, and his new colleague Draper. On the evidence now available, Wolcott won the race by October 7 with the use of a concave reflector instead of a lens.[4]

If Morse and Draper heard at the time that they had been beaten, they forgot about it in later years. They went on experimenting in the gloomy University building on Wooster Street, with its Gothic chapel sandwiched between crenelated battle towers.[5] Draper's laboratory was a small, unventilated back room, where the light fought its way past Venetian blinds and Gothic mullions.[6] Through a hole in the ceiling he elevated to the pulpit of the chapel above a tea tray of apparatus for his daily lecture in chemistry. In the cramped quarters below, he kept busy from seven in the morning till midnight. Morse fared no better in the Northwest Tower, where he worked, slept, and often got his thin meals in "a perfect shower bath" of a room with sweating walls.[7]

Since both men were busy through the fall in attempting portraits, perhaps with each other's advice, it is now difficult to establish their respective claims to priority. As late as November 19, however, Morse wrote to Daguerre that he had been experimenting "with indifferent success."[8] Professor Robert Taft, the historian of American photography, can find no evidence that Morse succeeded between this date and the end of 1839; and Carleton Mabee, the latest biographer of Morse, fails to challenge this statement.[9] But an equivocal remark by Draper indicates that he made a portrait at least as early as December of that year.[10] "The first portrait I obtained last December [i.e., 1839] was with a common spectacle glass. . . ." If E. L. Morse, the author of a life of his father, was right in conceding the priority of Draper by a matter of "hours only," we cannot now push the claim of either man further back than December.[11] But, unlike that of Morse, Draper's rests on contemporary evidence now available.

In any event, as soon as he read the London reports in September, Draper went back to the attempts at portraiture which he had begun in Virginia.[12] With a lens five inches in diameter and seven in focus, he adjusted the length of the camera to the "chemical" focus of the violet rays.[13] So far, he was merely following his experiments at

Hampden-Sidney. He still had to throw a painfully intense light on the sitter.

If Dorothy was already posing for her brother, she took in good part a recent piece of interference in her personal life.[14] In order to help out her sister-in-law, who stayed in the South for the birth of a third child in December, she rented and furnished their first New York home on Charles Street. While doing this she met Andrew H. Green, a rather hungry-looking clerk of nineteen, and fell in love with him.[15] But Draper doubted that the boy could support a wife, and Dorothy obediently broke off the match. As it turned out, Green quickly made his fortune; and he became perhaps the ablest civic leader New York City has ever had—the father of Central Park, the reformer of the municipal finances after Tweed, and the sponsor of the political union of the boroughs.[16] He saw Dorothy only once again, nearly fifty years later; neither of them ever married.[17] There is no way of telling how she felt as she watched him rise. On the surface she bowed quietly, as she always did, to her brother's strong will.

In the fall of 1839 it took the form of her posing before the camera. He began by dusting her face with flour, only to discover that the forehead, cheeks, and chin were first to impress themselves on the plate even without cosmetics.[18] He found that the darkest clothes left their mark besides. But his first "portrait" consisted of white spots for the forehead, cheeks, and chin.[19] To catch the whole face he increased the light and exposed the plate longer. Out-of-doors the sun made it possible to take photographs with an ordinary spectacle lens fastened to the end of a cigar box, but the strain on the sitter's eyes proved intolerable. They registered so poorly as to spoil the proof.[20] Indoors Draper needed lighting almost as brilliant, and Dorothy had to hold herself rigid for a longer time.

By the end of March 1840, when he sent the first report received in Europe of anyone's success in taking daguerreotype portraits, Draper had reduced these annoyances in several ways.[21] He increased the sensitivity of the plate by keeping it in the dark from twelve to twenty-four hours after coating it with iodine—a procedure Daguerre had especially warned against—and if not yet, then very soon, he combined chlorine with iodine, later the accepted means of speeding up action.[22] He also spared the model's eyes by filtering the direct or reflected sunlight through blue glass or ammoniaco-sulphate of copper.[23] And he began to use a chair with a staff at the back, ending in the movable iron ring or head-support soon to be familiar in all "Daguerrean parlors." [24] Wolcott claimed that the last two improvements were his, and Professor Taft seems to feel that Draper probably imitated them without giving sufficient credit.[25] Of the filters at least, one may point out that Draper had experimented much earlier with the growth of plants under different kinds and colors of glass and glass troughs filled with chemicals.[26]

Wherever he got his methods, he noted in his letter of March 31 to the *Philosophical Magazine* that he achieved portraits with "all the beauty and softness of the most finished mezzotint engraving" in "from 20 to 45 seconds." [27] These brief sittings contrast with a nearly universal impression, which Taft has not altogether dispelled: that people who sat for the camera in the spring of 1840 (and even later) invariably had to keep still for several minutes and owed their characteristically grim look to this martyrdom.[28] A famous likeness of Dorothy, taken in sixty-five seconds, has been thought, on this account as well as others, to date from no earlier than the summer of 1840.[29]

The year had hardly begun when the feasibility of portraiture, as shown by Wolcott, Draper, and Morse, led G. W. Prosch to advertise on February 21 the manufacture and sale of the needed apparatus, with the endorsement of the last two.[30] At the beginning of March, Wolcott and a partner opened their "parlor" to sitters who paid a fee.[31] Morse and Draper followed suit, probably in April, by crowning the architectural confusion of New York University with a glass studio on the roof.[32] "As our experiments had caused us considerable expense [Morse later wrote] we made a charge to those who sat for us to defray this expense." [33] They appear to have done "splendid" business among "the very best people of the City" at a minimum of five dollars a portrait and "very small even at that price." [34] They also gave instruction to student daguerreotypists, who were going to move around the country if Draper had his way (whether he had in mind amateurs, as well as professionals with pack on back, he failed to make clear).[35] For their benefit he described how a small proof could be placed in the full light so as to bring out lights and shadows distinctly; the camera could then produce a duplicate of larger size.[36]

During last winter [that of 1839–1840] I made many copies of my more fortunate proofs, with a view of ascertaining the possibility of diminishing the bulk of the traveller's Daguerreotype apparatus, on the principle of copying views on very minute plans, with a very minute camera; and then magnifying them subsequently to any required size, by means of a stationary apparatus.

This was not only a vision of the kodak, but also the first mention of an enlarging process.[37]

Morse and Draper began operations with the latter's non-achromatic lens, four inches in aperture and fourteen in focus.[38] Against the authority of Daguerre and Sir John Herschel, Draper argued that portraits could be taken successfully without correcting the chromatic aberration so as to transmit light free of color.[39] Since the maximum action on the daguerreotype plate came from rays in the blue region of the spectrum, a skillful operator could set the focus for blue light, use only these rays and end the exposure before the red and yellow had time to take effect. Though Draper got in this way reproductions of copperplate engravings which showed the marks of the tool under a magnifier, the partners were soon importing French achromatic lenses as well as plates.[40] To protect the plate its frame was grooved so that a small tin sheet could be slid from in front at the last moment in place of opening the French-model folding doors (which sometimes stuck).[41] The lens was mounted in a barrel which by projecting beyond the aperture cut off side lights and by narrowing formed a species of diaphragm.

The sitter who climbed to the roof of the University building sat in a chair so arranged that the lines running from his head to the camera and from the head to a mirror reflecting the sunlight formed an angle of ten degrees.[42] Otherwise the eyes would come out indistinct, "the shadow from the eyebrows and forehead encroaching on them." With these precautions, however, all the space below the eyebrows was lighted and the nose cast a slight shadow. The partners had discovered that if two mirrors were used—one to reflect the sunlight upon the other, which in turn threw the light on the sitter—the length of exposure ran from forty seconds to two minutes; but with only one mirror, the time was cut by a quarter.[43] On a bright day, with diffused light, the portraits took as long as from five to seven minutes; and on the day after a rain or a day of rapidly melting snow, results were either poor or worthless.[44] It was best, therefore, to pick a dry day with clear blue skies and brilliant light.[45] Draper and Morse guaranteed to help the customer's eyes through this ordeal by sunlight with filters of blue glass or of ammoniaco-sulphate of copper in a large trough of plate glass.[46]

Women were told not to try dresses "of strongly contrasting tints." [47] If a man wore a black coat and an open waistcoat of black, his white shirt fell under the ban, as likely to appear blue or even black by the time the plate registered the face and the fine shadows from woolen clothing. The proprietors undertook to cover the shirt with a temporary drab or flesh-colored front. The collar seldom caused trouble: there was less surface, and it caught the light obliquely.

With his clothing adjusted the client sat down in a chair from three to six feet in front of a drab-colored blanket, and rested the back or side of his head against the iron ring.[48] If he happened to cross his hands over his chest, Draper or Morse explained that his

breathing would spoil the veins on the back of the hand, "which, if
. . . held motionless, are copied with surprising beauty." [49] In the
midst of these peremptory dealings, however, the sitter had the right
to introduce "a vase, an urn, or other ornament" to enhance the
setting.[50] If so, the cameraman made a final check to see that both
the urn and the human figure appeared perfectly distinct on the
obscured glass.

Then, perhaps with a prayer of gratitude for lacking moles,
freckles, and warts which would come out as "ludicrous" black dots,
and another of supplication that the iris register sharp and clear
with "the white dot of light upon it," the sitter fixed the lens with
his stare.[51] Only now the operator slid the tin sheet from in front
of the plate, and quiet fell over the studio for perhaps two minutes.

At least in the earlier days of their work together, Draper and
Morse made the image permanent by Draper's special process.[52]
Putting the plate in a strong solution of common salt, he touched
a corner with a piece of zinc scraped bright. The zinc and the silver
surface formed a simple voltaic couple. The former took oxygen
from the saline solution, the latter evolved hydrogen. The hydrogen
uniting with the film of iodine formed hydriodic acid, which was
easily washed off with water. But the proofs tarnished, so that Daguerre's hyposulphite of soda was commonly used for bathing the
plate.[53]

By July of 1840, Draper had taken the famous portrait of his
sister Dorothy: a narrow face, with firm lips and nose and dark eyes,
framed by black hair, inside a round bonnet decorated with cloth
flowers and tied under the chin.[54] This fine daguerreotype, often
reproduced as the first portrait ever made, hardly deserves the title.
In sending it to the English scientist Sir John F. W. Herschel, Draper
wrote:

We have heard in America that all attempts of the kind had been unsuccess-
ful both in London and Paris, but whether or not it be a novelty with you,
allow me to offer it to your acceptance as an acknowledgement of the pleas-
ure with which I have read so many of your philosophical researches.

This portrait, which is of one of my sister [sic; sisters?], was obtained in a
sitting of 65 seconds, the light not being very intense and the sky coated with
a film of pale white cloud. It is not better in point of execution than those
ordinarily obtained. I believe I was the first person here who succeeded in
obtaining portraits from the life. This plate will show how the art is progress-
ing—a close examination will at once give satisfaction that no aid whatever
of an artificial kind—no touching with the pencil is resorted to, but that the
proof remains in the same state as brought out by the mercury. If, sir, you
should find time to look at the paper I have alluded to, you will see a reference to a remark of yours in relation to the propriety of using an achromatic
lens for the photographic camera. This picture was procured by two double

convex *non-achromatic* lenses set together, each lens being of 16 inches focus and 4 inches aperture—the indistinctness which may be detected in some parts arises mainly from the inevitable motions of the respiratory muscles—a slight play of the features, and the tedium of a forced attitude. Where inanimate objects are depicted the most rigid sharpness can be obtained.[55]

Herschel found the portrait "beautiful and exquisite," "by far the most satisfactory . . . which I have yet seen," but he refused to yield on the necessity for using achromatic lenses.[56] "For instance the bright speck in each eye [of Dorothy's portrait] *ought,* if the figure were rigid and the camera perfect, to exhibit a picture of the external landscape as seen through the window of the apartment. But this may be considered as too severe a test for a living figure." As Taft remarks, it is certainly so severe that most recent lenses could not measure up to Herschel's demand. Many years later, in exchange for the sober likeness of Dorothy Draper, her brother received a copy of the fine, fierce portrait of Herschel taken by Julia Margaret Cameron about 1867.[57]

Important as Draper's work with photographs from life may have been, he had to share the credit with Wolcott and Morse. But in the range of applications for photography which occurred to him, he had no American rivals and perhaps no European. In what must have been the busy winter of 1839–40, he found time to take the first known photograph of the moon, and launched, in a very modest way, the great age of astronomical photography.[58] For his first effort he made the rays of the moon pass by reflection from the mirror of a heliostat through a lens four inches in diameter and fifteen in focus. With an exposure of half an hour he got an image one-sixth of an inch in diameter; but this was apparently too long a time, because the plate began to blacken.[59] But he succeeded in getting another image, when the moon was seventeen days old, by using two lenses and exposing the plate for three-quarters of an hour. Though the result was "deficient in sharpness," mostly on account of trouble in making the heliostat follow the course of the moon accurately, Draper got "distinct" representations of the position of the dark spots or lunar maria.[60] Either this or a similar result must have led him to announce his success to the New York Lyceum of Natural History on March 23, 1840.[61] At about the same time he also began taking daguerreotypes by artificial light: images from the flame of a gas light, from a "grotesque" on the slide of a magic lantern with a lamp inside, and from a lime-pea in the oxy-hydrogen blowpipe of his old friend Hare.[62]

These investigations quickly took Draper out of Daguerrean parlors and back into physics and chemistry. He found these subjects of greater interest, and by the spring of 1841 he left to Morse the

delineation of "each button, button-hole, and every fold" of paying sitters' clothes.[63] But he never failed to take up the challenge
that other people had made the first photographic portrait. "It
will soon be twenty years [he wrote in 1858] since I took the first
one, . . . and I have not learnt that there was any question upon
the point." [64] Yet there had always been very great question. These
issues of precedence, however, can hardly have damped his pride
on learning in 1879 that his name was still heard among the itinerant
photographers who toured the countryside.[65] It was then exactly
forty years since he had raced with Wolcott and Morse.

Chapter IV

"THE AMERICAN DAVY"

In 1841 Draper joined Valentine Mott, John Revere, Granville S. Pattison, Martyn Paine, and Gunning S. Bedford in founding the medical school of New York University.[1] In an age of proprietary medical colleges, the only link between the new faculty as such and the University proper consisted in the purchase of diplomas from the Council. Draper, however, remained as collegiate professor of chemistry.

Mott, a bluff, insensitive man, sacrificed a cock to Æsculapius on a tour of the Near East after delivering "a brief clinical discourse" on the victim, and in the same relentless spirit dwelt in a memorial address on a colleague's "free and abundant muco-purulent expectoration" before death.[2] The best surgeon of his day in America, he was perhaps the first one to make a million dollars by his profession.[3] He performed a long series of brilliant and dangerous operations, particularly in resecting and tying the blood vessels, that had seldom or never been done before.[4]

Mott was good-natured in a rather bumbling way; John Revere, who had translated Magendie's *Physiology,* was not.[5] Even in a funeral tribute it slips out that he "never forgot the high-toned Revolutionary blood from which he descended" as "the youngest son of Colonel Paul Revere, a distinguished mechanic of Boston." [6] Under this weight—and Longfellow had not yet taken a hand in the matter—he kept up "a certain rigid courtesy." By his attack on the national effort to raise the standards of medical education, he proved to be backward-looking in another way.[7]

A third professor, Pattison, had been turned out of his chair in the University of London when Draper was a student there.[8] Not even Mott's sacrificial cock filled as much space in the New York press as Pattison's "travels by request." He seems to have left behind him for good a biting controversialist's tongue, his dueling pistol, and the last-minute appearance before his class in pink riding-coat and boots.[9] Now he expressed a languid interest in lengthening the medical school-year, and somewhat more in seeing the opera firmly established in New York City.[10]

Martyn Paine, who had first taken notice of Draper, later played a large part in lobbying at Albany for legalized dissection.[11] At examination time his students put their faith in the one response: "The treatment is bloodletting, sir." The remaining teacher, Bedford, is said to have advanced gynecological instruction in the United States.[12] On the whole, the faculty was respectable; in the case of Mott and Draper, a good deal more.

The success of the school turned on Mott's unrivaled reputation, heavy enrollments from the South, and the squaring of requirements with the low American standard.[13] The original intention had been to imitate the University of Paris in the golden age of French medicine, but, in fact, the New York school graduated students after three years' apprenticeship, two four-month lecture courses, and the writing of a thesis.[14] In 1843 the faculty even stuck to its brief terms, when a number of schools tried to lengthen theirs. Early, if fumbling, use of clinical instruction, and coöperation with the College of Surgeons and Physicians on the visiting staff of Bellevue Hospital from 1847 forward, may have raised the standards somewhat above the average.[15] But the chief attraction was the presence of Mott and Draper on the staff. When the former resigned as president in 1850, Draper succeeded him.

Unluckily the school fell into the bad graces of James A. Houston, an Irish immigrant who put out an American *Lancet* for Bennett of the *Herald*. Mott, a rambling speaker, vainly took Houston to court to stop the publication of his lectures.[16] For over a year the editor avenged himself by impudent accounts of the ill will between Mott and Pattison and of the defects of all the teachers except Draper.

Dr. Pattison's Clinique, as usual, poorly attended.—There were, however, a good many old women and ricketty babies present, to whom the learned Professor lectured with his usual energy and good sense; he also scarified an inflamed eyelid with remarkable dexterity and steadiness of hand. . . .[17]

Another time the *Lancet* would tell of a patient in Dr. Bedford's obstetrical clinic, attended by ten or twelve students "to the great and justifiable annoyance of the poor patient and her friends," and then entered on the records as ten or twelve women delivered.[18] There was running wit about the location of the school in the former Stuyvesant Institute lecture-hall, which "the great metropolitan medical college" shared with a ladies' shoe store, a grogshop, and a druggist.[19] But most of all Houston struck at a really vulnerable spot, the self-congratulatory spirit of the professors. Their annual announcement confused good intent with real practice, and turned all sorts of brute necessities to the advantage of the best possible school in the best possible city. When they rented rooms to the pharmacist "Dr." Sands, he emerged in their circular as an instructor in "practical pharmacy."[20] Now, Houston remarked, the students could learn at the source how to mix the "Infallible Remedy for Salt Rheum," the "Sarsaparilla Panacea," and other compounds advertised by the doctor before his elevation.

In all this flood of invective, however, Houston left Draper untouched as an individual: "[he] . . . is destined to become the Sir Humphrey Davy of the United States."[21] On this account Draper had better reason than his colleagues to think of Bennett as an ally in making a medical center of New York.

. . . if the medical celebrity of New York [he said later] is to be attributed specially to any one person, it is to James Gordon Bennett. And not only this . . . he made . . . [the *Herald*] the steadfast friend of Science, when the friends of science in New York were few.[22]

Draper might fairly have added that with its large Southern enrollment, his school profited from the doughface editorial policy of the *Herald*. But it must have been irony which led him to say that the *Lancet* "brought the University in a most prominent manner before the public."[23] When it was being published he joined the other professors in trying to divert this prominence to Houston himself. He was, they said, a trouble-making Irishman fresh off the boat.[24]

This appeal to prejudice is interesting in view of the nativist movement of the 1830's and 1840's in New York City.[25] Draper's friend and colleague S. F. B. Morse had published a classic of American nativism in 1834.[26] This was before Draper's time at New York University; and so was Morse's campaign for mayor as the "American" candidate in 1836. But Draper was there in 1841 when Morse ran again, and in 1844 when the nativists helped Theodore Frelinghuysen, the chancellor of the University, get second place on the ticket with Henry Clay. It may therefore be that the gibe at Houston expresses Draper's general sympathy for a cause in which his friends were active. But nothing of this importance ought to be deduced from a single statement, issued not by Draper alone but by the medical faculty collectively. By all accounts he was a-political, at least in later years; and as a recent immigrant himself he can hardly have swallowed nativism whole.[27] (It is, of course, true that the bugbear of a man like Morse was not the English Protestant of good education.) But in the absence of Draper's correspondence for this period, these questions must be left hanging in air. Nobody who lived in New York when he did and read the newspapers could help following the controversy with more or less interest. But when he began criticizing the Catholic church his arguments were distinctly different from those of Morse.

Perhaps Draper may be excused for joining the attack on Houston. Since his salary and fees from the academic department were always threatening to dry up, only his interest in the medical school enabled him to live.[28] But he reaped the advantages of a good time for professional people of limited means. At the end of the forties he moved to Hastings-on-Hudson, a country village in Westchester. Here he bought an old Dutch farmhouse at several removes from Washington Irving, in Cooper's *Spy* country, with large grounds and a superb view looking across the river to the Palisades and stretching away into the Tappan Zee.[29] At one edge of his land he built and rented three "cottages." [30] He also got modest royalties from Harper's on his textbooks—an American edition of Sir Robert Kane's *Elements of Chemistry* (1842), a *Text-book on Chemistry* (1846), and *A Text-Book on Natural Philosophy* (1847).[31] He forwarded Kane $207 as the author's share, but the editor's is unknown.[32] Of the new texts, between twelve and twenty thousand were sold by March 1853 at ten cents a copy for Draper.[33]

By these means he balanced a budget in the heroic tradition of underpaid Wesleyan preachers like his father. Besides keeping his wife and six children, he provided a home for two unmarried sisters, hired a gardener and maids, and helped his brother-in-law Daniel and his wife (Sarah Draper) and their big family.[34] Draper seems, indeed, to have thrived in the midst of a large circle of dependents. For this reason one would like to know more about the family rebel, his sister Elizabeth. When her eight-year-old nephew William was dying, she hid a devotional book which he cried for, and after his death laid it on Draper's breakfast plate.[35] He met this cool challenge by ordering her out of the house. Though he never forgave her, she passed a happy, unrepentant life as a Catholic convert in Bridgeport, Connecticut.[36] Perhaps her religious leanings lay at the bottom of the whole incident. If so, the experience may have helped to sour Draper on the Catholic church; but there seems to be no surviving evidence on this score, one way or the other. His oldest sister Dorothy went on getting up at dawn to watch over the fine linens, richly patterned silver, and San Domingo mahogany, after uterine prolapse had made Mrs. Draper a semi-invalid.[37] The children's "Auntie" took up flower-gardening for a hobby, but when her brother decided that the flowers were too much work, she broke off abruptly as a matter of course.[38] It was almost as though Draper pledged that if the members of his family never tried to stand on their own, he would see that they never needed to. If this impression is at all sound, he kept his bargain faithfully, and loved and protected them in about equal parts. At any rate, he broke with the sister who meant to have a mind of her own, cut ruthlessly across the plans of the sister who would put up with it, and kept all but one of his surviving sons and daughters close about him till the end of his life. There is, however, plenty of evidence for the love that Dorothy and the children bore him. He may simply have been the man with brains and charm who dominates without especially intending to do so.

Draper commuted from this tight little patriarchy to his work in New York, first by boat and then by train. Until the early 1850's he gave less time to medicine and physiology than to physics and chemistry, to judge by his publications from New York University. They are the record of about fifteen years of fairly steady work in "pure" science, which petered out toward the end of the fifties. The view that the social environment in the United States was then notably unfavorable to this kind of enterprise seems to be a little uncritical (which is not the same thing as untrue). But Draper and his contemporaries met with obstacles that add to the interest of the substantial body of research which he carried through. This interest grows when Draper is examined as a member of perhaps the second generation which showed a marked tendency toward making a professor out of the average American scientist—the tendency to give a man his pay for teaching but not to hire him unless he showed the stirrings of an impulse toward research, upon which the routine of teaching might then seem an intrusion.[39] Apart, therefore, from the intrinsic importance of his work, his career throws some light on the social relations of the research man.[40]

If a society breeds (or in the case of an immigrant like Draper does not stifle) an interest in research, two issues display the relation of science to its environment—money and technology. (Social prestige, the nutrient medium in some degree of every learned profession, is most concretely apprehended in terms of money.) For the support of research, and the dissemination of its results, where does the money come from, how much of it is there, why is it given, and why asked, and on what terms? Along with this goes the question whether technology, in its economically viable form, provides the apparatus for the experiments which a man has in mind.[41] So far as Draper is concerned, the evidence on these matters is distinctly scattering.

It is plain, however, that New York University, then quite poor, made little direct contribution to Draper's research. But by one of the emerging equivocations in the life of the American university, he was not hired as a research man—not exactly, and not exactly not. He spoke in 1853 of the appropriation over some undefined period of only $125 a year for chemical apparatus, for research and teaching purposes both—and "of late, even that has ceased." [42] This may help to account for the vigor with which he fended off the efforts of his colleague Elias Loomis to lay hold of some of the meager equipment. "The instruments we have have been here for a long time (almost from the beginning of this College) and many of them are worn out. I wish you could interest the Council to make a new supply and furnish all that both of us want." [43] But nothing seems to have come of this. In 1858 he was repeating his old complaints: "wear and tear and corrosion" had spoiled the small stock of apparatus over a period of twenty-five years; and the Council ought to appropriate a minimum of $1,000 for badly needed equipment.[44] On at least two occasions, in 1853 and in 1858, he said that practically all the expenses of the chemistry department were coming out of his own pocket: [45] ". . . during the last fourteen years [preceding 1853], the actual expenses incurred have been many thousand dollars; and it may, with perfect truth, be said that the entire sum has come, not from the City, not from the University treasury, but from the private resources of a single individual." [46]

This money must have come from Draper's salaries in the collegiate and medical faculties (never high), from the royalties on his textbooks (which represented a good many sales but not much return), and from the rent on his cottages. Exactly what provision was made, and by whom, for a student-helper is not clear. Draper had one for a while at least in the early forties; and in the next decade he had an unpaid assistant and co-worker in his son Henry, from the time the boy entered his teens.[47]

When Henry Draper began to make some money of his own about 1858, he probably shared in the cost of the college laboratory and of his own and his father's research.[48] The famous observatory built in 1860 on their grounds at Hastings and enlarged in 1862 must have come from the private funds of either or both.[49] Ironically enough, after the father had taken up other work, Henry married an heiress who took a great interest in science; and he soon came into the management of her fortune.[50] It comes as a rather poignant note to find that toward the end of the elder Draper's career the University library had stopped taking *Nature* and he was borrowing a copy from his wealthy son.[51]

Draper sometimes had occasion to ask the public to lend financial support to the University, no doubt in the hope that his own work would benefit. It is a striking fact that he couched his appeals almost entirely in terms of *applied* science—in terms of Morse's telegraph and his own daguerreotype portraits.[52] Just what construction ought to be put on this is hard to say. It may be that he himself was always leaping ahead to the practical consequences of research; or he may simply have fallen in with what he judged to be

the temper of his audience (in which event it is an interesting judgment). His appeals do not seem to have had much if any effect.

The existence of channels for publishing the results of research
is another financial question, of almost equal importance with the
support of research itself. Here Draper was fortunate. He seems
to have had no trouble in getting every article he wrote accepted
by one of four good journals, the *Journal of the Franklin Institute,*
the *Philosophical Magazine,* the *American Journal of Science,* and
the *American Journal of the Medical Sciences.*[53] All of these were
privately sponsored, they found enough subscribers to keep going,
and they supplied a window on the world for the men of Draper's
generation. By and large, this matter of scientific periodicals is one
of the better pages in the record of nineteenth-century laissez faire,
in the sense that no good writer was likely to go unpublished. (The
trouble toward the end of the century, at least in the medical field,
was a proliferation of journals beyond the needs of scholarship, and
the overpublication of inferior work.) [54]

Apart from the necessity of financing research and research publications, the problem remained of getting the required apparatus
even if one could pay for it. The history of scientific equipment in
the United States is mainly still to be written; and it is hard to
weigh with any conviction the scattered evidence about Draper. In
any event, he devised much of his own apparatus and tracked down
the man to make it—often Joseph M. Wightman of Boston.[55]

> The great difficulty which we have in New York [he wrote to Wightman]
> is to get things like this [accompanying order] done when we want them[.]
> There is always too much delay[.] I hope your engagements will permit you
> to send it to me in a few days, and if the work be done well as I feel assured
> it will be I will trouble you with further orders[.][56]

Draper must have had to rely in good part on equipment brought
in from Europe, or built on European models; and the long distance from the centers of precision instrument-making must have
had some effect on the character and the tempo of his research. But
these plausibilities need to be cleared away, and their place supplied by facts. Of these there are not many: Draper imported some
photographic supplies from France at the beginning of the forties;
and he spent a good deal of his time in London in 1870–71 shopping
for apparatus.[57] But at a time when Paris was only just beginning
to yield its place as the capital of science, French equipment was
used everywhere, including the other countries of Europe, and
especially for photographic work. And a scientist will look at in-
struments whenever he gets the chance.

This survey of the social climate of Draper's research will not bear up, therefore, under much theorizing. But his record is all the better for the obvious difficulties which he encountered. It is the product of an act of the will renewed from day to day in the face of obstacles—a moral as well as an intellectual construction.

Practically all of this work that is of any enduring interest arose out of the invention of daguerreotypy (and the similar processes thrown up at about the same time by the law of multiple invention). His research is an instance of the ramifying influence of some major innovation in scientific technique. Probably no other man did as much to measure the furthest reach of photography as a means to knowledge. (Photography must here be understood in its broadest sense—the leaving of some sort of permanent record by the action of light.) If, with certain exceptions, his work was mainly the starting of hares, there were a good many of them; and it is a real feat of the scientific imagination to have laid hold of so many possibilities connected with photography. If the history of science were broken up into epochs defined by the introduction of new apparatus and new techniques, Draper would be more highly regarded. His distinction in sketching the outlines of photographic investigation would then be seen as the other side of a temper uncongenial to many scientists —a temper more wide-ranging and suggestive than deep-mining and exhaustive. But apart from this, a number of Draper's discoveries are striking by the ordinary standards of the historian of science.

His research bore mainly on three broad issues. What happens when radiant energy strikes an object and changes it? What is the full range of the spectrum? And what "light" does the spectrum reflect back upon the source of radiant energy?

Draper began the more important of his studies by taking a fresh look at an old observation. If, say, a coin is placed on a clean piece of glass and then taken off, its image can be brought back for some considerable time by simply breathing upon the glass. The phenomenon is variously known as the "roric image" or the "Hauchbild." Both Draper and the Königsberg professor Ludwig Moser associated these images with those produced by daguerreotypy.[58] Moser then put the process forward to support the view that in photography the plate is physically, rather than chemically, altered.[59] On behalf of this thesis he cited an experiment of Draper's—which did not prove what Moser thought.[60] In this roundabout way Draper entered the vigorous European controversy terminated by the proof of Choiselat and Ratel in 1843 that there is a chemical change.[61]

At about the same time (1841) that Draper was studying the roric images, he laid down the one cardinal principle for which he spoke consistently from youth into age: that only the absorbed rays produce chemical change.[62] With this he associated the thesis that the

36   JOHN WILLIAM DRAPER

optical qualities of sensitive material affect its absorptive response.[63] The major principle here, the effectiveness of the absorbed rays only, is now known either as Grotthuss' law, from the German scholar who formulated it in 1817, or as the Grotthuss-Draper law.[64] But it seems clear that the idea fell dead from the press in 1817; more, indeed, than Avogadro's hypothesis, because Grotthuss' law made its way into the consciousness of the scientific world entirely as the independent discovery of Draper.[65] The principle was in fact long known simply as "Draper's law." Eder, the Austrian historian of photography, in his relentless pursuit of the origins of everything in Central Europe, then discovered at the close of the nineteenth century that the law had previously been stated by Grotthuss. This is so; but the viable life of the idea was due to Draper's publications, which happened to be taken account of as Grotthuss' were not. The whole story bears on the ethics of scientific attribution, the involvement of chauvinism with the history of science (with a result unobjectionable in itself), and that part of the sociology of knowledge which deals with the falling of the same discovery now on barren ground, now on fertile. If informed opinion must be "ready" before taking up a theory, the consuming interest in photography obviously accounted in great part for the impression which Draper made and Grotthuss failed to make. Grotthuss was twenty years too soon.

The time of day in the history of science is not, however, the whole explanation. Draper went beyond the point where Grotthuss left off, and made the basic law of more interest.[66] He earned his public by having more to offer. He split the gross principle up into finer relationships; and he advanced a good way toward quantitative analysis.

Draper plainly surpassed Grotthuss by showing that a given chemical effect is associated with rays of a certain wave-length.[67] This discovery was congenial with the resonance theory of the dark lines in the absorption spectrum, first expressed by G. G. Stokes in his lectures at Cambridge before 1850.[68] These lines represent the stripping of color from the spectrum owing to the harmony between the frequency of such color and the frequency of the vibrations of the atoms in some substance that lies across the path of the light. The intervening medium, so to say, drinks up the frequency in question, and drinks full. The explanation turns on making the effect of radiant energy a function of the thing it strikes (in terms of the matching of frequencies). Why the resonance theory should hold—and the emission and absorption of colors by atoms always occur at the same wave-length or frequency—was first explained in the twentieth century by the application of the quantum theory to the

Rutherford-Bohr model of the atom. The resonance theory (necessarily cut off in the nineteenth century from this rationale) formed the basis of Draper's law. But he did not grasp the implication; and there is no occasion for supposing that Stokes was in his debt.

The attention to wave-lengths introduced one quantitative element into photochemistry. The measurement of the time which it took for light to produce a change, and how much light and how much change, introduced another. Here Draper did striking work. He discovered photochemical induction, "the lapse of an appreciable time between the absorption of light by a system and the occurrence of the resulting chemical reaction"; and he constructed a tithonometer for measuring the intensity of light.[69] This "tithonometer" made use of the fact uncovered in 1809 by Gay-Lussac and Thenard that light causes hydrogen and chlorine to combine progressively.[70] The seminal work in this field remained to be done by Bunsen and Roscoe beginning in the mid-fifties. They proved what Draper's work strongly suggested, that the amount of photochemical change is proportional to the amount of light energy absorbed, or proportional to the intensity of the absorbed radiation multiplied by the time during which it acts.[71] Their actinometer, built after rejecting Draper's instrument as inaccurate, made use of exactly the same phenomenon.[72] Draper has therefore some claim to being if not the founder, then the prophet—and something more than the prophet—of photometry.

After Bunsen and Roscoe in the 1850's and 1860's, no general principle of the first importance was laid down in photochemistry till Einstein formulated his "photochemical law of equivalence" in 1912.[73] This represents the extension of the quantum theory to photochemistry. One way of putting the law is to say that the shorter the wave-length the greater the energy is for working chemical change.

If care is taken to give Grotthuss his due, there are three "generations" in the effective tradition which shaped the basic laws of photochemistry—Draper, Bunsen and Roscoe, and Einstein. Draper is not of the same stature with the others; but this succession defines his claim to a more than respectable place in one of the major lines of physical thought.

If we look to the past, the Grotthuss-Draper law struck a damaging blow at the whole doctrine of the imponderables—the parceling out of the incidents of radiant energy among a set of discrete forces, chiefly light, heat, and actinism.[74] These and other weightless fluids led a less and less palpable existence from generation to generation in the nineteenth century and wound up at its close as the ether of Michelson and Morley's experiment. But after helping bring the fluids into disrepute, Draper cast much of his work for the rest of the forties—in the mold of these imponderables. He announced, in fact, the discovery of a new one which he thought accounted for photochemical change.[75] He called his find "tithonicity," on the ground of a parallel with the myth of Tithonus.[76] The variations on this term represent his mark on the unabridged dictionaries of the English language. If they are the relics of an exploded theory, some perfectly sound observations came of holding it. Part of the myth of Tithonus, as Draper tells the story, is the ebbing of his strength; and this represents metaphorically the sound discovery that the "latent" image in photography will disappear if kept in the dark.[77] The value of the tithonometer, shaken loose of its connection with the imponderables, has already appeared.

At the time when Draper was propounding the theory of tithonicity with great enthusiasm, he had already begun to inch his way forward to the repudiation of all the imponderables (except for the ether, always a special case). With the help of a grating ruled for him by the famous mechanician of the United States mint, Joseph Saxton, Draper took in 1844 what seems to have been the first photograph of the diffraction spectrum.[78] At about this time he insisted on the wisdom of referring, at least for precise purposes, to wave-lengths rather than colors.[79] He also emphasized the way in which the prism crowds together certain regions of the spectrum and "dilates" other regions.[80] If attention is paid to the wave-lengths, this distortion will appear in its true guise. It is easier to avoid the distortion altogether by the use of a grating. When a diffraction spectrum is secured in this way, the thesis that the maximum of luminosity and the maximum of heat do *not* coincide is overthrown.[81] It was the thesis commonly held in the middle of the nineteenth century, and it told on the side of separate principles at work in radiant energy —on the side of the imponderables. Draper was nibbling at the correct view in the mid-forties; he stated it clearly in 1857; and he drew the proper conclusion from it in 1872, when he read a funeral service over all the imponderables (if the ether is left aside).[82] This conclusion sprang from actual experiments which did not, however, approach the delicacy of S. P. Langley's work with the bolometer.[83]

Draper's work in photographing the diffraction spectrum took him to the edge of a whole universe of study: the mapping of the spectrum. Questions of priority are at least as difficult here as anywhere else in the history of science and technology. But it seems that Draper was the first to take with any precision a photograph in the infrared region, and the first to describe three great Fraunhofer lines there, which he called alpha, beta, and gamma.[84] His discovery of these lines was subsequently confirmed by Foucault and Fizeau.[85] He also photographed lines in the ultraviolet at about the same time as Edmond Becquerel.[86] If, as seems true, Becquerel preceded him, Draper does not appear to have known about it.

Draper may fairly be described as one of the chief, if not the chief, of the pioneers in pushing with the techniques of photography beyond both extremes of the visible spectrum. In addition he secured some of the earliest photographs of Fraunhofer lines between these extremes—though here again he seems to have been just anticipated by Becquerel.[87] Draper's work was crude by comparison with the exquisitely delicate photographs of the spectrum which were being taken at the end of his life, by his own son Henry and by the Englishman Abney. But he had a shrewd grasp of the sort of thing that needed to be done, if not always the patience to do it supremely well. Aside from this, his discovery of lines in the invisible regions is a contribution which stands free of the quality of his photographs.

Inside the visible range Draper showed in 1842 that the red rays will bleach the latent image on iodized silver plates which have been exposed but not yet developed.[88] The basic principle is known as the "Herschel effect," from the discovery by Sir John Herschel in 1839 that silver chloride paper is darkened by the concentrated light of the solar spectrum but bleached by the oxidizing action of red light.[89] Draper's contribution lay in broadening the application of this discovery to the iodized silver plates of daguerreotypy. Both Herschel and Draper speculated about the existence of "negative" rays (that is, red) acting in an opposite way from the blue and the violet, but it must be said that Draper rather backed and filled on the issue.[90] The principal importance of the Herschel effect has been in the field into which Draper introduced it: it bears on infrared photography, and the production of direct positives.[91]

In the work which has been described to this point, Draper focused his attention primarily on the spectrum itself and on the character of the radiant energy producing it. In one of his most important memoirs, published in 1847, he shifted his focus and dealt with the source of the energy and with the process by which it is discharged. He showed that all solid substances (and probably liquids as well) became incandescent at the same temperature (his figure was 977° F.), and that with a rise in temperature they emitted rays of increasing refrangibility.[92] He argued, correctly, that incandescent solids produce a continuous spectrum; and, incorrectly, that this is also true of gases (which he sometimes found to have bright lines superposed). Draper drew his conclusions from experimental observation. Deducing from theory about ten years later those of Draper's principles which were sound—and he made only the one important mistake—

Kirchhoff was able to set them in the context of thermodynamics, of the resonance theory of absorption which we now know to have been thought out by G. G. Stokes, and of astrophysics.[93] The gain in the elegance of physical theory was enormous; and Draper's contribution was by comparison altogether modest. With regard to astrophysics, for example, perhaps his furthest reach was to say in 1857 that the study of the spectrum was the key to knowledge about "the physical state of the sun and other stars." [94] The article from which this remark is taken shows that he had no idea of explaining the Fraunhofer lines in terms of resonance.[95] But it ought not to be forgotten that well within Draper's own lifetime Auguste Comte himself had fixed upon the chemical composition of the stars as a thing which could never be known and ought not even to be discussed. Moreover, Draper had pioneered in both of the techniques which revolutionized astronomy and gave the lie to Comte: direct photographic records and spectroscopy.

The memoir on incandescence, which he could not "place" as Kirchhoff did, showed nevertheless that Draper was a brilliant *experimentalist*. This is probably the note that ought to be struck in assessing the whole of Draper's work in pure science, if we add the proviso that it is a matter of emphasis.[96] The man with no skill in "theory" could not plan a good experiment, or state the results. But it is undoubtedly true that Draper held a good many theories (some of them crucial) which have gone under; and some of his best work has to be disengaged from much of the theory with which he clothes it. This comparative weakness loomed larger when it followed him into fields which did not provide the strong disciplines and the validating procedures of the laboratory tradition.

Over the same period in which he was doing his best theoretical work, Draper also lent a hand to applied science. In 1841 he published one of the earliest successful methods for copying daguerreotype originals.[97] Two years later his old partner Morse appealed for help in connection with the telegraph. Draper always remembered his first acquaintance with the invention in 1839.

. . . there stood upon the floor of the Chemical Laboratory . . . a pair of old-fashioned galvanic batteries. Like the cradle of a baby, they worked upon rockers, and so the acid might be turned on or off. A gray-haired gentleman had been using them for many years, to see whether he could produce enough magnetism in a piece of iron at a distance to move a pencil and make marks upon paper. He had contrived a brass instrument that had keys, something like a piano in miniature, only there was engraven on each a letter of the alphabet. When these were touched, the influence of the batteries were [sic] sent through a copper wire, and a mark answering to a letter was made a long way off.[98]

Now Morse wanted to know the mathematics of long-distance telegraphy.[99] Did the conducting power of electric wires vary inversely as their length and directly as their section, as Moritz Jacobi contended? If this was so, William Ritchie had objected, the signal must die away at no great distance. Draper showed that Jacobi had the right of the dispute, without imperiling the telegraph as a business investment. "When a certain limit is reached the diminution of the intensity of the forces becomes *very small*, whilst the increase in the lengths of the wire is vastly great." [100]

Encouraged by this, a party of gentlemen went with the inventor of the telegraph to a rope-walk near Bloomingdale, one summer's morning, and there tested the truth of these conclusions on lengths of wire varying from one to some hundred miles. The losses of the currents were measured by the quantity of gas set free in the decomposition of water. The result was completely successful, and telegraphing for any distance became an established certainty.[101]

With the addition of physiology to his chair at the medical school in 1850, Draper made the last of his contributions to photography. In preparing the illustrations for a textbook, published six years later as *Human Physiology,* he had his son Henry, then thirteen, photograph slides through a microscope.[102] In the book they appeared as engravings; printing from camera plates had not yet begun. But Draper pioneered once more, certainly in America and probably in Europe, in exploiting the full range of photography. His was an imposing achievement—portraits, photographs of the moon, spectrographs, photomicrographs, and techniques for enlarging and multiplying. This grasp of ends which the camera might serve and of ways for increasing its use marks his real distinction rather than claims to absolute priority. But he had these as well.

The appearance of his *Physiology* on the eve of the Civil War largely ended Draper's career as a research scientist.[103] He was then only forty-five, with dark, wavy hair, full face, large nose, incipient double chin, and sideburns.[104] At the mercy of the camera which he helped to put in their hands, he sat, clear-eyed and unpretentious, for Brady, but another photographer conceived the bad idea of posing his short stocky figure in front of a thick column.[105] In the resulting portrait there is a monumental heaviness about both of them. But perhaps it took self-composure of this order to give a good part of twenty years to pure science in the native land of the pragmatists. Yet underneath the marble of Draper's assurance, a tug-of-war was being fought.

Chapter V

THE NET OF CREATION

ONE half of Draper, buoyant, self-assured, and confident of the benefi-cence of science, belonged to the age of philanthropy and progress. In this character he was an American who believed in rushing in to fill the vacuum of the past with modern civilization, a college pro-fessor who thought that the graduates of the proper kind of school would set the world to rights. The other half of Draper bowed down before Fate, in its nineteenth-century guise of scientific determin-ism. Unlike Tennyson groping in the darkness, Draper never beat his fists against the decrees of science (as he took them to be). But time and again he ignored their implications. It was his way of crossing the tight rope from Wesleyanism to Darwinism.

In the religion that Draper knew as a boy, the Methodism of the early nineteenth century, he found a set of values stretching back into European history. By these standards the individual knew that he was significant: free to improve the world, and directly effective in realizing his purpose if he had wits and energy. By keeping in mind the fundamental premise of God's creation, the individual Methodist could deduce that the whole of human and natural history served a still greater purpose. And it must be part of this purpose to gather back to Himself some of His creatures, partly by their own choice.[1] The world was built on some plan, benevolent in the sense of putting no insuperable obstacle in the way of the mediation by men's faith and works between their yearn-ing for God and His extending salvation. Prying intellect was no substitute for saving grace, but the reason could study the rational, orderly world of nature as a testimony to the power behind na-ture. Since the Father of the Christians was also dispenser of rocks and fossils, there was no prospect of discovering through science that the natural world was altogether hostile, and effectively hostile, to men. Reason and faith at peace, Evangelicals like the elder Draper strode forward, scattering tracts to the civilized, missions to the heathen, and optimistic individualism to their children.[2]

From this background Draper had gone up to the University of London.[3] University College was an alliance of have-nots: Dissenters

42

kept out of Oxford, and out of the honors and degrees of Cambridge, by the tests, plus Utilitarians and scientists rebelling against
a curriculum inherited from the Middle Ages. Bred in Dissent,
Draper gulped down the science courses he needed to become a
doctor, and sampled Benthamism in the form of John Austin's course
in jurisprudence.

So far as he came under the influence of the Utilitarian temper,
Draper discovered the same focus on individualism as he had already
encountered at home, with civil war between the economists and
the jurisprudents as to what would come of letting the free individual go his way. Approached from either side, Benthamism recognized effective human purpose—sometimes rejoicing to see it lodged
with the unrestrained economic man, sometimes working to hold it
in check through the efforts of the jurisprudents.[4] Utilitarianism and
Methodism also converged in their reliance on a priori rationalism.
In place of positing God, and then deducing that His attributes
would be mirrored forth in the natural world, the mass of the Utilitarians tended to deduce from the premise of Benthamite human
nature as much as the logical traffic would bear.[5]

At University College Draper also came within the orbit of an
unsystematic Positivism—not the full-blown and conscious doctrine
of Comte, but its emotional core, faith in the infinite possibilities of
science. From still a third source Draper could buttress his conviction that individual men were free to effect their purpose, in
this view exclusively through science. On the surface the Positivistic habit of mind was radically empirical; it swept on to the rubbish heap anything unconfirmed by direct experimental observation. Yet this empiricism rested on a priori reasoning. Like Methodism or Benthamism, Positivism laid down a great postulate, the
all-sufficiency of "immediate" scientific observation. Every part of
experience must fit within the framework of this fiat. The Positivists
took an empirical attitude toward everything but empiricism itself.
It was this changing of a provisional technique into an article of
faith which revived among the Comtians the theological party spirit
which they had attacked in others.[6]

When Draper arrived at New York University in 1839, from London via Hampden-Sidney, outside of the laboratory he was an in-
curably deductive thinker, systematizing downward from some great
monolithic principle—the existence of God, the nature of Utilitarian
man, or the sufficiency of science—to the minutest particular. His
schooling had added to this way of thought a set of values: individualism, liberty, and progress by means of science and technology.
From 1840 to 1860 he was busy testing whether he could keep the
elements of his intellectual stock—his deductive temper, his scien-

tific curiosity, and his allegiance to humane standards—from flying apart.

His emotional commitments were the disruptive force. Somewhere he had picked up a fear of arbitrary power, and he set his views of the natural world to revolving about this fear. When he talked in religious terms he thought that it was the worst offense against the divinity of God to speak of His meddling in the affairs of the world in place of laying down natural laws for its self-operation. Of the two opposing religious tendencies of the eighteenth century, symbolized by Wesleyanism and Deism, Draper looked back in this way to the latter. It was the tradition which men like his father had meant to crush underfoot. In Deism the younger Draper could have found a master mechanic who set the watch ticking and withdrew, letting His power lapse by disuse. But Hume had already shown in spite of Paley that the logical end of Deism was to drop the mechanic. Even for less rigorous logicians God the mechanic must have sunk further and further into the emotional background. In both ways a path was blazed for the Positivists, who would say in time that nothing lay behind the scenes or beneath the surface of nature (or at least nothing more than that old spook metaphysics).

No one was more likely to feel the force of this claim, whatever its historical roots in his own experience, than Draper. As an emotional rebel against the arbitrary division of the world between the physical and the spiritual, he felt the compulsion to reduce this dualism to a monism in the manner of the Positivists. As a chemist and physicist connected with the medical school of New York University, he saw the practical advantage of this attitude. Like so many of the leading French disciples of Comte, he felt himself balked in the study of physiology by the "vitalists." [7] Many people of different views have gone by this name; Draper seems to have meant by "vitalism" the throwing around bodily processes of a fence intended to keep physico-chemists out and to keep mysterious vital forces inviolate. He properly regarded this view (which may be a caricature on the subtler brands of vitalism) as destructive of medical advance: an island of obscurantism floated on an ocean of mechanism by lazy minds. He often seemed to stop here, to consider the vitalist position mere bad tactics, a priori submission to ignorance.

This approach brought Draper to the point where the scientist might still choose between merging with Positivism and keeping free. But Draper was driven irresistibly forward by his effort to conceive of God as a singularly clear-headed engineer who went about the task of sustaining a world with the greatest economy of means. In this light God would be sensible by the standards of human

sense, without the lapses of human intellect and human power—
the greatest of watchmakers, who need not maintain a celestial
repair-shop. The perfection of the universal mechanism would lie,
for an intellectual, precisely in the absence of regions or kinds of
knowledge discontinuous one from another. By this route Draper
arrived at a genuine philosopher's puzzle. It was the "radical inconsistency" of which Alfred North Whitehead later spoke (adding
that it accounted for "much that is half-hearted and wavering in
our civilization").[8] Could a mechanistic physics and purposeful
organisms go on subsisting side by side, in mutually exclusive compartments, as the vitalists seemed to argue?

The answer was yes, if an arbitrary Providence intervened to save
purpose from drowning in physics. But all of Draper's instincts re-
belled against taking comfort in the alleged perversity of God—
His waste of energy in decreeing contradictions and then thrusting
in His hand to make the defect good. By Draper's account divinity
could only reside in a shrewd Workman who built to avoid friction
—and perpetual repairs. If God was such a mechanic, the scientist
need not regard experimental observation as a mere strategy for research, with unknown possibilities. Instead he could look upon it as
the certain means of reducing the world to intellectual unity, the
basis for a sweeping deduction concerning the whole of nature. Positivism consisted in just this switch from a technique to a faith, from
a jumping-off place for investigation to a point of repose for the
emotions of the investigator. The universe *was,* as Draper needed
to feel, of one piece, intellectually tractable by man:

> . . . by degrees, the rapidity with which all the great branches . . .
> Mathematics, Mechanics, Chemistry, were advancing, caused things to be
> seen in their right proportions . . . and men at last began to suspect that
> the world is not governed by many systems of laws, or one part of it cut
> off and isolated or even at variance with the rest, but that there is a unity
> of plan obtaining throughout; and that whether things be living or inani-
> mate, they are mutually dependent and equally obedient to the same
> rules. . . .[9]

The words "unity of plan" vibrate with emotional gratification, but
they also dispose of the logical conflict between nineteenth-century
physics and purposeful organisms—by choosing the former. Another
reply to the same difficulty, the organismic theory of physics, still
lay ahead. ("The only way of mitigating mechanism is by the discovery that it is not mechanism.") [10]

In his view that mechanistic physics must swallow up the human
organism, Draper belonged to a special era in the history of science.
But in his faith that science would spring the lock on every door, he
belonged to the great enduring current of Positivism. He belonged

also, in however equivocal a form, to an older tradition; and for him the assurance of finding a natural law to fit every piece of experience depended on the First Mover's original decree. It was in fact a cluster of theological concerns, approached for their bearing on the rationality of the natural world, which drove Draper forward to optimism about the intelligibility of the universe. But he came out at much the same place as the Positivists. He and they put their faith in the general proposition that scientific method would bring all experience under control. This method was direct observation, by which Draper meant observation of God's work. This work he took to be of a kind which would yield up all its secrets to the observer. He and the Comtians asserted that the success of the Positivist method to date guaranteed its success in all enterprises extending into the endless future of human learning. The sample which they had already taken was infallibly characteristic of what they had yet to learn. It may be that this is the psychological condition of persistence in the scientific pursuit. If so, we must take account of an atmosphere of sustaining warmth stoked up by prophets of the sufficiency of science.

To maintain this faith in science, Draper had the authority of a distinguished research worker and the temper of a strong rationalist. Impelled by his conviction that the cosmos was orderly and mechanistic physics its ordering principle, Draper proclaimed the physiological gospel according to Comte. "There is no mystery in animated beings, which time will not at last reveal." [11] His remarks implied that not much time would be needed after all. Where the seventeenth century struck him as laying the basis of astronomy and the eighteenth of physics and chemistry, "It is the office of the nineteenth to discover the laws which obtain in the complicated structure of animated beings, those laws which give rise to the mysterious phenomena which we call life." [12] But it was the function of the Positivizing spirit to banish mystery from the world, to drench the world in intellectual sunshine without shadow. It was not so much the uniqueness of life which obsessed Draper as the insecurity of distinctions between the organic and the inorganic. He wanted to trace the chemistry and physics of the human body, and account for its operation exclusively in such terms. The order of nature, he said, necessarily laid down a common principle for the circulation of blood in animals and of sap in plants.[13] He believed he had discovered the principle experimentally as well.[14]

Swept forward by his deductive temper, Draper tried to rub out the line between the organic and the inorganic in the interest of a monistic universe. He arrested the interplay of the environment and the organism at a given instant, and pronounced the world to consist of but one great process on a single, physical plane. But was natural *history* a sequence of these planes, sharply differentiated by the introduction of new species?

To answer this question Draper must pass from the early morning of the nineteenth century as heir to the Age of Progress, to the noonday of the Age of Evolution. Where the eighteenth century had given the individual a flock of natural rights in politics, the nineteenth was giving him an almost excessive number of natural rights in personality. But the zest for the human enterprise which bred these patents of right could not help feeling for better or worse the effect of scientific theory. The advance from the eighteenth century in terms of biological conceptions was largely a matter of one step prolonged into another; but the advance of theory upon the lay consciousness was not so slow or so steady. Rather suddenly, as it seemed, the jungle turned on man, encroached on his sphere of influence, and mocked at his freedom. But even the proximate ideas which ended by spreading this sense of malaise were not the work of Darwin and Wallace alone, but of the older tradition which they shared with Draper—the tradition of Lamarck's giraffe stretching to reach the banana, of the German *Naturphilosophen,* Robert Chambers's *Vestiges of the Natural History of Creation,* and Charles Lyell's *Principles of Geology.*[15] What Darwin and Wallace did was to provide a convincing rationale of how the species evolved, once the catastrophic theory of geology and the idea of discrete creations had been thrown overboard.

This distinction is well illustrated in Draper's career. At least as early as the publication of *A Treatise on the Forces Which Produce the Organization of Plants* in 1844, he asked:

Are we . . . to regard the Author of these wonderful forms [of successive geological epochs, as symbolized by the trilobite and man] as operating in each one of these instances by the same law, and, from small beginnings, evolving and transforming the most elaborate by a successive passage through those which are inferior? or are we to understand that at particular and unconnected epochs, the broad hand of an overruling Providence is to be discovered, fashioning and framing each class of created forms, irrespective of external physical forces or agents, and giving birth spontaneously to unconnected tribes of animals and plants, which bear no sort of relationship to one another, and are not parts of one common plan in which there is a unity of design? [16]

Draper's own answer is plain, and it is the answer of the future. Here he was already providing an out for religious people interested in saving the good name of God the constitutional monarch. This is what one would expect of a man who thought that the greatest glory of God was to have instituted the world on a principle of perpetual motion requiring no interference to make it go. A true son of what passes for the eighteenth century, Draper could not breathe in "a mysterious and emotional world, rich in insoluble riddles, and needing a mediatory and miraculous Church to give a mystical clue." [17]

If God's plan for the world lay embodied in natural laws open to discovery by man, this ought to have been a warm, comfortable doctrine for Draper. In a way it was. But there were chinks in the discipline of a benevolent despot like the Christian God, and none in the operation of a perfect machine. As Draper began to see this, he took a bold, intransigent stand, as if he had made a very good trade: if men did not like this new incarnation of Fate, they must make the best of it just the same, for it was so.

In the system of the universe an individual is not known, but action takes place on masses. Nor are the laws of Nature ever bent to give benefits to or bring punishment on any individual. They go into effect with an inexorable decision.[18]

And yet, he could not be at peace with this ravenous natural world closing in upon the individual, the environment not so much at war with the individual as totally unmindful of him.

Science, as he thought, commanded him to look steadily at this prospect and call it fair, but a rebel within him refused to recant his high spirits, his pride in his profession, and his ambition to improve the world. Something of all this appears in a lecture of 1845 when he passed blithely from early nineteenth-century evolution to eighteenth-century progress as if they were identical; whereas historically the latter is shot through with a conviction of man's power, which hardly revived among the social evolutionists, in its full vigor, before Lester Ward.[19]

The whole creation is bound together like a net; the various objects of it, and we ourselves among them, are the knots. We talk about liberty of action and freedom of will, it is the liberty and freedom of those knots. They too can move from side to side as chance or circumstance directs. You may throw them into ten thousand positions—you may twist them together, and spread them out, and what does it avail? Are they not all the while under the same relation to one another as at first? There are invisible lines that hold in their proper position the different objects of nature. There are also invisible lines which retain us in a certain social position. In our times there is but one condition which can compel men to acknowledge distinctions—that condition is intellectual superiority. Neither birth, nor wealth, nor connexions, can retain a man in any elevated position in which he may chance to be cast; and in the medical profession, as well as in all others, it is shining abilities alone which can command lasting success.[20]

It is hard to make cold sense out of these strong convictions heaving to communicate themselves. But one may infer from the context that the distinction of the informed physician and scientist rests on usefulness in promoting the ends of society; and this usefulness is not a mere fact but a merit. Yet the good deed is hard to disengage from the free will. Creation, then, is a faultless net of predetermination (for it is difficult to see what squeezing the knots could really mean)—but the scientifically trained medical-research man somehow slips through. Logically the contradiction is preposterous. But it takes on poignancy from laying bare the conflict between the emotional impact of scientific laws which inhibit and hedge man about and the exuberant sense of freedom belonging to the men who discover the laws. The sense of this conflict stuck with Draper through the rest of his career.

The single strand of his thought had unraveled. From his necessity to believe in God as an efficient mechanic economical of His means, Draper had deduced a monistic view of the universe. He applied this view to physiology, with the effect of engulfing the individual human spirit in mechanistic physics. In addition, he came naturally to believe in evolution as part of the monistic intelligibility of the world. But his allegiance to certain standards of human conduct, rooted in the freedom and effective purposefulness of the individual, could not legitimately survive the voyage of exploration into this new scientific climate of his own choosing. The advance of science (as he construed it) had made the place of individual man altogether too comprehensible, and smashed to bits the naïve faith that the world would be proved a genial setting for the activity of Western man. Inadequate physics and one-sided evolutionism professed to show what the world was really like, the great discovery being that it had never turned on the pivot of the free, effective individual. The new scientific fruit was in direct line of descent from Eve's apple. The question now was how to shore up human standards robbed of their accustomed support. Without playing science false, Draper had to try reconstructing the emotional climate of Wesleyan man.

The immediate concern which forced this problem upon Draper was his effort to make physiology an exact science. Not till the publication of his textbook on *Human Physiology* in 1856 does it appear for sure that he had read Comte. Perhaps, indeed, he read merely the competent précis by Harriet Martineau, the study of Comte by G. H. Lewes, or the partial translation of the *Cours de philosophie positive* by the American W. M. Gillespie.[21] But however this may be Draper now echoed the vocabulary, as well as the general tone, of the Frenchman: physiology was passing from a "speculative" to a "positive" science.[22]

To put physiology in its broadest setting, and lay the basis for a "positive" approach, Draper had to decide how the body was formed. His evolutionary thinking led him to reject any barrier between man and the other organisms: "we must dismiss the vulgar error that the physical conditions of existence vary in different tribes [genera, etc.], and that man is not to be compared with lower forms." [23] But what generalization would pull together the greatest variety of these comparisons? Draper's response was the cellular theory of Schwann and Schleiden. "The primordial germ being in all instances alike, its mode of development will depend on the physical agents and conditions to which it is exposed. . . ." [24] Gliding from simplicity to simplicity, Draper seized on Meckel's theory of "recapitulation": ". . . the development of the various animal tribes . . . takes place under the operation of a far-reaching and common law, . . . the particular condition which any species presents . . . is a manifestation of the degree or extent to which that law has been carried out." [25]

Between the words "primordial germ" and the word "species," there is room to insert a wedge. Suppose the environment to shape the species beyond appeal, the individual cell, expanded into an organism, may deviate from the main line of development. Indeed, "the main line" may simply be the direction taken by the preponderant body of the cells that survive and propagate. Draper backs and fills on this question of the "statistical" computation of scientific laws. Frequently he seems to argue that the environment taken as a single unit, will force all cells to accommodate themselves equally. But he often cast about for means of gratifying an emotional appetite for individual freedom. And he thought that he had found them in the work of the great statistician L. A. J. Quetelet.

. . . M. Quetelet . . . has in an interesting manner extended the methods of statistics to the illustration of the physical and moral career of man, and impressed us with the facts that in the discussion of the phenomena which masses present, individual peculiarity disappears and general laws emerge. The actions which seem to be the result of free will in the individual, assume the guise of necessity in the community. [26]

This (very dubious) statistical rehabilitation of freedom, with changes dictated by the geneticists, has had a long life. [27] But it was a thin reed for Draper to lean upon until the mind was firmly inserted into the evolutionary process. It would still have been poor comfort for a man who wanted to save the whole Evangelical man, to prove him effectively purposeful as well as free. For this end it was no good pooling individual purposes, to catch the main drift of the purposive instinct, and discarding the rest—especially if one held, as Draper mostly did, that this main drift was externally defined from the beginning.

For a physiologist, there was another recourse. Draper might talk, as he did, of the *balance* of activities in the body, and so return to the old problem of vitalism. When he asserted that the body was a physicochemical system, the fact remained that it showed a marvelous common effort forwarded by countless adjustments. The vitalists attacked the nature of this stubborn marvel with the wrong weapon. (They ended by saying, "There is something different about organisms, and this difference is different-ness.") The *milieu interne* of Claude Bernard proved a more fruitful line of attack; and in the last twenty-five years the cutting edge of Bernard's approach has been sharpened by the work of W. B. Cannon with the concept of "homeostasis." [28] When, therefore, Draper fastened on the word "equilibrium," he at least got hold of the distinctive problem in the study of the more complicated organisms. He did more by focusing attention on "the circulating liquid" and the complementary "withdrawing" of "supplies" by different parts of the body.[29] Moreover, he had a good deal to say of "vicarious action," that is, the attempt by one part of the body to take up the work of another which has got out of order.[30]

If Draper had pressed the implications of this idea, he might have anticipated one of the major traditions of the twentieth century and so have found a seeming exit from determinism, of the kind for which his emotions appear to have been looking on a subterranean level. For the more and more delicate organization of organisms may be regarded as raising man above the level of the rest of nature, without the need for invoking vitalism. Under the name of "emergent evolution," this idea has put the development of the mind, with its sense of purpose and its assertion of freedom to mold the future, into the evolutionary sequence.[31] From Draper's point of view, this thesis would have mended the intolerable break between the "physical" world and the human. But he failed to work out this line of argument. Even if he had succeeded, he would merely have had a "natural history" of the mind without the assurance that the mind works its purpose. For this he needed what was curiously lacking in much thought of his time, the knowledge that men are logically entitled to maul the environment as much as it mauls them; that they are reflected back upon themselves through the medium of the environment. In any event, Draper did not progress to the point of formulating "emergent evolution."

As a last resort there remained only blind, unanalyzable exuberance, floating in mid-air on no visible foundation. Without saying that science was wrong, Draper could repudiate in practice its emotionally intolerable conclusions. His repudiation took the singular form of reasserting the old, and one would have supposed for him, logically shattered faith that scientific discoveries *must* prove psychically and physically beneficent.

This is what he did at every turn. Confronted with the progress of modern medicine and technology, he simply shook off the burden of resignation and determinism. Surveying American problems, he proclaimed that doctors could end the waste of life in the slums and on the frontier—if properly grounded in science.[32] Indeed, an institution like New York University must be measured in terms of men of science given the opportunity to transform the world: "positive" physicians; men like Morse, who had revolutionized industry and commerce and made it possible for the government at Washington to rule over an entire continent; or Draper himself, who had brought into being an army of ten thousand photographers and put a new calling at the disposal of women shifting for themselves.[33] Wherever he looked, he saw miracles brought to pass by investigators and technologists: "[The steam engine of James Watt] . . . has produced within the last thirty years, such a political revolution as this world never saw before. It has re-arranged the geography of countries, and re-distributed the elements of society. It has thrown into movement masses of men that in old times were stationary." [34] "Look what is its effect among us: the United States are now absolutely smaller than was the State of New York forty years ago."

Charged with the explosive energy of nineteenth-century America, Draper cast his vote with the reforming Brownson against Channing and Emerson, in the great campaign between souls and institutions. Where the Concord transcendentalists worked at fanning the inner flame, Draper was busy sweeping the hearth. Chastising the humbug fringe of the tractarians, he quarreled with the whole effort to save souls instead of reforming institutions.[35] He therefore assigned the doctor a central role in making the community a fit place for the growth of healthy bodies.[36] When this idea is cast in the imperative mood, it becomes the cry wrung from the conscience of the nineteenth century by yellow fever, malaria, and cholera.[37] But the cause of sanitary improvement had a sharp edge to it, a firm outline, which made it the reform of people who were scared of sentiment and impatient of moralizing. It was the cause, in Draper's own formula, of letting up on the conversion of Burma and bearing down on the vaccination of America. The chief way to take the pulse of this problem of disease in an urban society is to keep statistics; and we know that Quetelet's work struck Draper as supplying a kind of new dimension to society. There is, however, no evidence that he ever took an active part in the movement for sanitary reform. But he cheered it on, made a stick of it for beating at the missionary temper, and built it into his social philosophy.

If he did not argue that everything needful would follow from the right environment, he forgot to make a point of his reservations. He showed the same skepticism of moral transformations by arguing that quacks would not be got rid of by "legal enactments" or "ethical codes" but by a better anatomy and physiology to save the physician the need of working in the dark.[38] The remedy was technological unemployment for the quacks, not responsive readings of a Hippocratic catechism. He called not for a moral revolution but for enough knowledge to make the honest practice of medicine easier than the dishonest. But like the reformers from within, Draper gave himself up to belief in the progress of mankind; this belief was one of those intellectual bonds which go unnoticed between sworn enemies in debate.

Indeed, the chief significance of Draper's remarks on the doctor of the future is their aura of confidence—the common assurance of the most diverse nineteenth-century thinkers. Draper's words fairly breathe the conviction that men will lead longer, healthier lives, with all that this implies for giving man the upper hand over the menacing environment. Where his father might have looked to Wilberforce as the type of the free, purposeful, and significant figure in society, Draper now set the "positive" physician in the place of the philanthropist. By a piece of warmhearted inconsistency, Draper shrugged off the fatalism which science had seemed to lay like a great stone on his shoulders. But it symbolized one of the revolutions in intellectual history that, to rid himself of intolerable scientific conclusions, he gave himself up to faith in the scientist. He was taking part in the process by which the scientist got a corner on zest and the sense of freedom.

In Draper's view, man, like Humpty Dumpty, had had a great fall. There he had sat, a free agent, important in himself and effective in the world, and here he lay, a set of loose members—freedom, significance, and utility. Could any consulting king's men put him together again? Quetelet, perhaps? Lamarck, or Darwin? But Draper's native buoyancy would get the upper hand, and cry, Nonsense! Humpty Dumpty-man was still on top of the wall, all in one piece —but the wall was really a laboratory or a clinic. In this way Draper fluctuated between trying to put Humpty together again and denying that he had ever had a fall.

The statistical man, *l'homme moyen,* of Quetelet, seemed to avoid determinism for the individual without restoring effective purpose to his life, unless he happened to be going the same way with a great many other people (and Draper tended to argue that the only possible "way" of this kind was already defined from outside the human race). The idea of evolution came down for Draper on much the same side, of magnifying the environment at the expense of the individual organism, for he took scarcely any account of the influence of the organism on the environment.

The environmentalists offered no theory of the "natural rights" of individuals held back safe from the pressure of history and society. A man's natural right was to get into accord with his environment (in other terms, to join a majority). Yet this, with *l'homme moyen*, is not at all the emotional impact of Watt's, Morse's, and Draper's innovations, or of the sanitary reforms of Edwin Chadwick and Lemuel Shattuck—the work of single men who boldly remake the environment. Draper was like those reformers of his age who proposed to improve institutions rather than souls—to produce a change of scene in place of a change of heart. Both they and he, however, supported an initial rebellion against the environment and looked for it to prosper. If this is not by their own terms a contradiction, it is at very least a drastic shift in emphasis. Draper by mixing evolution and the statistical computation of scientific laws might conceivably have provided for an area of tolerance within which Nature threw up its malcontents; but he would have been hard put to show how they could turn the evolutionary stream. And in fact he does not seem ever to have discussed these issues.

Draper reflects in this way a persistent tension in the thinking of scientists, between coming to terms with things as they are and finding out how they are with an express view to making them different. If he had shaken his ideas down into consistency, he might have had to abandon his reforming impulse. But he had a saving inconsistency. Instead of looking backward to rights not to be violated by the present environment, he looked forward to a more nearly perfect environment of his own making. Nevertheless he reserved to himself and to all who could be induced to join him—other reformers and professionally competent scientists—the inalienable right to be at war with the environment out of inner conviction.

By letting consistency flag in this fashion, Draper escaped sounding the depths of the tragedy for which he supplied the terms. He was saved by old habits of mind which kept their surreptitious hold upon him, in spite of neglect. But for men of his temper it remained to be seen how long the motives of conduct could do their work, with the logic knocked out from under them. If the effort were not to lapse for some people at least, the churches must sift their teachings; and the churchmen must find if they could the germ of religion borne along in the thought of the scientifically minded. But Draper soon had evidence that the bulk of the clergy in his time, ignorant of science and proud of it, would miss their chance.[39]

Meanwhile he himself found the consolations of faith by kneeling at the altar of something like Comte's Humanity-served-by-Science. There is no evidence of his actually joining Comte's church—most of which Draper would have found distasteful—but such a faith was the effective residue of the hopefulness which he had brought with him from a Wesleyan parsonage. He could not reconcile mechanistic physics and free, purposeful individuals, but it was better for native buoyancy to override the contradiction than for bad logic to "gloze it over with phrases." [40] Draper left the antithesis unresolved; he either bowed to mechanism or got altogether carried away by confident individualism. In so far as he seemed to lose himself in the species or the statistical "pool," he shared in the moral paralysis which has since overtaken many individuals-as-individuals. In so far as he preserved the zest of a scientific innovator for making the world over, he escaped from the very determinism which he spread in the name of science. He illustrated in this way the disjunction, in him rather gross, in others almost impalpably subtle, between the content of science and the emotional climate which it breeds.

Chapter VI

THE TURNING POINT *

THE last pages of Draper's *Physiology* pointed the way to nearly all of his future work. It was a milestone in his career when he made a speech on the same ideas to inaugurate the Cooper Union on July 1, 1859.[1]

> . . . it has pleased God to place the government of this world in its onward progress under the same laws as the development of man.
>
> [With regard to these natural laws governing the development of society:] Ask the Historian what is the impression[,] the final conclusion to which he has come, from his examination of the life of Nations. He has still the same story to tell. Nations like Individuals are born, run through an unavoidable career, and then die, some earlier, some more maturely, some at a still later date. In their infancy some are cut off by mere feebleness, some are destroyed by civil diseases, some commit suicide, some perish of old age. But for every one there is an orderly way of progress—the same pursued by the individual and assigned to the Globe.[2]

From this point forward Draper in his published work left the exact sciences behind, and made it his business to reduce the historical and cultural ramifications of these sciences to comparable exactness. Why did the straight line of his career veer off at right angles?

It looks at first glance as if he had been misplaced by history. He had a wide streak in him of the eighteenth century, or perhaps the Middle Ages, or the Renaissance—an aching need to be a whole man and take in the whole of knowledge. But the effect was a Georgian front faced over with brownstone. He was very much like a solemn Ben Franklin, or better still, Thomas Cooper—one of the last of the "universal" men. But where such men had once been praised for breadth, the nineteenth century now cut a vertical cross-section and observed that they had spread themselves thin. When Draper began to teach at New York University, Cooper had just died; when Draper himself died, the German Ph.D., monograph, and seminar had already taken out first papers at Johns Hopkins.[3] And, of course, Draper belonged to both traditions—with his mind to the new and perhaps with his heart to the old. On the one side, he has every claim to being the principal founder in New York University of professional training, other than medical, and of graduate study.[4] He proposed in 1853 a course in "Practical Chemistry," to be given in "other hours than those of the regular course"; and he was teaching the subject to evening classes in the medical school building at least as early as January 1854. This seems to have been a private undertaking down to 1858. By that time the title had swelled to include analytical chemistry; and the University then began to register the students and give them diplomas. Draper seems also to have been the moving spirit behind the plans for instruction in civil engineering which were laid (after a lapse of twenty years) in 1853. In 1855, probably under his influence, the Council authorized the degree of bachelor of science, for which no Greek or Latin was required; and it would be fair to consider this as a sign of his professionalizing temper. Under the most ambitious of all his proposals, the University first granted (what was called) the degree of doctor of philosophy—five times between 1867 and 1872, after which the enterprise seems to have petered out with Draper's advancing age. The recipient of this degree had to present an A.B., a B.S., or an M.D. (with a certificate in this event of "literary attainments" issued by a college), and then complete satisfactorily two years of study in analytical and practical chemistry.

In this way Draper did his best to seal up scholars in air-tight professional compartments of smaller and smaller dimensions. But he himself burst all walls, and made a great discursive *Wanderjahr* out of the last third of his life.

At the end of the fifties, then, Draper appeared in a new light. From beating the drum for experts he turned to playing the part of a universal man—in just the wrong climate of opinion for universal men. He started to write history, and showed his insensitivity to historical fashions. The reasons why he fell decisively out of step are hard to determine. But the initial fact is clear that Draper did his most important scientific work from twenty-five to thirty years before the flood tide of Ph.D.'s came in.[5] He lacked, what might have kept him to the task, the stimulus of graduate students, with a few exceptions in his later middle age. He had therefore to content himself in great part with rubbing the illiteracy off undergraduates.[6] Even his medical students had little interest in research. Moreover, in a day when instructors in science ranged from one end of "natural philosophy" to the other, he got every encouragement for parceling out his efforts among chemistry, physics, physiology, and geology.[7] Merely to rehearse the outlines of so many subjects, and try to keep up with the mushrooming literature on them, must have been a deterrent to close investigation. If this was not enough to make him slacken in his own research, Draper felt that this work had not paid off in prestige. This feeling is the framework for his sharp, querulous letters to the *Philo-*

sophical Magazine in defense of his priority over European scientists.[8] Perhaps if he had had the sense of a sufficiently respectful European audience following his articles, they would not have dwindled away at the end of the fifties. But when of all of this is said, one has just nibbled at the edges of the question why Draper substantially ended his laboratory research by 1860 and never repented.

One thing which conditioned without causing the change was the fact that he had no consciousness, so far as one can judge, of making a sharp turn. It was possible for him to become a universal man because he continued to be part of the great tradition of modern science —its effort to swallow up the whole of learning. If Draper's new work had appeared to leave science behind, he could hardly have stuck with it. He needed the assurance that he belonged to a respectable tradition; and for him there was only one, the scientific. He thought of himself as proceeding from the base to the outposts of a single theater of operations.

By extending his lines in this way, he hoped to find a fresh, nine-teenth-century encyclopedism—not the filing of intellectual bits and pieces by alphabet but the ranging of experience by logic. At bottom what he got was the Positivism of Auguste Comte.[9] Newman, Comte, and Draper agreed on the necessity for some counterpart of the me-dieval hierarchy of learning. Newman meant to continue (or revive) theology in its old place as queen of studies. Comte and Draper, on the other hand, felt as great need for unifying knowledge as Newman, but looked for natural science, rather than theology, to turn the trick. Draper was happiest in measuring the gamut of the naturalistic tech-nique instead of pursuing intensively, as more and more people did, some small segment of learning. His instinct was to rise above particu-lar disciplines and see the relation between them. In this work he found—what he wanted to find—that the study of history ought to be regarded as a branch of natural science. Draper had a strong sense for the right issue, if not always the common sense to make the right point about it. As he saw, the Positivistic temper would stand or fall by its success in handling the least tractable problem before it: how to make a science of history. The compulsion to answer this question supplied Draper with his new subject-matter. But he had still to de-cide what it meant to make a field of study scientific.

If the body of "scientific" historians is taken as a whole, the weight of Positivism came down mainly at the two extremes of smashing the materials of history into as small bits, or building them into as large systems, as possible.[10] On the one side—it was not Draper's—this meant that history, like biology or physics, had its minute "facts"; and these could be isolated and disinfected of the subjective response of the historian. This attitude had the good effect of tightening up the canons of historical evidence. But though data need to be cleansed of fraud and bias, there is after all no datum, apart from the universe as a whole, to be had except by asking for it; and once data are chosen on some principle they must still be sifted and put together for some purpose (not necessarily the original purpose of selection). To have seen this need for *composing* facts into history—and not merely to have acted upon it—is the strength of a systematizer like Draper.

Comte had, of course, his particular way of stringing the facts of history on a thread of system. If there was a science of society, as there was, it must have its laws—so to say, Newton's laws of society. The business of the historian then became to file his materials according to the logic of these laws. This is exactly the spirit in which Draper wrote history; but it was not the only thing which he borrowed from Positivism. Comte laid down three stages through which the thought of the individual passes, from the theological through the metaphysical to the positive; and he said that society went through the same stages.[11] Draper agreed. But he added to this theory the proposition that society *was* a man, or at least a small group of men, the "nations," with the states of health and the different ages of a man. "Nations like Individuals are born, run through an unavoidable career, and then die. . . ."[12] Saint-Simon, the master whom Comte repudiated, had played about with this idea; and some of his minor disciples put the matter almost exactly as Draper did. In Comte himself the fascination with physiology as in some way the key to a science of society had not yet worn off. But he mostly escaped from the uncritical identification of a man's body with the body of men. Except for this one issue there would be no good reason for supposing that Draper knew the literature of Saint-Simonianism; whereas he obviously did know Comte, from whom the idea might have been gathered (if not rigorously, then again not implausibly). Wherever Draper got the notion, it is a really curious instance of physiological imperialism, the effort of physiology to swallow up history and politics.[13] He gave the final twist by assimilating the man Society to the biological organism of Darwin, shaped by the environment.[14]

Draper found a parallel, and left an allegory. But he did not think of it as an allegory. His was not the effort of the popularizer of science to strike off the telling comparison—the ether quaking like a jelly, or the energy of the quantum theory getting off a railroad train at the appointed stops only. Draper accepted on the basis of a very close analogy between man and society propositions that would otherwise have had to be established independently.[15] And this is the pragmatic test of not knowing an allegory for what it is. Draper was, in fact, a victim of semantic confusion in the grossest form. Jonathan Edwards put up a much better fight against the seductions of language; and the gain in sophistication was distinctly equivocal when the best side of the religious tradition dropped into the void with the worst.[16]

It would be easy to say merely that Draper got drunk on analogy, and draw back in embarrassment. But a man has his own way of behaving in drink; and the use Draper made of his analogy is an index to his felt needs. Some of these needs could not be satisfied—not as much or as openly—in his laboratory research. They might have been answered to some extent inside the laboratory, but they would always be receding to the edges of his consciousness or dropping between the logical interstices of his scientific memoirs. But for grappling straight-out with these needs, there was ample license in the tradition of historical writing. They help therefore to answer the question why he took up new work in mid-career. They are nothing like the whole content of his later work, they take their turn with plain statement and bare exposition and, it cannot be emphasized too strongly, with counterneeds; but they supply the distinctive note.

E. L. Youmans, the popularizer of science among American laymen, turned up a significant clue: "[In Draper's writings] . . . accurate and profound instruction is so often and happily blended with the charms of poetic eloquence." [17] It seems clear that he was in some degree a poet *manqué* constrained to appear as a scientist. He was able to manage this all the better because he had done experimental work of real interest. Now, however, the poet often got the upper hand, partly because he had always been there and partly because the scientist grew discouraged. It need hardly be said that such a man would set his poetry in the context of science—like the Tennyson of "nature red in tooth and claw" or the Melville of *Clarel*.

Draper had also a strong sense for conduct and demeanor which was always making itself felt in his historical writing. One manifestation of this, the sorting out of heroes and villains, friends of science and enemies, bulks large. But this process, extremely important in accounting for the satisfaction which he got from history, is at once common and easy to follow. It is not so easy to disengage another process, the mingling of the aesthetic and the ethical impulses, to make of him a kind of ethical, almost a religious, poet.

These impulses are compacted together in his allegory of the life of Society, along with the use which he makes of it. On the one hand, it embodies the form, shapeliness, and harmony of the world—the life-history of the individual man running parallel with that of the great social being, the human enterprise fully assimilated to its environment, the writ of scientific law holding for society as well as the climate, and the basic principles of the universe shaken down into a gratifying simplicity. In this way the idea of the life of Society calls up for Draper the likeness of nature; and he makes of nature a conduit for draining off the emotions. (One must agree for this purpose to mean by "nature" not particular discriminated areas in the scheme of things but the scheme as a whole.) Here the ethical mode insinuates itself, to keep the emotions from going wrong, and to command that the formliness of nature shall get the response which it deserves.

One need not suppose that Draper set out in cold blood to spend his emotions on the form of nature; even less that he meant to declare war on the scientific spirit. There is nothing to suggest that he wished to justify men in forming sentimental stereotypes of nature and refusing to give them up. Quite the contrary; a man ought to surrender old conceptions of nature as soon as informed scientific opinion provided new and provisionally better ones. He ought to know the world as well as he could and keep his aspirations within the range of this world. In this attitude, which is more pervasive than explicit, Draper was in the main line of descent from the Enlightenment. The chief sin is to nurse unsound theories because they have come down in the family—whether from Adam and Eve, or Ptolemy, or Saint Paul.

If the duty of men is to find out their fix in the universe without sentimental reservations, what room does this leave for playing a stream of emotions on nature as a whole? Draper's implicit reply was that a good part of the psychic fund can be paid out in aesthetic responses to nature, *as it is described by the best authorities*. Their description, with its testimony to the elegance, simplicity, and form of the basic scheme, Draper embodied in his allegory of the life of Society. As it happened, he thought that he found the authorities on the side which he preferred. Darwin was providing, or so Draper thought, new evidence of as orderly and simple a universe as Draper could wish—and in this direction his appetite was nearly insatiable. Yet the whole tenor of his remarks would commit him, if need be, to adjusting his demands to some other theory less congenial to his own temper.

The great men of the Enlightenment would have gone along with Draper in telling men to find out their situation and let their will range to the edges of this situation and no further. But Draper added something to this. He seemed to feel that men ought to map the exact scheme of natural possibilities and *warm* toward the whole of it besides; not only to admit it but to infuse the admission with emotional gratification. In this view, Margaret Fuller had after all the better of the famous exchange about accepting the universe.

What point was there in Draper's and Margaret Fuller's turning the stream of preferences and choices on the universe as a whole? Why should he show by his example that men ought not only to find out what nature is like but also persist in asking, do I like the aspect of it, such as it is? Why is there implicit in his poetizing on science a kind of Stoicism heated by emotion?

One answer would be, because his attitude is in fact a variety of Stoicism, the pursuit of free will inside determinism. Man has got to accommodate himself to nature, but if he does so of his own free will, he earns a dividend of emotional gratification. Here Draper by his practice strikes off a rule of conduct: tip the scales back again in favor of human dignity by choosing what is thrust upon you. But if by the drift of his remarks on science Draper made it an ethical precept to rush out and embrace necessity, this bound him logically to the superior proposition that men ought properly to train their emotions on nature one way or the other. (The other, Byronic storming against the universe, would be temperamentally uncongenial to Draper himself.)

There is another explanation of Draper's persistent taking of attitudes toward nature. For his own part, he is nowhere explicit about the point, but he was showing by his example one way out of the old conflict between religious people and the scientists. Much of the conflict arose out of the fact that the new scientific theories seemed, on a quick survey at least, to spoil the natural world, to make it disagreeable—indifferent to men, radically dissevered from their interests, and out from under the control of the God of men. Draper would never have agreed to save Christian dogmas at the expense of Darwinism. But if the dogmas must go, Draper showed by his example (instead of his precept) that a man could take the soundest available theory, and then rebuild the structure of psychic gratifications inside the limits of the new idea.

Draper felt the need for what John Dewey calls the "wholesale justification" of nature ("to assert that [specific values generated by concretely knowable conditions] . . . are justified only when they and their particular causes and effects have all at once been gathered up into some inclusive first cause and some exhaustive final goal").[18] For this purpose, both Positivism and evolution as construed by Asa Gray lay at hand.[19] What Draper appears chiefly to have got from the old religion of his childhood was the conviction that the world bore witness to God's design, and the key word is design, not God; that the whole of nature was through and through orderly. There was form to it, and a rather *simple* form. But the same repose which Draper got from this conviction as a boy could be got back again within the bounds of nineteenth-century science—or so he thought. The same emotions which he had been able to gratify inside the conventional Christian theology (and some which he had not) found a new outlet, instead of being dammed up in a great reservoir of unreasoning resistance to the advance of science. It was his own response to the situation which has transformed liberal theology and made it partly a matter of keeping up with science, throwing overboard the intellectual luggage which prevents the clergyman from staying abreast of the scientist, and then discovering that the latest theory is merely the best confirmation yet of what one was already preaching when it came into sight.

Draper knew that the inertia of the affective impulses ought not to hold research back. But he also showed by his example that he could not help looking on science as a consolation that would have to be prolonged by emotion. It was well enough to be crisp and clear-eyed in finding out what nature was like, but he wanted to relax and brood over the likeness once he got it in mind. It was this desire that drove him forward from science to poetry. Hungry for recognition as he was, he could now get in touch with the unscholarly students at New York University and with the whole community of laymen who knew an emotion if not a spectrum.

In the process of showing by his example that the natural order could be made an aesthetic object, Draper lapsed into the ethical mode. By his practice he defined the limits beyond which the sense for beauty *must* not range; and he implied that the opportunity to gratify this sense *must* be seized. But there is a profound tension here. Draper appears to get the sharpest apprehension of the form of nature from his allegory of the life of Society. But after all the desire to mold conduct and demeanor can only be directed toward actual men and women. Stow them away in the great social "man," and they still remain the only thing on which the ethical impulse can lay hold. And sometimes Draper wanted to lay hold of them, and dress them down—for their laughable self-assurance, their indocility, their aimlessness, their willful diversity, and their general intractability as objects of scientific prediction.[20] But in doing this, he stumbled over the plain fact that though individual human beings might be made up statistically into scientific laws, there was something in the universe out from under strict control. Indeed, when he wanted to point up the form and harmony of the basic scheme, he often resorted to chiaroscuro—at bottom everything is extremely neat and tidy, and to see this and take the satisfaction in it that one ought, only look at the frantic disorder of concrete life. (But he would not have used the word "concrete.")

The idea of the "man" Society commends itself to Draper as falling in with the theory of evolution. In fact Society becomes the biological organism of Darwin, with a rather physiological cast to it. In this sense Draper keeps up with the fashions in science. But in his vexation at human activity, he prolongs the temper of a much older age in science, and more the temper of physics than biology. It is the attitude of an exact scientist, who throws up his hands on meeting with ineradicable diversity and irreduceable quality. For Draper, men ought to be a middle term between the law-abiding atom and the orderly society; and if the issue had been put to him directly, he might sometimes have hesitated to say that they were not. But in a rather different context, he does say so. A good deal of his political writing then takes the form of urging men to put themselves in touch with the fundamental orderliness of the world, to fit themselves into the terms of a scientific law. This counsel does not change the fact that, added together and averaged out, they are all going the legal way anyhow.

The reader who enters sympathetically into Draper's books on history and politics will find himself going about in this way—from admiring the form of nature, to straining after conduct, and back. His writings belong in part to the secret life of the poem—and the sermon. But they are meant to belong to the history of science, and this is the intellectual tragedy of Draper's career. He was entitled to raise a paean to nature or to scold mankind. He was not entitled for this purpose to put forward an allegory as a scientific proposition. But he did not think of it as an allegory; or he would not have made the use of it which he did. It was scientific light that Draper wished to throw about him, not mere psychic warmth (or cold). This steady consecration, often betrayed in practice, made Draper feel that the end of his career was continuous with the beginning, the writing of history with the study of the spectrum.

Chapter VII

ROCK-PIGEONS AND APES

In 1843 Draper remitted the author's royalty on an American edition of Robert Kane's chemistry, and got an invitation in return:

> I wish very much you would come over to the Meeting [of the British Association for the Advancement of Science] at Cork in August. I expect [J. B. A.] Dumas, and Arago will be with us. Do not attend to what the English journals say about disturbance. The people are determined to keep quiet, and after the meeting when you should come with us to Killarney and the Shannon, you will find yourself almost at home steaming on a river 200 miles from the sea, passing from Lake to Lake as if you were looking at America through the wrong end of a telescope.[1]

Draper sent a paper for Kane to read at Cork, but kept out of the reach of Young Ireland.[2] It was nearly twenty years before he went back to Europe. Perhaps the desire to go was whetted by the visit of his sons John and Henry in 1857.[3] After finishing their medical studies at New York University, they had gone abroad for a year. They attended the British Association at Dublin, and Henry got from the Earl of Rosse's observatory at Parsonstown the idea of building his own.[4] He had begun to do so on his father's grounds in 1860.

As the summer vacation of that year approached, Draper wrote to Alexander Dallas Bache, the superintendent of the United States Coast Survey, asking for a letter of introduction to George M. Dallas, Buchanan's minister to Great Britain.[5] "Expecting to spend my vacation there and in France," he would like "to be so provided if occasion should arise." With or without the letter, Draper, his wife Antonia, and their daughter Virginia sailed on June 6 from New York harbor on board the *Persia,* bound for England—"where I have not been for nearly thirty years." [6] But he had been there often in spirit—trying to keep up his American home according to the standards of an English gentleman (the roast beef was dry and the silver was laid in the English manner), aiming his memoirs at an English audience by way of the *Philosophical Magazine,* and sending his daguerreotypes to the great Herschel.[7]

They talked together at last; and Herschel sent some advice to Henry about the telescope at Hastings.[8] But this was an agreeable by-product of Draper's main purpose. He was being sucked to the Oxford meeting of the British Association at the end of June, by the whirlwind of Darwinism. By this time the Association had split into armed camps. Ink had been shed in the quarterlies, and members were falling in behind the bishops or the biologists according to an intricate system of alliances. It was recognized on both sides that a great deal turned on gaining the moral ascendancy in Section D, the organization of the life scientists (with whom Draper now classed himself). The advantage lay with the anti-Darwinians, who could swamp their enemies in a great crowd of amateurs from this and other sections. For just this reason, the evolutionists shied away from a debate: "a general audience, in which sentiment would unduly interfere with intellect, was not the public before which such a discussion should be carried on." [9] There was nothing left for the clergymen and their scientist friends but to infuriate their opponents into replying regardless of better judgment: "there were facts [it was said] by which the public could come to some conclusion with regard to the probabilities of the truth of Mr. Darwin's theory." [10] Anyone could judge the bearing of the fact that the brain of the gorilla "presented more differences, as compared with the brain of man, than it did when compared with the brains of the very lowest and most problematical of the Quadrumana." [11]

On Thursday, June 28, this remark of Richard Owen, the acerb controversialist who was priming the clergy with data, stung T. H. Huxley into a "direct and unqualified contradiction"—but not a debate.[12] Huxley would "justify" himself elsewhere. But his enemies had no intention of letting the weight of uninformed public opinion be lifted off the scales by settling the issue in scholarly publications. Both sides must be forced to submit the quarrel to the general public in Section D. There was a lull on Friday the twenty-ninth, but on Saturday Draper was down for a paper in this section "On the Intellectual Development of Europe, Considered with Reference to the Views of Mr. Darwin and Others, that the Progression of Organisms Is Determined by Law." Word went out that Samuel Wilberforce, Bishop of Oxford, would seize the occasion to "smash Darwin."

Darwin, who stayed at home, would as soon have died, he later wrote, as "tried to answer the Bishop in such an assembly." [13] His lieutenants on the ground felt the same way. Huxley decided to go join his wife on Saturday morning, and so cut Section D altogether.[14] But on Friday he ran into Robert Chambers, the author of *Vestiges of Creation,* and let himself be talked into "having his share" at the session next day, rather than seem to desert his friends. Joseph Hooker, the young botanist who had been collaborating with Darwin for almost twenty years, had been taking moonlight "saunters," dreaming over the Radcliffe Camera, and sleeping in the drowsy college gardens, with but one firm purpose—not to attend the Association.[15] But on Saturday morning he walked along to the sections with an old friend from the Ross Antarctic Expedition. Still another Darwinian got swept along to Section D. "Johnnie" Green, the future historian, met a friend on his way to the Lecture Room of the University Museum "to hear the Bishop of Oxford smash Darwin." [16]

"Smash Darwin! Smash the Pyramids," said I, in great wrath, and muttering something about "impertinence," which caused Jenkins to explain that "the Bishop was a first-class in mathematics, you know, and so has a right to treat on scientific matters" . . . .

With rising excitement spectators poured into the Lecture Room of the Museum till they threatened to burst its walls, and the session was transferred to the Library in the same building.[17] At least 700 people pushed into this long "west room" to steam in its suffocating atmosphere.[18] Along the windows on the west side the members' women were packed together, with white handkerchiefs in readiness to signal the victor.[19] Mrs. Draper and her daughter were among them.[20] In the middle of the room the clergymen made a great mass of white chokers and black coats ready to bear down on the Darwinites with still blacker looks.[21] A little knot of undergraduates, clustering together in the northwest corner to cheer for the other side, made a poor showing by comparison.[22]

Along the east side between the two doors, the president of Section D, John Stevens Henslow, professor of botany in Cambridge, took the chair in the center; thirty years before he had recommended Darwin as naturalist on the *Beagle*.[23] In the audience Admiral Robert Fitzroy, captain of the *Beagle*, reflected on the waywardness of his former shipmate.[24] On Henslow's far left sat Mr. Dingle, "a clergyman from Lancaster, near Durham." Joseph Hooker slipped into a seat in front of Dingle, on the assumption that the meeting could bore him no worse than idleness: a narrow face in its early forties, more sensitive even than the general run of Richmond's sitters, with sideburns merging into chin-whiskers, disproportionately bushy brows, and disheveled hair.[25] Alongside Hooker sat John Lubbock, then in his early twenties, fair, fine-featured, and overlaid by sideburns, mustache, and two-horned beard.[26] Nearer the center Lionel Beale, the microscopist from King's College, and old Sir Benjamin Brodie, nearly eighty, a former surgeon to William IV and Victoria, with obligations to God, Church, and Queen, sat close around Huxley.[27]

Clean-shaven except for sideburns, with a great mane of black hair, excessively dark brows, piercing dark eyes, large nose tilted up at the end, and thin mobile lips, Huxley despaired of getting a grip on the

JOHN WILLIAM DRAPER

smooth slippery surface of "Soapy Sam" Wilberforce.[28] Arriving late, the bishop thrust his way through the crowd with the decision of the man who had revived the power of the Convocations—brisker than his father the philanthropist and on better terms with established opinion.[29] Much of a physical type with Huxley, Wilberforce took his seat to the right of Henslow, alongside the official speaker of the day, John William Draper.[30]

After Henslow brought the meeting to order, the section ground at a majestic pace through its business of the day: a report on dredging in Dublin Bay, an account of an insect of "anomalous character," an invitation from Professor Charles Daubeny to visit the experimental garden under his direction in the vicinity of Oxford, another report on dredging, an announcement that the first part of Blackwell's British spiders was completed, and a paper by Cuthbert Collingwood "On Recurrent Animal Form, and Its Significance in Systematic Zoology." [31]

At last it was time for the principal paper. Draper now had his revenge for years of comparative neglect by European scientists. He was the focus of all eyes as he rose, dark, with mutton-chop whiskers, grave dignity triumphant over a plumpish sort of figure mounted on short legs.[32] His address took considerably more than an hour to deliver. As the general restlessness grew, the audience had at hand the worst of insults: he was a "Yankee donkey," he was pouring forth a great torrent of "nasal Yankeeism," he was asking in his "American accents": "Air we a fortuitous concourse of atoms?"—he was delaying Wilberforce.[33] Impatience would have found some other vent if the listeners had known that Draper was originally North of England. (His family and his students in New York also thought that he had a distinct accent—British and about halfway to Scotland.)[34] If nothing more, he droned—"droned out his paper, turning first to the right hand and then to the left." [35]

If the speech seemed dull gray to the audience, it must have pulsed with emotional gratification for Draper. Once more he was protesting against the notion that the world was a toy in the hands of a capricious tyrant.

The author introduced his subject [the annual report of the British Association recorded] by recalling proofs of the dominion of law in the three great lines of the manifestation of life:—first, in the successive stages of development of every individual from the earliest rudiment to maturity; second, in the numberless organic forms now living contemporaneously with us, and constituting the animal series; third, in the orderly appearance of that grand succession, which in the slow lapse of geological times has emerged, constituting the life of the earth, showing therefore not only the evidences, but also proofs of the dominion of law over the world of life.[36]

This was well enough, but Draper also wanted to build a science of society. He thought that his work in physiology at New York University had brought him to the very doorstep of this science:

. . . it is physiologically impossible to separate the individual from the race, . . . what holds good for the one holds good for the other too, . . . man is the Archetype of Society, and individual development the model of social progress, . . . both . . . under the control of immutable law; . . . a parallel exists between individual and national life in this, that the production, life, and death of an organic particle in the person, answers to the production, life, and death of a person in the nation.[37]

After assimilating history to physiology in the manner of the Saint-Simonians, whom there is otherwise no reason to suppose he knew, and of Comte, whom he almost certainly did know, Draper then pushed ahead along the lines laid down by Comte: from the example of the ancient Greek "nation," it was possible to determine a law of variation in Greek opinion, "and to establish its analogy with that of the variations of opinion in individual life." [38] "Passing to the consideration of Europe in the aggregate, Professor Draper showed that it has already in part repeated these phases in its intellectual life." [39] And passing to the controversy which he was supposed to clarify, he concluded by sounding the note of evolution.

He showed that the advances of men are due to external and not to interior influences, and that in this respect a nation is like a seed, which can only develope [sic] when conditions are favourable, and then only in a definite way; that the time for psychical change corresponds with that for physical, and that a nation cannot advance except its material condition be touched, this having been the case throughout all Europe . . . ; that all organisms, and even men, are dependent for their characteristics, continuance, and life, on the physical conditions under which they live; that the existing apparent invariability presented by the world of organization is the direct consequence of the physical equilibrium; but that, if that should suffer modification, in an instant the fanciful doctrine of the immutability of species would be brought to its proper value. The organic world appears to be in repose because natural influences have reached an equilibrium.[40]

Draper had flung the challenge to his neighbor Wilberforce, and the tension was building to an explosion.

Henslow announced that no one would be allowed to speak unless he had valid arguments on one side or the other.[41] But this did not deter "a layman from Brompton," belonging to the new Economic section of the Association, or the Reverend Mr. Richard Greswell, an old Oxford don, Gladstone's election chairman, and "re-founder" of the National School Society, or the Mr. Dingle of deplorable memory.[42] The layman from Brompton spoke out for theology in a loud

voice, Greswell denied in a thin pipe that any parallel could be drawn
between the intellectual progress of man and the physical development of lower animals, and Dingle rushed boldly to the blackboard
to sketch a diagram.[43] "Let this point A be man, and let that point B
be the mawnkey." [44] The rumbling discontent with these "vague dec-
lamations" now swelled into a raucous whoop of "Mawnkey! Mawnkey!" [45] The chairman had to say that he would tolerate no further
arguments which did not rest on scientific grounds.[46] Evidently he
meant by this that he would hear no one but established scientists or
pretenders to the title, for old Sir Benjamin Brodie rose to repudiate
Darwin, credited man with the unique possession of self-conscious-
ness, and equated this with the "Divine Intelligence"—which could
not have originated in lower organisms.[47]

With the audience already in a frenzy of anticipation, Wilberforce
got up in response to cries for his opinion—and yielded to Professor
Beale, who called for a fair discussion but denied that he was competent to take part himself.[48] At last the bishop took the floor and
kept it for half an hour.

His voice was musical, his manner was plausible, and his sentences
were graceful, in the opinion of an unfriendly observer, Joseph
Hooker.[49] In fact the bishop was sweeping the audience along with
disastrous ease on a tide of light, scoffing, fluent ridicule. He mocked
at the long-legged sheep of which the Darwinians talked, he laid down
the proposition that rock-pigeons, from the beginning of time to the
end, shared the same uniform rock-pigeon-ness, and, reaching for another triumph in the line of sarcasm, turned to ask Huxley a question.[50] There has never been perfect agreement on the form of the
question, but the point was plain: was it Huxley's grandfather or his
grandmother who transmitted the line of descent from an ape.[51] Huxley slapped his knee and whispered to Sir Benjamin Brodie, "The
Lord hath delivered him into mine hands," of which the venerable
old gentleman made less than nothing.[52] For the moment the Lord
had delivered Wilberforce into the hands of his sympathizers who let
out a great roar of approval or waved their white handkerchiefs according to sex.[53]

Huxley waited for the tumult to die down and then responded to
calls for his reply.[54] He spoke drily till he drove home his thrust that
he would rather descend from an ape than a shallow rhetorician ap-
pealing to religious prejudice.[55] A great gasp followed, broken up by
Lady Brewster's fainting and having to be carried out.[56] It came as a
poignant anticlimax for Admiral Robert Fitzroy, the captain of the
Beagle, to cry out that he had often rebuked his former shipmate Darwin for running counter to the first chapter of Genesis.[57] Lubbock and
Hooker, however, got the discussion back on the main track by fur-

ther exposing the weakness of the bishop's argument.[58] The meeting then broke up. Draper and the other supporters of Darwin left the room under the pressure of "fierce party spirit" and "looks of bitter hatred" from the majority of the audience.[59] "As we passed through the crowd we felt that we were expected to say 'how abominably the Bishop was treated'—or to be considered outcasts and detestable." To the end of Draper's life the whole scene must have been the validating image for him of intellectual conservatism—fine ladies and educated gentlemen trying to roll the weight of fixed opinions over a new idea and then dispatching what was left of it with the weapons of social intercourse.

Many of the leading participants went the same evening to hear post-mortems in the rooms of Professor Daubeny.[60] Draper was almost certainly among them, for his second published memoir had dealt with some of Daubeny's work and correspondence between the two survives.[61] If so, Draper saw the black coats and white cravats of Oxford reluctantly conceding that Huxley had the better of Wilberforce in manners if nothing more. But Huxley did not seem altogether happy with his triumph.

I gathered [one of the guests later wrote] from Mr. Huxley's look when I spoke to him at Dr. Daubeny's that he was not quite satisfied to have been forced to take so personal a tone—it a little jarred on his fine taste. But it was the Bishop who first struck the insolent note of personal attack.[62]

Yet Huxley by replying in kind, only better, had risen at last to the bait offered by the opponents of evolution. He had appealed to the court of general public opinion, and so helped to bathe Darwinism in emotional imprecisions.

Wilberforce had sinned against fair play, and Huxley rapped him across the knuckles. By the bishop's unexpected lapse from urbanity, something had been saved for the Darwinians. But from their point of view the day's battle had been fought out on altogether the wrong ground. In this respect Draper was almost a worse offender than Wilberforce. Indeed, the issue between them was curiously equivocal.

Draper had spoken out for Darwin, and the bishop had "smashed" him and his works; but they met with much the same response from the inner circle of Darwinians, a kind of restless contempt for men out of their depth. Draper and Wilberforce spoke on opposite sides, but they did not escape their common heritage and the tone of the age. In spite of everything, they *would* examine Darwin's theory in the light of its effect on the average Western man of the nineteenth century. The hardheaded scientists had the right to protest that this would open the gates to a flood of sentimental nonsense, on the order of Wilberforce's own address. It is far from certain that Draper's effort to see all the ramifications of evolution was either irrelevant or unneedful; but the effort left something to be desired in point of skill, and he chose his occasion badly.

Both men saw, or at least sensed, that the emotions would feel the impress of the new theory. It was not for them a limited-liability enterprise, but an assault, for better or worse, on the whole intellectual, emotional, and ethical structure of the European world. The theory of evolution could not be quarantined; it must spread its contagion from one end to the other of human thought and through the whole range of final commitments within which thought operates. Draper and Wilberforce insisted on facing this fact; but strategically it was not the part of wisdom for the Darwinians. The more they fought free of emotional implications, the better for the acceptance of their theories. It does not detract in the least from Isaac Newton's sincerity to say that his figure of having gathered merely a few pebbles along the fathomless ocean of knowledge was just the thing for injecting the theory of gravitation quietly into the curriculum of Harvard College. But in the long run it was of no use: the whole beach was turned over in his name, and the Deists launched countless ships on the great sea itself.

Draper—and, as a debating stratagem, Wilberforce—meant to play the same role to Darwin which the Deists had played to Newton. They came forward to insist on holding up to the light the furthest implications of Darwinism. One of these was the place of man in the universe. Wilberforce made the error of crying out that Darwin had degraded man, and must on that account be wrong. Draper accepted the theory, and tried to point out its consolations. There can be little doubt that, confused and sometimes quite mistaken as they both were, they had fetched up a real problem: the affective response of human beings to scientific theory, not so much for its particular content closely examined as for its imagined bearing on the zest of the whole human enterprise. Never mind about the details of natural selection, Wilberforce said in effect, but wouldn't it be disgusting to have come of a long line of monkeys? And isn't there some kind of emotional reflex which tells you that you didn't? For his part, Draper in failing to show persuasively what natural selection had to do with his "laws of society" was not so much examining Darwinism as raising a paean to any new evidence of a scientifically constructed universe.

To the great mass of people who were trying to make out whether they should be cheerful over evolution, or downcast, Draper offered the comfort that the world was at least intelligible to men. It was built to be understood by man; maybe not to preserve or cherish him, but to meet the demands of his intelligence and of his sense for form. Draper could at least offer the solace—when it came to facing the issue, he always declared for its consolations—that behind the prevailing winds and variable water levels of omnipotent Nature, there was some kind of sustaining force acting in ways comprehensible to men (in fact, rather simple). One must know his background to see that this is not so much a neutral statement of fact as a means of feeding a great emotional hunger for apprehending the form of the universe as a whole. It was perhaps unscientific of him to heed this appetite, but he had a surer instinct than the cautious intimates of Darwin about the historical role of the theory of evolution. So had Wilberforce. But Draper accepted the probable explanations which science could offer, and struck out honestly to see if he could find any comfort attached. The intelligibility of the universe was his solution to the problem, but (on rather preposterous grounds) he added the shrewd proviso that this would not satisfy forever.

If he accommodated himself to Darwinism as well as he could, he still rubbed the real experimentalists among Darwin's friends the wrong way. He was helping to throw to all the sleeping dogs of Christendom the great bone of contention: the change in *man's* status effected by Darwin. Instinctively they would rather have piled evidence on evidence till men cried, "it is so" than raised at the outset the whole of the question "what does it *mean* for us who found it out? what does it mean for the emotional and intellectual habitat of ordinary Victorian man?"

Chapter VIII

THE WEB OF HISTORY

THE full-length history of European thought, projected by Draper in his *Physiology* of 1856 and sketched before the Oxford meeting in 1860, had a complicated history of its own. In his original preface, dated 1861, Draper wrote of *The Intellectual Development of Europe:*

> In the Preface to the second edition of my Physiology, published in 1858, it was mentioned that this work was at that time written. The changes that have been made since in it have been chiefly with a view of condensing it. The discussion of several scientific questions, such as that of the origin of species, which have recently attracted public attention so strongly, has, however, remained untouched, the principles offered being the same as presented in the former work in 1856.[1]

This is clearly designed to meet the challenge that he cribbed from Darwin, after the publication of the *Origin.*[2] It may, or may not, be intended to show also that Draper had finished his book before the appearance of the first volume of H. T. Buckle's *History of Civilization* in 1857.

On both points, it seems fairly certain that Draper had arrived at his conclusions independently. Belief in evolution and interest in the historical bearing of the physical environment go much further back than either Darwin or Buckle. Without question both ideas had taken firm root in Draper's thinking at least as early as the beginning of the 1850's.[3] When it is added that the resemblance between the three books is not at all close, one would be hard put to avoid the conclusion that Draper, for better or worse, copied neither of the others. Neither Darwin nor Buckle wrote to the accompaniment of piano selections from Bellini's *La Sonnambula;* but Draper says that *he* did.[4] And this is not a bad index to the radical difference in tone. The three men shared in a common European tradition, which it is no stranger to find bursting out everywhere at once than a rash of mechanical inventions of the same kind.

The dates of publication, however, of Draper's book gave him the appearance of bringing up the rear behind Darwin and Buckle. His old publisher, Harper's, waited till 1863 to issue the new work (copyrighted in 1862); and the British edition did not appear till 1864. Trübner wrote in June 1863 offering to import sheets but not to print a new edition, but Draper preferred "one of the great publishing houses." [5] "What I seek is an extensive circulation." In the interest of baiting the hook, he sent seventy-five copies to a graduate of the New York University Medical School, then in London, for distribution among the leading scientists and philosophers.[6] The response was disappointing. Herbert Spencer read the table of contents and some of the marginal heads, and he thought that when he got around to it the text would "interest" him.[7] "It bears on the face of it, an aspect of scientific comprehensiveness, which I am glad to see showing itself in the treatment of the subject—a subject which has hitherto been left in the hands of men who were little more than learned gossips." But owing to bad health, Spencer never read a book unless it bore directly on his writing of the moment; and Draper would have to wait. John Tyndall, of the Royal Institution, wrote to say that the book—which he had not had time to read through—took "courage as well as ability on the part of its author." [8] He hoped the time was coming when the word "courage" would not "need to be applied to any undertaking which consists in the earnest utterance of a man's convictions." But if Draper expected one of the recipients to thrust his book on an English publisher, he was mistaken. His personal agent took the work to John Murray and the Macmillans, but Murray refused at once and, after taking several weeks to think the matter over, Macmillan also turned it down.[9] Meanwhile Draper got no word from the agent, and then got direct word from Bell and Daldy of London that they would meet £250 of the cost of publishing, if he would meet the remaining £100, with an equal division of any profit.[10] This proposal was, in fact, the doing of his agent, on whom Draper now vented his exasperation at not making a better bargain.[11] But he took the offer, and Bell and Daldy brought out the *Intellectual Development* in 1864, with a careful excision of American spelling and some American allusions—"as you wish it to appear as an English book by an Englishman." [12] So far as one can make out Draper was always proud of coming from England. But it was merely good business to play down the origin of his book at a time when the educated classes abroad had seldom been more hostile toward the United States.

In order not to lose sight of the single impetus which carried Draper forward from his *Physiology* to his Oxford address and the publication of the *Intellectual Development,* it seems best to treat the history in succession to the address. Stripped of Darwinian terminology, the speech to the British Association must have resembled quite closely the sketch with which Draper began to write his book. It therefore seems logical to proceed from a kind of table of contents, in the Oxford paper, to the text; though historically the order seems to have been reversed.[13]

Draper tried to write the history of Western thought from the beginning of civilization to his own day. The emotional climax of the book is the vain effort of Roman Catholicism to hold back the universal dominion of the scientific spirit. The popes appear as the heads of an enormous bureaucracy tyrannizing over the minds of men, and sacrificing the advance of reason and science to the cause of continued faith in the supernatural. The chapters dealing with earlier history are best approached as a kind of backward extension of this conflict.

If not arbitrary, Draper's allotment of space is highly selective, in keeping with his thesis about the great tug-of-war in the history of thought. By far the largest part of the book deals with Greek philosophy, the rise of Islam, the worst days of the popes, and the history of science and technology (mainly from Galileo forward). In treating these subjects Draper made no pretense of independent research, but neither did he provide footnotes for his sources.[14] Among historians and philosophers of history he mentions only Bodin, Bunsen, Niebuhr, Macaulay, and Froude.[15] Buckle, next to Comte the man whose temper was closest to Draper's, makes no appearance. If Draper had read Grote, the rehabilitation of the Sophists carried no conviction.[16] But no one can doubt that Draper founded his book on the bedrock of *The Decline and Fall of the Roman Empire,* and it is curious to find no reference to Gibbon—except on the premise that this debt was self-evident. In any event, Draper was trying to construct out of the soundest scholarship available, not a text with citations, but a new synthesis.

Perhaps it would be fairer to admit that the synthesis went before, wagging the data behind it; but for Draper it was their appointed destiny to bring up the rear behind the particular thesis which he was defending. He did not limit himself to one, or rid the book of gross contradictions.

In the main, however, Draper tried to sketch the pattern of history after the manner of Auguste Comte, with one curious addition. The great collective person Mankind passed through the ages of thought as individuals passed from youth to death. Pascal was right: ". . . 'the entire succession of men, through the whole course of ages, must be regarded as one man, always living and incessantly learning.' "[17] Like the individual, the race passed from theology through metaphysics to positive, that is, scientific, thought. But generally Draper does not mean the whole human race, but some organic portion of it, say, the ancient Greek "nation." Indeed, given Draper's line of argument, there had to be a *succession* of these different social organisms. They are born, if their luck is good they reach their prime, and they surely die. Unless the human race were to peter out, others of these collective, but more than collective, beings would have to spring up. Draper's science of history is therefore not unfairly to be described as the result of mixing up together Shakespeare's seven ages of man and Comte's three stages of thought. But, in fact, one cannot mix the oil of cyclical theories with the water of the theory of progress (prolonged by Comte into the law of three stages). Comte did not expect that the positivistic temper would be snuffed out; once the management of society, or any part of it, got into the hands of mature men and women, themselves in the third stage, there was no intrinsic reason for having to slip back. Indeed, a good deal of Draper's own writing speaks the conviction that one can make good the intellectual advance of mankind—reach the ground he preferred, take one's stand, and hold fast. But when he was true to his own peculiar thesis, the nineteenth century could not regard enlightened science as a secure possession forever; within the cycle progress occurred but failed to sustain itself. Civilizations rose, but they also went under.

Apart from this adaptation of Comte's law of three stages, Draper explored the relation of the environment of peoples to their history, and made of enveloping Nature the compulsive force behind all of history. By this standard the biography of a nation consisted in its adjustment to its natural setting. This idea, with its Darwinian connotations, may not be radically incompatible with the three stages of Comte, and the physiological stages of Draper. The environment may conceivably be as rigorous a systematizer as Comte or Draper—or God. But no one would recognize in such a trim and calculating Nature the haphazard old sloven of Darwin. If Draper had always accommodated his laws of history to his environmentalism, he would have been guilty of an astonishing multiplication of hypotheses and rending of traditions to very little fresh advantage. Naturalistic evolution is a substitute for the anthropomorphic God who laid down orderly decrees; and the law of three stages is a secular version of these decrees, in a limited area. Put them together, and the combination is a rather infertile transposition of old ideas, which if torn apart could shake the world. Draper does sometimes put them together, but by no means always. On this score it would be better to convict him of a recurring contradiction than vindicate his consistency altogether. And he does often seem in practice to be swinging back and forth from evolutionary biology to Positivistic history. In the main he cut with the knife of each theory in alternation; but this was better than always trying to wield them together, and never cutting at all.

In addition to these two major issues, Draper let himself be swept along by a want of thesis, in the tradition of earlier historians. If he drew on them tendentiously, he did not always lop off their irrelevancies regarded from his own point of view.

No one today would read the *Intellectual Development* for the light which it throws on its subject.[18] But it is full of prescriptions for setting the right value on historical events and attitudes. For the most part these prescriptions amount to the necessity for the reader's seizing an idea, tearing it up by the roots, and transplanting it in the nineteenth century. Ideas out of the Middle Ages either wither in the new climate or survive by being falsified from the start. But Draper was not indulging in capricious distortions cut off from the felt wants of his time. Indeed, he came to terms with all of history by an exaggerated response to his own day. This response had the double effect of making his temper profoundly unhistorical and his book a quarry for the historian of nineteenth-century ideas. It is a nexus of Victorian traditions concerning the European past—history brought abreast of current thought and action.

It will be convenient to disentangle as far as possible three great traditions in Draper's thinking: Christian theology, the Enlightenment projected forward into nineteenth-century liberalism, and science as he construed it. If the point is not pressed too far, one might with some justice identify these traditions, in their origin but not in their duration, with stages in Draper's own career—his youth in a Wesleyan manse; his meeting with the temper of the Enlightenment prolonged in a most selective way by the Utilitarian founders of University College and by Comte; and his research in radiant energy and his teaching of physiology in the medical school of New York University. But great care must be taken not to discriminate these traditions, as they existed in Draper, too sharply. It will be evident in some cases (and demonstrable in others) that the language of the *philosophes* and the biologists served only to mediate between Draper and residual theology—to clothe old yearnings in new respectability. But even if one should grant that *all* the strains in his thought took their common rise from Christianity, one could not ignore the role of mediating traditions in bringing about real displacement from one view of the world to another. Indeed, it is a sufficient innovation merely to select particular ideas from any given whole and discard the rest. In this way Draper selected out God the engineer from God the father and God the judge. But he was also overly thrifty of the lessons he had already learned, so that something new, like Darwin's theory of evolution, was often assimilated to something older, like the stages of Comte, and the particular impetus of one idea deadened by the other. Much of the interest of the *Intellectual Development* now consists in this mingling and dissevering of traditions. A form of natural theology bore Draper along into the main current of the Enlightenment; the Enlightenment extended into liberalism made an appeal of its own; and ideas which he took to be scientific qualified his liberalism in the profoundest way. But this qualification was already implicit in the theological side of his temper.

Among the Christian dogmas transmitted by Draper full-strength, the most important was the comprehension of the world at a gulp. He crammed his zest for scientific innovation well within the bounds of basic security about the nature of things. From change and confusion he pointed to stability and order: shook off the distaste for life by going "behind" it.

If from visible forms we turn to directing law, how vast is the difference. We pass from the finite, the momentary, the incidental, the conditioned, to the illimitable, the eternal, the necessary, the unshackled.[19]

I am to lead my reader . . . from the outward phantasmagorial illusions which surround us, and so ostentatiously obtrude themselves on our attention, to something that lies in silence and strength behind. I am to draw his thoughts from the tangible to the invisible, from the limited to the universal, from the changeable to the invariable, from the transitory to the eternal; from the expedients and volitions so largely amusing the life of man, to the predestined and resistless issuing from the fiat of God.[20]

It is a paean to life and nature wrung dry of their human significance and valued for unlikeness to themselves as known to men. In this mood Draper was a victim of "metaphysical pathos,"—in the form of a craving for infinity, eternity, and stability.[21] The swarming diversities of life are written off as illusions. There is, indeed, a nervous overcertification of the fraud, as if the capacity to be cheated were flooding back. But his lapses from conviction do not remove the *will* to conviction—the will to "justify" the world of sense all together and all at once. This resolve is almost the critical test of the theological temper.

It need scarcely be added that Draper constructed a kind of godhead to subsume the principles of order in the universe. The great difficulty in defining God is to avoid whittling Him down for the purposes of discussion—to show Him the sum of many attributes, and something more—the perfectly elusive mystery, and something less; to keep from putting limitations on divinity, and yet stay just this side of letting the idea float away in a cloud of in-definition. Draper cannot be said to have solved this insoluble problem. But he meant to rid the notion of the "Almighty Being" of as many limitations as he could. In particular he rejected the attribute of persistent activity on the order of human beings.

. . . it is a more noble view of the government of this world to impute its order to a penetrating wisdom, which could foresee consequences throughout a future eternity, and provide for them in the original plan at the outset, than to invoke the perpetual intervention of an ever-acting spiritual agency for the purpose of warding off misfortunes that might happen, and setting things to rights.[22]

To operate by expedients is for the creature, to operate by law for the Creator; and so far from the doctrine that creations and extinctions are carried on by a foreseen and predestined ordinance—a system which works of itself without need of any intermeddling—being an unworthy, an ignoble conception, it is completely in unison with the resistless movements of the mechanism of the universe, with whatever is orderly, symmetrical, and beautiful upon earth, and with all the dread magnificence of the heavens.[23]

In the setting of evolution, the effect of this is to leave the history of the world as much shot through with purpose as ever. But teleology now shifts from the intermittent proclamations of God to the physical environment. In a sense, God has been emptied out upon "nature." (There is a strong, if not rigorous, strain of pantheism in Draper.) Draper's position here approaches very nearly that of Asa Gray—nature as the chosen instrument of the primary cause. But Draper accommodates theology to science, not as an ingenious second-best to the old religion but as the only view of the world compatible with the "wisdom" and "nobility" of God. It is an excellent example of the reassertion in the noonday of Victorianism of a stubborn theologian's problem: how to conceive of God "worthily," to delimit the illimitable. It is at least curious that this persistent concern in European thought (which Draper felt as far back as one can trace his opinions) should end by helping to earn for him the reputation of an advanced thinker.

In the same tradition which predisposed Draper to embrace Darwin, much of Protestant theology drew back from describing God's form. Draper rebukes Milton for producing in *Paradise Lost* "a dreadful materialization of the great and invisible God." [24] And he quotes with evident relish from the General Scholium at the end of the third book of Newton's *Principia*:

The Supreme God exists necessarily, and by the same necessity he exists *always* and *every where*. Whence, also, he is all similar, all eye, all ear, all brain, all arm, all power to perceive, to understand, and to act, but in a manner not at all human, not at all corporeal; in a manner utterly unknown to us. As a blind man has no idea of colors, so have we no idea of the manner by which the all-wise God perceives and understands all things. He is utterly void of all body and bodily figure, and can therefore neither be seen, nor heard, nor touched, nor ought to be worshiped under the representation of any corporeal thing. We have ideas of his attributes, but what the real substance of any thing is we know not.[25]

If we ask, then, what God is like, the response is that we hardly know, but "not at all human." At every turn Draper vents his scorn on "anthropoid conceptions" of God.[26] This is partly his effort to differentiate the creator from the created. But he seems also to be indulging his intermittent contempt for the distinctively human aspects of existence. At very least he inclines to a dispassionate view of human concerns; at times he spends on the short lives and small pleasures of men the indignation and scorn of an ascetic. If man could see the whole of nature, "well might he ask what had become of all the aspirations and anxieties, the pleasures and agonies of life." [27] "Well might he incline . . . to question . . . whether beneath the vastness, energy, and immutable course of a moving world, there lay concealed the feebleness and imbecility of man." [28] It is "outward phantasmagorial illusions" that surround and engross man; and his attention moves "in a reluctant path" from "the expedients and volitions so largely amusing the life of man, to the predestined and resistless issuing from the fiat of God." [29]

It was part of the same mood for Draper to sketch the role which science has played in affecting the view which men take of themselves.

Is the earth the greatest and most noble body in the universe, round which, as an immovable centre, the sun, and the various planets, and stars revolve, ministering by their light and other qualities to the wants and pleasures of man, or is it an insignificant orb—a mere point—submissively revolving, among a crowd of compeers and superiors, around a central sun? The former of these views was authoritatively asserted by the Church; the latter, timidly suggested by a few thoughtful and religious men at first, in the end gathered strength and carried the day.

Behind this physical question—a mere scientific problem—lay something of the utmost importance—the position of man in the universe.[30]

The result of the discoveries of Copernicus and Galileo was thus to bring the earth to her real position of subordination and to give sublimer views of the universe.[31]

This view that the astronomical revolution shook the self-esteem of the men who witnessed it is probably a myth.[32] But it is an extremely tenacious myth in recent times, so that it must gratify a felt need for self-abasement. Just so, for Draper it was the glory of science to have given man a properly low estimate of his own importance.

. . . when he looks upon the countless multitude of stars—when he reflects that all he sees are only a little portion of those which exist, yet that each is a light and life-giving sun to multitudes of opaque, and, therefore, invisible worlds—when he considers the enormous size of these various bodies and their immeasurable distance from one another, [he] may form an estimate of the scale of the magnitude on which the world is constructed, and learn therefrom his own unspeakable insignificance.[33]

And a good thing, too, because this experience defines the progress from error to truth: "from anthropocentric ideas, which in all nations and parts of the world have ever been the same, to the discovery of . . . [man's] true position and insignificance in the universe."[34]

It is hard to escape the conclusion that this view of science springs from the flagellation of man and the denigration of earthly existence in the Christian tradition, with an effort to make of man's place in the drama of the universe as much an occasion for humility as anything else about him. Yet there is just room, both in Christian determinism and in Draper, for men to slip through with their best gifts intact; just room for Draper to elude the full force of John Dewey's taunt that the theological temper legislates intellectual irresponsibility.[35] Thus Draper ends by protesting that in spite of everything we are wrong if we suppose that science has really degraded man:

It might appear that . . . [astronomical revelations] must necessarily have for their consequences the diminution and degradation of man, the rendering him too worthless an object for God's regard. But here again we fall into an error. True, we have debased his animal value, and taught him how little he is—how insignificant are the evils, how vain the pleasures of his life. But, as respects his intellectual principle, how does the matter stand? What is it that has thus been measuring the terrestrial world, and weighing it in a balance? What is it that has been standing on the sun, and marking out the orbits and boundaries of the solar system? What is it that has descended into the infinite abysses of space, examined the countless worlds that they contain, and compared and contrasted them together? What is it that has shown itself capable of dealing with magnitudes that are infinite, even of comparing infinites together? What is it that has not hesitated to trace things in their history through a past eternity, and been found capable of regarding equally the transitory momen. and endless duration? That which is competent to do all this, so far from being degraded, rises before us with an air of surpassing grandeur and inappreciable worth. It is the soul of man.[36]

Modern science humiliates man, but then it is his own creation; no other form of life could calculate its significance at all. It is a reminiscence of the old conjunction in Christian theology—consciousness, and consciousness of sin—now transposed into knowledge, and knowledge of one's smallness. If the power of taking thought, and diminishing the thinker, is the highest reach of men, Draper would have them pay the price, rise to their potentialities, see the world straight—and see themselves small. His whole book is saturated with the assurance that the only way to do this is by an independent effort of the individual.

By this insistence on shaking down his opinions for himself—with its theological roots in the obligation of men to be all that they were fitted to be—Draper joined hands with the Enlightenment. He was also its heir independent of the direct theological tradition. Both in content and tone, the *Intellectual Development* bears in great part a striking resemblance to Condorcet's *Esquisse d'un tableau historique des progrès de l'esprit humain,* the last proclamation of the *philosophes.*[37]

New tyrants and old tyrannies, old superstitions and fresh believers, lay between Condorcet and Draper; but one side of Draper's temper kept faith with the Enlightenment. De Maistre had said of it that it was "the insurrection of the individual reason against the general reason," "the enemy at bottom of every belief common to men, and therefore the enemy of the human race." [38] But Draper preserved intact the spirit of the Encyclopedia. He glorified the crumbling of the medieval unity so much lamented by De Maistre, glorified it in the perspective of a still untarnished opportunity to make a new whole out of the diversities of European thought. He wanted to blow on the fever of controversy, cool thought into new canons of faith and security.

Draper would have made De Maistre a free gift of one of chief indictments brought against Protestantism by its enemies:

It was in the nature of Protestantism from its outset that it was not constructive. Unlike its great antagonist, it contained no fundamental principle that could combine distant communities and foreign countries together.[39]

For the attainment of his aims the Protestant had only wishes, the Catholic had a will.[40]

But this was the best thing that could possibly have happened: "The predestined issue of sectarian differences and dissensions is individual liberty of thought." [41]

If, then, the Reformation marks the onset of free inquiry, Draper makes the American Revolution the beginning of the second great epoch in the war for liberation. For "Macaulay and others who have treated of the Reformation have taken too limited a view of it, supposing that . . . [toleration] was its point of arrest." [42] The new departures dating from the Declaration of Independence, the Constitution, and the Bill of Rights, praised and attacked on many grounds, now fall into place as ushering in freedom of opinion—with the equal conflict of creeds the last concession wrung from the old regime.

[Free trade in ideas] . . . made another enormous stride when, at the American Revolution, the State and the Church were solemnly and openly dissevered from one another. Now might the vaticinations of the prophets of evil expect to find credit; a great people had irrevocably broken off its politics from its theology, and it might surely have been expected that the unbridled interests, and instincts, and passions of men would have dragged every thing into the abyss of anarchy.[43]

Yet none of this has occurred, and religion itself thrives on voluntarism.

Given perfect freedom of thought, Draper turns to the portrayal of the great universal society within men's reach. It is the same community already found to be just *out* of reach of Condorcet and Tom Paine—with the serpent Unreason stuffed as a trophy. The presiding deity is Progress (by Free Schooling out of Sentimentality).

. . . I come to the conclusion that in the unanimous consent of the entire human race lies the human criterion of truth—a criterion, in its turn, capable of increased precision with the diffusion of enlightenment and knowledge. For this reason, I do not look upon the prospects of humanity in so cheerless a light as they did of old. On the contrary, every thing seems full of hope. Good auguries may be drawn for philosophy from the great mechanical and material inventions which multiply the means of intercommunication, and, it may be said, annihilate terrestrial distances. In the intellectual collisions that must ensue, in the melting down of opinions, in the examinations and analyses of nations, truth will come forth. Whatever can not stand that ordeal must submit to its fate. Lies and imposture, no matter how powerfully sustained, must prepare to depart. In that supreme tribunal man may place implicit confidence.[44]

The difference between this and millenary Christianity is very great —and quite small. The immediate affinity, however, is with the blander spirits of the Enlightenment. Draper had a good eye for the worm in man, but not the devil. Voltaire would have praised him for a poker-faced satirist in writing of physicians and lawyers—in the prime of Daumier and the young manhood of Anatole France!— [45]

. . . they never sought for a perpetuation of power by schemes of vast organization, never attempted to delude mankind by stupendous impostures, never compelled them to desist from the expression of their thoughts, and even from thinking, by alliance with civil power.[46]

If the great men of the Enlightenment would mostly have choked on this passage, an Apostle's Creed of the minor Illuminati might nevertheless be compiled from the *Intellectual Development*. Polish up a man's wits, and morality will take care of itself. "The morality of man is enhanced by the improvement of his intellect. . . ." [47] Trust that superstition will vanish like fog before sunshine some morning very soon. "Who is there now that pays fees to a relic or goes to a saint-shrine to be cured?" [48] Put your faith in machines. "Good auguries may be drawn . . . from the great mechanical and material inventions which multiply the means of intercommunication, . . . annihilate terrestrial distances." [49] Above all, rest very certain that men

will tax their minds if only given the chance: ". . . the more opportunity men have for reflection the more they will think." [50] Taking
his stand on these sure foundations of faith, Draper balanced the accounts of the Age of Reason.

There has not been a progress in physical conditions only—a securing of
better food, better clothing, better shelter, swifter locomotion, the procure-
ment of individual happiness, an extension of the term of life.[51]

There has been [also] a great moral advancement. Such atrocities as those
mentioned [earlier] . . . are now impossible, and so unlike our own manners that doubtless we read of them at first with incredulity, and with difficulty are brought to believe that these are the things our ancestors did.
What a difference between the dilatoriness of the past, its objectless exertions, its unsatisfactory end, and the energy, the well-directed intentions
of the present age, which have already yielded results like the prodigies of
romance.[52]

All of this has come of free trade in ideas. It is a Sursum Corda of
utilitarian liberalism—a projection into the nineteenth century of
certain elements in the Enlightenment; Draper's substitute for the
common faith of the Middle Ages. The object of this new faith is the
inevitable triumph of free inquiry as the means to happiness—soon.
Yet in retrospect the easy confidence of Draper's book—not the thesis
but the superb assurance—makes him not so much the prophet of the
coming age as one of the last untroubled voices of the old.

The *Intellectual Development* is in this sense a kind of first draft
of the last testament of the Age of Mazzini and Mill. Men want to be
free, if you set them free they will rise to the occasion, and they would
rather think than feel their way into the future. The shrewd reviewer
for the *Continental*, recognizing Draper's book as an eloquent statement of the liberal formula, put his finger on what the formula left
out; and his criticism is worth reading as a direct inversion of Draper's own thought.

There are but comparatively few individuals . . . so highly developed in
their intellectual and moral capacities . . . to be a law unto themselves
in the general conduct of life. The great mass of mankind, even in the most
advanced communities, need still the guiding hand of a wisely constituted
and really paternal Government, and the religious admonitions of a true
priesthood.[53]

The degradation, squalor, ignorance, disrespect, dishonesty, and moral
blindness of the middle orders; and the apathy, heartlessness, unscrupulous-
ness, selfishness, cupidity, and irreligion of the upper stratum of Society,
are alike due to the absence of a rightly organized State, which should
command the allegiance, and of a rightly constituted Church, which should
absorb the devotion, of the whole community.[54]

Church and State do their best work in acting as a drag on the progress of individual liberty of opinion.

Much of this review must have affronted and shaken the side of Draper that was uppermost in the *Intellectual Development*. It was a reminder of the misuse and the mistrust of self-reliant reason, and the recuperative powers which they gave to authority in the face of attack. But Draper mostly had the assurance to thrust such reminders aside. The desire to know the truth on one's own would make its way —and bring social healing with it.[55]

It was part of Draper's confidence to advocate free trade in opinions, and to defend the right of the wrong to be heard. He never argues for any sort of hindrance to Roman Catholicism other than the kind of open debate which he thinks will show it up. He seems to have no apprehension at all that an idea could descend into the marketplace of opinion, and then prosper by proposing to shut the market up. Anxiety on this score must turn in some degree on the conviction that there is a great fund of unreason to be tapped and an immense fatigue with thinking to be assuaged. It follows that none of these fears could assail a good Victorian who believed in the unconquerable will of mankind to fight its way toward the truth. And the author of the *Intellectual Development* was the nearest of Draper's personae to the core of nineteenth-century liberalism. Yet the book was an effort to accommodate history to science; and the way in which Draper put the two of them together displayed the sharp limits and the radical equivocations of his liberalism.

In the scientific thought of his time Draper set the most store by Positivism and evolutionary biology: the former with its vision of all learning reduced to science, the latter with its close rationale of the new faith. This subordination of Darwin to Comte is unmistakable. When the *Origin of Species* appeared, between the writing of the *Intellectual Development* and its publication, Draper's response was a kind of bland complacence, as if Positivism had drained off the capacity to be shocked by Darwin. (The equanimity verging on indifference of another Positivist, George Eliot, is an interesting parallel.) The book proved to be too long for the publisher's taste, and had to be cut accordingly; but Draper does not seem to have crossed out, watered down, or ripped up any part of his manuscript on Darwin's account. Yet from Draper's point of view natural selection proved altogether too much: the oneness of the universe (which he was glad to have); plus the moral aimlessness of the great unity (and he wanted no part of this).

For Comte and Draper the universe was neither "open" nor neutral. In the *Intellectual Development* Draper adapted from Comte— without credit—the law of the three stages through which the indi-

vidual and society were bound to pass. Draper grafted on to this law
his own notion of historical cycles, but inside their appointed limits
they both held that history was unfolding according to plot. And
recognizable human values were subserved by the plot. Draper had
rejected the proposition that God was improvising, but he could not
tolerate the third possibility that there was no compulsive blueprint,
of human significance, at all. This would have left him with the very
same confusing world of sense which he had made up his mind to see
under the aspect of eternity.[56] He seems not to have grasped—and
would not after all have welcomed—the possibilities of natural selection for a radically "un-anthropoid" view of the universe. He spent
the last twenty-five years of his life in the atmosphere of Darwinism—
one of its most famous champions—untroubled, so far as we can
judge, in his serenity that the universe was as much steeped in higher
purpose as it was at the noontime of the medieval church. (This does
not change the fact that in expounding his environmentalism he often
appears to be—not *shaken* in his sense of cosmic purpose—but *forget-
ful* of it.)

On this side Draper may not have profited as he ought from nineteenth-century theories of evolution; but he took to heart the idea
of the encroachment of physical surroundings on the development of
men. The modern interest in physiography as a conditioning factor
of history and politics is at least as old as Bodin, a good deal older
than Montesquieu, Turgot, and Fichte, and very much older than
Draper, Buckle, or Ratzel.[57] The new work left to be done by the
nineteenth and twentieth centuries was minute investigation of the
effect of sharply defined physiographic factors on the history of particular communities at particular times. This work Buckle and Ratzel
may have forwarded, but Draper did not. In the *Intellectual Development* perhaps the only plausible case-history which he offers to prove
the effect of physiography is the ejection of nomads into Europe by
changes in the geological level of the Near East and the consequent
drying up of rivers.[58] It was Draper's role instead to help popularize
the geographical factor in history, and to capitalize for this purpose
on the climate of opinion created by Evolution.

The word "evolution" yields the echo "Darwin." But for the historian of biology the echo is equivocal and serves as a reminder that
evolutionary speculation was no late growth in the nineteenth century but a vigorous perennial with its roots in the eighteenth—the
legacy of Erasmus Darwin as well as Charles. The grandfather sym-
bolizes the persistent tradition of nature-philosophizing to which
Draper really belonged (in this context)—a great loose rag-bag of a
tradition into which natural selection was dropped without too much
inspection. In Draper this tradition took the form of compounding

together respect for the advance of scientific biology and delusive facility in composing biological analogies.[59]

As Benedetto Croce said of Taine, Draper belongs in this respect to the history of "cultural fashions"—"a typical representative of the fanatical interest in the natural sciences, and especially in medicine, which, after 1850, filled a good forty years of European life, accompanied by . . . efforts to remodel the whole of culture on a similar basis." [60] The new element was the conviction that biological analogies were not mere aids to communication or objects of contemplation—metaphysical or aesthetic counters—or even analogies at all, but validated truths of empirical science.

In Draper this "fanaticism" made history a branch of physiology, in the line of descent from the Saint-Simonians and Comte (without the saving reservations of the best minds among them).

The life of an individual is a miniature of the life of a nation.[61]

The equilibrium and movement of humanity are altogether physiological phenomena.[62]

If, indeed, history is the story of great social "organisms," a physiologist will wish to know what constitutes health for such patients. Draper replies, "the attainment of a correspondence with the conditions to which the type is exposed." [63]

If from its original seats a whole nation were transposed to some new abode, in which the climate, the seasons, the aspect of nature were altogether different, it would appear spontaneously in all its parts to commence a movement to come into harmony with the new conditions—a movement of a secular nature, and implying the consumption of many generations for its accomplishment.[64]

Here Draper belongs to the pertinacious current in Western thought which has filled the magical word "nature" with the wildest variety of meanings and intimations of meaning, and then found repose in contemplating this great entity as the normative force in history.[65]

In this fight for health, a new kind of social diagnostician can lend a hand—such a man as Draper himself. This practitioner must be intent on getting the whole body politic to pull together. The individual cells and organs strike the physician as being of no importance except for their bearing on the continued existence of an organic whole. Just so, Draper found in society that superior end, rich in significance and purpose, which gave a point to the aimless individuality of particular men.

It may be offensive to our pride, but it is none the less true, that in his social progress, the free-will of which man so boasts himself in his individual capacity disappears as an active influence, and the domination of general and inflexible laws becomes manifest. The free-will of the individual is supplanted by instinct and automatism in the race.[66]

It is by no means certain that this passage communicates any intelligible idea, but the animus behind it seems fairly clear—the resolve to lend to society, instead of the individual, the meaningfulness and dignity which Draper associated with "the dominion of law."

Here Draper was taking his share in one of the great enterprises of the nineteenth century—the rehabilitation of society as against the contractual man of the eighteenth. But for him (in this context) the individual did not so much diminish as dissipate into thin air. The personality of whom *he* had a vivid apprehension was the social organism; and this organism has the appearance of a kind of natural datum handed down from above, on which the will of particular men and women could never lay hold. A great many people were busy vindicating the claims of society; Draper breathed life into it and allowed it to devour its old enemies, the men of Locke's contract. His book helped in this way to breed the monstrous, willful Leviathan which took to itself in the twentieth century the old respect for the human personality. His was more the case of failure to explore the logical implications of his thought than of conscious dissent from liberalism. But his recoil from individualism—from the radical want of system in the human race below the level of the social organism which somehow knit up into scientific law the confusions of free activity—was explicit, and hostile to much of the liberal tradition.

In this way Draper put together in one book his strivings after natural theology, his commitments to freedom, and his genuflections before science. But the theologian in him, and the scientist, were sometimes inclined to despise the ragged discipline of the free. This need not, however, obscure the vindication of free inquiry which is the characteristic note of the book.

If it is possible to make out all kinds of internal strains in the *Intellectual Development,* and profound equivocations in Draper's liberalism, he himself had very little consciousness of the fact. He had no fears that his thought would fall apart, but simply that the coherent ideas for which he stood would meet with resistance from people lagging behind in the intellectual progress of the nineteenth century. For his own taste he had made a gratifying whole of science and liberalism, and pursued their congenial principles as far as they led. The question was: had everyone the same courage and insight? When he received a flattering letter from Robert Chambers, the author of the *Vestiges of Creation,* in return for a copy of the American edition of the new history, Draper thanked him and added:

In America the work has had in one sense a great success having passed to a third large edition in a year but as you very well know it was not to be expected that such views could be presented without opposition[.] And accordingly it has had in some quarters opposition of a malignantly bitter kind—But that has only served to bring it under the protection of a more intelligent class who have done this as much from a sense of duty to the [last two words doubtful] cause of truth as out of friendship to me.

The final success will however depend on the success of the reprint which is being issued by Messrs Bell & Daldy in London. In America we are still to no small extent colonial in literary matters, the verdict of English critics determines public [illegible; "opinion?"] here[.] And so I look forward to the treatment it will receive on your side of the Atlantic with no little anxiety, hoping that the sentiment [?] which has so powerfully intervened in its behalf here will intervene there too. And that the more advanced thinkers to whom its shortcomings & defects will be plain enough will treat it with generosity in consideration of the end it has in view and the social risks its author has not hesitated to encounter in the cause of liberty of thought.[67]

The book met with a mixed response on both sides of the ocean, but the most favorable notices in major journals came from England. The *Westminster Review,* the great organ of the Utilitarians, George Eliot's old journal, praised Draper's work, with reservations about the biological analogy, as "graceful," sometimes "eloquent," "indisputably true" in its general principle, and "for the most part correct and felicitous" in "the particular exemplifications" of his thesis.[68] The *Anthropological Review* claimed the book for its own, "a valuable contribution to the science of anthropology." [69] The *Saturday Review,* on the other hand, struck out at "coarse" and "rank" materialism, unprecedented in European thought.[70] After a sneer at Draper's having let the book go to press unaltered by the outbreak of the Civil War—"It is perhaps only characteristic of the American mind that formulas previously laid down should stand absolutely unaffected by the revolution of the last few years."—the *Saturday Review* ended on a surprisingly gentle note.[71]

In the special portions of his history Professor Draper displays a remarkable industry, vigour, and skill. His narrative is accurate and graphic, and his grasp of historical truth powerful and tenacious. The work has thus a real value as a comprehensive summary of facts, apart from the particular theories of philosophy which it is intended to uphold. Indeed, it is surprising how little such abstract theories really affect the practical treatment of historical subjects.[72]

In the United States, the *North American Review* thought that Draper had not done his work with an "unerring hand," but this was hardly to have been expected in a task of such size.

To have made the attempt is of itself a great merit and a high achievement. His work must take its place as among the most truly original, profound, and instructive contributions of the age, in the department of speculative philosophy.[73]

The short-lived *Continental* ran a series of four articles which treated Draper and Buckle as important thinkers of great merit, both of whom overestimated intelligence as the mainspring of human conduct. The *Atlantic*, however, attacked Draper's book with great vehemence.[74] Its tendency was materialistic; and he showed "no tokens of an intelligence sufficiently subtile, penetrating, and profound" for the task which he had set himself.[75] But the reviewer added, curiously enough, that the analogy between man and society was "genuine," "a rich mine" making the book "of grave importance." [76] Only the *New York Times* among the commercial press seems to have attacked Draper without reserve.[77] The famous analogy was "not only a very old notion," but "very feeble and unimportant" besides. Moreover, Draper dealt with no historical problem on his vaunted "physiological principles." The book was an indifferent sort of hodge-podge: ". . . its main fault, aside from its feeble and stupid *theory*, is the utter lack of logical faculty in the author. There is in the book any quantity of material, but it perfectly responds to CARLYLE's definition of history: '*Dead rubbish shot here.'* "

The *Intellectual Development* was better received than might have been expected in the religious press of the United States. Draper got decidedly favorable reviews from the *Lutheran Observer* of Philadelphia, the Unitarian *Christian Register,* the Methodist *Christian Advocate and Journal,* the Protestant Episcopal *Christian Times,* and the *Presbyterian Witness.*[78] The *Christian Register* may have hit upon the explanation in remarking that Draper dealt with European church history in a spirit "entirely Protestant." [79]

On the other side of the fence, several religious organs found that Draper had sown his pages with free thought and heresy.[80] He avoided stating in so many words that Christianity had the same kind of "natural" history as other ideas; nevertheless, he failed in fact to demonstrate that Christianity differed from any other belief in its origins or sanctions; and he talked of the decline of peoples as the consequence of the revolving of historical cycles instead of faithlessness to Christian principles of conduct.

Every thing in man and in the universe [the Catholic, Orestes A. Brownson, interpreted Draper as arguing] is generated or developed by physiological or natural laws, and follows them in all their variations and changes. Religion, then, must be a natural production, generated by man, in conjunction with nature, and modified, changed, or destroyed, according to the physical causes to which he is subjected in time and place. This is partially true,

or, at least, not manifestly false in all respects of the various pagan superstitions, and many facts may be cited that seem to prove it; but it is manifestly not true of the patriarchal, Jewish, and Christian religion, and the
only way to make it appear true, is not to distinguish that religion from the
others, to include all religions in one and the same category, and conclude
that what they prove to be partially true of a part, is and must be true of
the whole.

The cause [for the decline of peoples] is in the loss of religious faith, in
the lack of moral and religious instruction, in the spread of naturalism,
and the rejection of supernatural grace—without which the natural cannot
be sustained in its integrity—in the growth of luxury, and the assertion of
material goods or sensible pleasures, as the end and aim of life.[81]

And Draper works for precisely this end. The heart of Brownson's
attack is his insistence that Draper measure scientific "truths" alongside the even better truths of revealed religion.

. . . no reason or argument [wrote another such reviewer] can be more
legitimate than the proof that the new [scientific] doctrine does not under-
mine the foundations of Religion or Morality: for it is the method of true
Science to compare truths together, and to test the unknown by the known.[82]

It is evident that revelation of the one God is the true "known." Of
this argument, it can only be said that it plays fast and loose with the
connotations of the word "science" in the nineteenth century, and
tries to strip it of all accretions since the Middle Ages. The critic who
wrote in this vein quite properly fixed on Draper as an enemy.

All these criticisms of Draper found their most compact dimensions
in the form of naming his kindred spirits: the book was "very Buckle-
ish," it showed "some leanings" toward Darwin and Lyell, it was a
compound of "the familiar odors, the nard of Comte, the cassia of
Buckle, and the frankincense of Grote," and for "superficial sophis-
try" there had been nothing comparable since that old heathen
Volney.[83]

Vituperation aside, the book was in fact a forerunner of two new
kinds of history: intellectual and "physiographic." Draper made very
little of the latter—and too much. On the side of extravagance, his
conviction that the environment had shaped human history suggested
that societies were a kind of biological organism. On the other hand,
Draper did much less than he might have done in offering specific
examples of the impact of the environment. The few which he cites
are weakly handled into the bargain.

He had got hold of an important thesis, destined to be fruitful, but
dependent for carrying conviction on the most patient discrimination
of historical factors. The task called for steady nerves, an infinite tolerance of the merely tentative, and the lightness of touch for sorting

out the filaments in the largest, finest cobweb ever spun. But Draper
was quick, bold, and insensitive—intent on chopping his way through
history with a great axe of a thesis to speed things along.

This thesis was the direct and unmitigated influence of the physical
environment. Yet even when Turner's Western man finds himself
flung backward in time, he is still bent on pushing ahead of him the
frontier of European civilization. But he finds that he could not easily
compass, even if he wanted to, the preservation in the wilderness of
the whole complex—silk knee-pants and Christian religion, Latin
grammar schools and laissez-faire, entail and the Paris mode—but
must pick and choose, exercise a kind of cultural economy in the face
of natural obstacles. This imposition of economies must often have
been what Draper had in mind in writing the *Intellectual Development*. But when he confronts the issue directly, he appears to say that
history is a rough, one-sided sport which consists in the irresistible
pummeling of mankind by the environment. It is the business of a
philosopher of history to make his ideas clear, and his clear ideas
sufficient. But when Draper's environmentalism is stretched to cover
the facts, it is no longer clear (hardly even overt), and when it is clear
it will not reach. He fed the interest in the physical setting of history,
but scarcely more.

In the field of intellectual history, Draper not only pointed the
way but made a respectable start.[84] This side of the *Intellectual Development* made many readers look back upon it as a crucial stage in
their education of themselves: the means for cutting loose from every
species of authoritarianism. The struggle between religion, symboliz-
ing all claims on the blind devotion of men, and science, freeing them
of any obligation except the honest pursuit of knowledge, is neither
the whole story of religion or of science, nor the whole history of European thought. But the fact that Draper claims too much for his
subject cannot destroy the force and eloquence with which he treats a
monumental theme.

In spite of grave faults and bitter criticism this theme carried the
Intellectual Development around the world in American, English,
German, French, Polish, Danish, Swedish, Spanish, and Russian editions.[85] The book had a long life on Harper's list; they were reprint-
ing as late as 1918.[86] To judge its impact, one must make the most of
scattered clues. Draper heard directly from a celebrated palaeontologist, Joseph Leidy (the best American book of a philosophical character he knew, it would "classify with" Buckle and Darwin), an unknown Austrian ("in my eyes you are an extraordinary waymaker
and reformer in historical writing"), and a famous historian, George
Bancroft, the Romantic poet of the American nation (who called the
book "great").[87] And he heard indirectly that when the son of the

great physiologist Rudolf Virchow (also the inventor of the word *Kulturkampf*) left home to pursue his studies, his father gave him one book only, the *Intellectual Development*.[88] Yet in Draper's own lifetime the influence of the book had only begun to ramify. The businessman-historian of the next age, James Ford Rhodes, who took Draper's course in geology at New York University, recalled from his college days that "I read two books that mark an epoch in my intellectual life—Buckle's 'History of Civilization' and Draper's 'Intellectual Development of Europe.' " [89] A New England college professor thinks that the book did more than anything else to set him to questioning as a boy the standards of a narrowly religious upbringing at the beginning of the twentieth century.[90] And a Southern lawyer who went into politics reads Plato's *Dialogues,* Grote's *Plato,* and Mill's *Autobiography* and *On Liberty.*

But there are two authors whom he has read even more assiduously: Jefferson . . . ; and John W. Draper, whose highly libertarian *Intellectual Development of Europe* he has read four or five times. The curious may even now turn to the *Congressional Record* for 1929 and read [Senator, later Mr. Justice, Hugo L.] Black's fervid speech against the Treasury bill for censoring books from abroad, in which he quoted Draper's account of the burning of the Alexandria library. . . .[91]

Chapter IX

THE REIGN OF REASON

Whatever may be our personal political leanings, we cannot mistake the signs of the times. We hear men speak of civil service bills, of the desirability of putting the right man in the right place. What does all this mean? Is it that we are blindly groping after something the necessity of which we urgently feel, but the substance of which we do not as yet completely grasp? Is it that we all instinctively realize that in human societies, as in the human individual, as the epoch of mature life is reached, all wishes and acts must be brought in subordination to intelligence, and that reason must rule? Is it because we all instinctively believe that a nation to be truly great must aim at something higher than its material interests; that the declaration of the Roman historian is as true now as it was in those old times when he said, "The pomp of wealth is delusive and transitory, but the glory of intellectual power is illustrious and immortal?"
—John W. Draper, *Address Delivered to the American Union Academy of Literature, Science, and Art* (Washington, 1870), pp. 13–14.

WHEN the Civil War broke out, the American Photographical Society of New York, of which Draper was the perpetual president, offered its services to the War Department, which intimated in the bad summer of 1861 that it had better things to do than investigate the military uses of photography.[1] This seems to be as close as Draper ever got to making a direct contribution to the war, unless he accepted the invitation of the Sanitary Commission, the predecessor of the American Red Cross, to inspect military hospitals.[2] There appears to be no evidence that he did; he was not, of course, a practicing physician.

Draper's youngest son, Daniel, whose health was thought to be too poor for the army, worked as an apprentice at the Novelty Iron Works in Brooklyn, where he helped to build the *Monitor*.[3] The two older boys, John Christopher and Henry, then twenty-seven and twenty-five, got commissioned as surgeons with the Twelfth Regiment of the New York State Militia, and went off to Fort McHenry and then Harpers Ferry for three months' service beginning in June 1862.[4] With trying to keep Henry, his favorite, up to date on the astronomical photographs taken at the Hastings observatory, and making a couple trips "in the cars" to see his sons in camp, the father found himself busy.[5] In October, however, Henry was mustered out with the "Chickahominy fever," which he had picked up in the swamps along the Monocacy.[6] He promptly went back to his important work at the observatory. It would be hard to imagine a greater contrast with the crowds of men, the dust of the march, and the threat of battle.

The surrounding country on the banks of the North River is occupied by country seats, on the slopes and summits of ridges of low hills, and no offensive manufactories vitiate the atmosphere with smoke. Our grounds are sufficiently extensive to exclude the near passages of vehicles, and to avoid tremor and other annoyances.

An uninterrupted horizon is commanded in every direction, except where trees near the dwelling house cut off a few degrees toward the southwest. The advantages of the location are very great, and often when the valleys round are filled with foggy exhalations, there is a clear sky over the Observatory, the mist flowing down like a great stream, and losing itself in the chasm through which the Hudson here passes.[7]

It was a good place for the son to take his photographs and the father to write his books—a place of "refuge and repose" as one correspondent wrote after the draft riots of 1863, "in the late shameful & lamentable riots which disturbed your great city." [8]

In terms of service the Drapers got off rather easily—though the boys did a great deal more than was socially incumbent on people of their class in the North. But the father felt the war, as Walt Whitman wanted him to feel it:

Through the windows—through doors—burst like a ruthless force,

.   .   .   .

Into the school where the scholar is studying.

The note struck by Draper's students in their recollections of him is more nearly respect than affection—he moves along the hall on his way to class, a little heavy around the middle and decidedly short in the legs, in his black clothes and silk hat, with a firm, deliberate step, repressing any hilarity en route—invariably polite but seldom familiar.[9] But he frequently saw to it that a poor boy had no tuition to pay.[10] (When one of these men tried to pay him back with compound interest for twenty years, he refused on the condition that the money be used to help some other student: "Go, do thou as I have done unto you." [11]) And there seems to have been a long-standing tradition of a New Year's reception at Hastings for his students.[12] He must therefore have felt some anxiety for them in wartime. Quite apart from this, the current classes at New York University shrank. This decline meant among other things less income in the way of tuition fees. For a time in the mid-fifties the collegiate professors got no salary at all, but merely divided the tuition among them.[13] In 1860, when they were once more getting a salary, $1,425 a year, they urged the Council to set up an endowment of $20,000 and drop tuition fees altogether.[14]

This would have been in line with a general tendency at that period to slash the fees or remove them entirely. A drastic cut by Columbia College made the issue pressing for its chief rival; but it was one thing to propose an endowment and another to find the money.[15] Apart from the nominal value of their pay, the faculty had to keep an eye on their real income. Along with the other professors in the college Draper appealed in December 1862 for a rise in salary to $2,000 on the ground that inflation was pinching them badly.[16] Draper must also have felt the serious decline in the enrollment of the medical school, which had always drawn heavily on the Southern states. So far as we know, he had steady tenants for his "cottages" in Hastings; at any rate Mrs. Farragut was one, and there was a good deal of running back and forth between the households by the young people, and some mild romancing between the Draper daughters and a Farragut boy.[17]

In addition to seeing his sons go into the army and the war industries and watching his income shrink, Draper had the special torment of being a native of Great Britain—and a strong Union man. He saw his two countries drifting further and further apart, and he seems in the end to have lost patience with the British attitude toward the war. When an unidentified British journalist asked him to write some articles to present the Northern case to the English public, Draper refused for want of time; but he added:

> If I thought I could be the means of bringing to the knowledge of English leaders a more correct appreciation of the state of affairs here and also of our mutual international relations I would find time notwithstanding . . . to write to you occasionally.

> It would affect you deeply were you here to find what an alienation has arisen since your visit[.] You would see it in every rank of society. It springs from a profound conviction that in our moment of [illegible; "greatest peril"?] England has been less true to us [canceled: "in a moment of national peril"] than even France or Spain.[18]

Robert Chambers, the fighting old evolutionist, writing to congratulate Draper on the *Intellectual Development of Europe,* inferred from the preface that

> you do not approve of the course which your country has pursued in regard to secession. If so, you have the great mass of British, indeed European[,] opinion backing you. Every step taken by your government since April 1861 seems to us a mistake, for gentle measures alone could win back such dissentients. While even the perfectest military success can only give you a wretched Poland to keep.[19]

Draper took this up with an obvious effort at moderation:

It has been my privilege to have more accurate means of forming a correct opinion respecting the troubles that have [illegible; "befallen"?] our Nation than have fallen to the opportunity of most persons. I have lived both in the South & in the North and have engaged the friendship of many of those who are prominent actors on both sides in these affairs. Never participating in political affairs but standing aloof from them I have endeavoured to look upon things with a philosophical & unprejudiced eye.

And this is the conclusion—Loyalty to the Government. I wish we could spend an hour together alone and I would ["irresistibly"?] bring you to the same result[.]

All this bloodshed and devastation will not be without its use[.] From being a people it is making us a nation[,] it is ridding us of slavery[.]

I look forward with hope to the time when American affairs will be better understood in Europe than they are now—and with confidence as to the issue. A great [illegible; "nation"?] can afford to wait[.]

Did you ever read the speech of Mr Stephens the present Vicepresident [sic] of the Southern Confederacy just previous to the outbreak of hostilities. If not the copy enclosed will interest you. He stands in the rebel ranks next to Jefferson Davis.[20]

Perhaps from fear of seeming wrought up, Draper canceled the paragraphs "All this bloodshed" and "Did you ever read." But they form as clear a statement as we have of his attitude toward the Civil War.

By far the most important consequence of the war for Draper was the impulse it gave for shaking down his views about politics (in the broadest sense of the term). Up to this point he had written rather loosely of a new science of history; now he began to apply the lessons of this science to American politics, which had gone wrong, as he thought, from want of skill. The landmarks are his "anniversary discourse" before the New York Academy of Medicine, *The Historical Influence of the Medical Profession,* of December 10, 1863; his lectures before the New York Historical Society on *The Historical Influence of Natural Causes,* delivered in February and March 1865; his expansion of these lectures into a new book, *Thoughts on the Future Civil Policy of America,* published in 1865; and his inaugural address as president of the American Union Academy of Literature, Science and Art in 1870.[21] They are so much of a piece that they can be treated as variations on a single theme.

In these writings Draper dealt with a tangle of related issues. How does one go about improving society? Granted that there is a science of society, what light does it throw on American history and politics? And what is the place of natural and social scientists in a democracy?

To the question, how can society advance, Draper returned the uncompromising answer: "To elevate or to depress a group of men, it is necessary to touch their physical condition." [22] It is impossible to judge how far this attitude is a revolt against the atmosphere of pietistic exhortation in which Draper grew up. He was breathing an altogether different atmosphere when he wrote: "We vainly attempt the improvement of a race, intellectually or morally, by missionary exertion or by education, unless we simultaneously touch its actual physical condition." [23] The man who wrote this would have joined with Robert Owen in proclaiming, "Man's character is made for, and not by, him." Both of them threw down the challenge to the eighteenth-century Age of Charity Schools which held that if the underprivileged would only impose a kind of moral strain on themselves, the social mechanism would go on turning quite well enough to make do.[24]

In this context Draper examined American history to see how it had been shaped by the physical setting. If his account is deficient in subtlety, it is clear and precise where the *Intellectual Development of Europe,* with its general propositions about the influence of geography on history, was vague and fuzzy.

Draper finds the key to American history in the amount of land and the methods used in cultivating it. "Agriculture has never been practiced in the United States. We are miners, not farmers." [25] Broad statements of this kind, history viewed from the mountain-peak, are common enough in Draper; but for once he had been in the valley himself, and had his own concrete experience as a control. He had lived in rural Virginia in the age of Ruffin (and owed his first job, with a Mineralogical Society, to the inspiration of Ruffin); his brother-in-law Daniel Gardner had written on agricultural chemistry within view of the exhausted soils of the Atlantic seaboard; and when Draper read, as he almost certainly did read, the discussion by Liebig of soil depletion in Virginia, he could descend from large theories to small particulars of his own observation.[26] This experience informs his parallel between mining soil and mining gold.

What, then, is the difference between the Virginian, who has been setting tobacco-plants to collect the potash from his land, and the Californian, who has been employing men to wash his soil for gold? Both have sold or sent to other countries the inorganic material that was their source of wealth. Both have impoverished their estates. Both are miners.

But the land is exhausted. What next? It will cost more than the whole produce has brought to put the potash back. Then restoration of the old fields is out of the question. New ones must be sought. What does that mean? Nomadic life.

If the estate is large enough, perhaps it may last the old planter's time. But, as his sons grow up, field after field is destroyed. Their eyes are set on untouched lands in the West. Why should they reverence or love the daily deteriorating spot? Their hopes are elsewhere. So, moral results of the profoundest kind are springing from the physical conditions.[27]

Consider, now, what has been going on for the last two centuries along the whole Atlantic coast; for what I have said is only a forcible presentment of what has been going on everywhere. It holds good for the cotton, the wheat, the corn. From the shoreline there has been an onward march up the gentle incline of the continent. Strand after strand of fertile soil has yielded up its wealth. The front of the vast phalanx has already touched those regions where the rains are uncertain, and therefore the seasons unreliable. Beyond them is the untrodden desert. It were well if we all realized thoroughly that great fact! [28]

There were, then, physical conditions of sufficient power to put an end to that period of tranquillity which our predecessors vainly imagined would be perpetual. There must be rivalries for the mastery of the promised lands of the West! [29]

Given the two conditions of abundant land and "mining" agriculture, Draper thus portrays the American people as necessarily set in motion toward the West. The number, however, of abortive Turners and aborted essays on the frontier ought not to be swollen further. The pertinence and skill of Draper's analysis need not be eked out by displacing to him the merits of a greater man.

Draper argued that "extensive" cultivation and the supply of fresh land on which it depended helped to make the American people both restless and individualistic. Their mobility was all to the good, for they were trying to make one nation out of many physiographic regions. The danger was that these regions would each evolve a civilization in keeping with its climate, and the Union fly apart. The South was in fact the region which had worked out the closest adjustment to its peculiar physical setting, and made out a claim to independence on the basis of this adjustment.[30]

Now, since there is an unceasing tendency to the modification of the human system by the operation of climate, and evils ensue both by a community coming into repose, which is politically falling into a stagnant condition, and by the antagonisms that arise between coterminous communities that have thus passed into different states, it is very plain that the thing of primary importance to be accomplished is, as far as may be possible, to prevent such climate actions from reaching their full effect. This can only be done by promoting locomotion.

It is therefore unwise to give legislative encouragement to any thing that may tend to make communities, or even families, too stationary. Fortunately, the intentions of the statesman, in this respect, are greatly facilitated by the established usages respecting the inheritance of property and the incessant breaking up of estates. Not less effectual is the system of agriculture, if such it can be called, that we pursue—our practice of killing land. A soil that has undergone exhaustion of certain of its essential ingredients, as bone-earth, potash, or the like, can not be economically restored. It is much cheaper to abandon the ruined estate and move to the

virgin lands of the West. That love of the homestead, so characteristic of
the settled populations of Europe, can scarcely be said to exist among us.
The children leave their father's hearth without reluctance, for he is perpetually anticipating leaving it himself. It might have been feared—perhaps
was feared by many observant persons—that this loss of local patriotism
would imply the loss of national sentiment, but the experience of the civil
war has shown the incorrectness of such a foreboding.[31]

Foreigners were perfectly right in calling the Americans "a nomadic race." [32] "It is well for our future that we are so." [33] Draper
therefore laid down as "a settled principle of American legislation":
"to encourage in every possible manner facilities for intercommunication, to repress in the most effectual way any thing that might possibly act as a restraint." [34] If, indeed, for the last ten years the South
had been "pervaded by an unceasing stream of Northern travel in
every direction, the civil war would not have occurred." [35] But the
American restlessness had not taken that turn; so much the worse.

The abundance of new land to be taken up had the paradoxical
effect in Draper's opinion of fostering individualism and proving its
insufficiency. Like Turner, Draper concluded that the habit of shifting for oneself in all things had been confirmed by the prospect of
quenching a man's thirst for land. "A greed for gain, a desire for personal independence, and emancipation from domestic control, invade
the fireside and scatter the family." [36] Draper made clear that this is
what comes of being set down "in the vast field of a new continent,"
with political traditions to match.[37] It was helping to make society
"a chaos of human atoms." [38]

If pushing back the margin of new lands had produced individualism, this very process showed up the fraudulent maxim "each man for
himself." [39] Draper argued that settling fresh country forces men to
reconstruct society from the start—and to bind themselves in pursuit
of liberty. Thrown back upon themselves, the American pioneers had
made of their social instincts the great resource for setting themselves
free. Built from the beginning, social institutions liberate instead of
crushing. Thus, the Americans have had repeatedly the chance to
begin again their government of themselves, and to learn, what comes
hard to Europeans, that democracy and collectivism can be made to
march together. But in Europe the democrats had to clear away old
institutions, at the price of identifying democracy with a kind of
creeping anarchy.

. . . the essential difference between democracies in Europe and America—
that the former are destructive, the latter constructive.

This constructiveness is strikingly seen in new-settled American states.
Where, but a short time before, there was an untrodden wilderness, population began to converge—a village formed. In an incredibly short time, or-

ganization of the infant community might be observed; its outward signs, the school-house, the town-hall, the church, the newspaper. These differentiations from the growing body spontaneously issued from the people; they required no stimulus from above. The village rapidly grew into a town. All round it, in precisely like manner, other towns were emerging. The instinct of cohesion I have referred to combined them together; an organized territory, a state is the result. Constructive affinity still continues to be manifested, and the new state merges in to and becomes an acknowledged part of the Republic.[40]

The instinct of self-government, so characteristic of the American democracy, thus leads to the formation of villages, towns, counties, territories, states—nay, even to the expansion of the Republic itself. So far from centralization and self-government standing in opposition to each other, as some authors have supposed, the former necessarily issues out of the latter. Self-government, instead of conveying the idea of absolute freedom, conveys, in reality, the idea of restraint—restraint spontaneously imposed. If, as must be the case in self-conscious communities, that restraint is organized by those who are intending to submit to its rule, centralization is the necessary result.[41]

Now Draper himself pointed out that the new lands had, in fact, bred individualism. But no contradiction was involved. He was deducing logically what *ought* to be the habit of mind of men who have had to throw society together out of their desperate need. Leaving aside the real path-breakers, stubbornly private men like Boone, Draper pointed to the American past as the warrant for relaxing individualism; or rather, for containing it within respect for the society which made it possible. By his account, it was just this accommodation of the two goods—individualism and social sense—which had marked the advance from the Atlantic to the Pacific. But along with this had gone prodigal waste of natural resources.

A Virginia planter grows tobacco on his land until he has exhausted it. Of what avail to him is agricultural chemistry, with all its great discoveries? It might cost him five hundred dollars an acre to repair the mischief he has done to his estate; but he can buy virgin lands in the West at a dollar and a quarter an acre. Agricultural colleges are of no use to him. And so, for miles together in the Southern states, there are desolated and forsaken tracts—old fields, as they are called. But, if land is worth little, labor is worth much. Whoever can invent a labor-saving machine will make money. So our improvements are not in the direction of agricultural chemistry, but of agricultural mechanism.[42]

Here, then, were three products of the westward movement: a raging fever for independence; in spite of this, the reconstitution of society; and the reckless draining off of natural wealth. Draper was trying to disentangle the elements in this mixed legacy and determine their value. With the last he had no patience, but he hoped that the others could be put to good use—though the use of independence seems mostly to be to give it up.

He appealed to the American people for common effort, on the ground that they would simply be profiting from the real lessons of their history. In terms of the recent past, they ought to put behind them the reckless misuse of their resources. In more general terms, they ought to spend their energies to the greatest advantage, on expert advice. Though he used no such language, Draper seemed to be groping toward a planned society and a positive state.

This wasted energy, which we so easily recognize in individual life, necessarily occurs in the national life. In the settlement of this continent, in the utilization of its resources, in making it the fitting abode of millions of men, how numerous the mistakes, how much energy must be wasted for want of information, for want of a guide!

At the close of this century the inhabitants of the United States will exceed one hundred millions. Vast tracts of territory, now a wilderness, will be seats of civilization. In the settlement of these lands there will be a great, a needless consumption of life; there will be undertakings unwisely engaged in, involving great loss of capital. Improvements which would accelerate the progress and add to the happiness of this host of human beings will be neglected, and legislation meant for their advantage will prove inadequate, or, perhaps, prejudicial.[43]

Among the proposals which Draper put forward for avoiding "wasted energy" were as much control of the railroads by the federal government as would keep the country one great volatile mixture; systematic investigation of climatic conditions in the interest of farmers; and a giant project for river-management.

Are we to suppose that the industry of this continent is to be forever paralyzed in the summer months through want of water in the rivers? There falls rain enough to keep them all in full stage throughout the year. The management of these streams, though they run through many thousands of miles, is simply an affair of hydraulic engineering—a great but not an impossible task.[44]

That there is propriety in giving public aid toward the proper conduct of agriculture, mining, manufactures, and navigation has long ago been recognized by both the General and State Governments. It was this that led to the authorization of the Coast Survey, the Observatory, the Patent Office, the Agricultural Bureau, the Light-house Board, and the numerous State geological surveys and exploring expeditions as as [sic] those of Fremont.[45]

Draper trod rather lightly in discussing the control of population by the government. He would have nothing to do with birth control as public policy; but if the goal was *more* population, the means were at hand for encouraging it.[46] "More food, cheaper clothing, better houses, are insured by increased remunerative labor, and this is instantly followed by increase of numbers. These also are things which fall within the scope of enlightened legislation." [47] What "enlightened legislation" on these questions would mean, Draper neglected to say.

We ought not to make him out a doctrinaire of the planning state, if we mean by this that he would have swallowed whole the twentieth-century Leviathan. But he showed less than no concern for hedging the state about with checks and prohibitions. His views ought not, of course, to be ripped from their context in an American society which had more to fear from political paralysis than from galloping authoritarianism. But there is more to his attitude than a healthy reaction from the Age of Grab. The Positivistic view of history and politics which Draper had been exploring bred an authoritarian temper of its own. If his remarks are taken one by one, they often seem to reflect merely the beginnings of the conservation movement and the fanning of nationalism by the Civil War; but something has been added to these ideas, the tradition of social science by way of Comte. No doubt Draper's thinking was influenced by the war, and the current elevation of the national government above the states. But he clearly thought that the war had come simply as a confirmation of views which he already held (and held on grounds other than its approach). Though a notable change of emphasis, a waning libertarianism, gives him in some degree the lie, he is nevertheless drawing in a rather different context on ideas which he had already proclaimed. The effort therefore to assimilate Draper to men like Francis Lieber and John C. Hurd would be on the balance unsound.[48] It is conspicuously Draper who set the activity of the national government in the context of science, and of the scientific expert; and there is more affinity here with Comte than with the American philosophers of nationalism. It would, however, be absurd to claim that Draper succeeded in disengaging his particular ends from those of the people around him. That side of the conservation movement which took fire from Liebig has some place in Draper, and by the middle of the sixties Liebig had become a fund of commonplaces. But neither this nor the rest of the nascent conservation movement is the whole of Draper's thought. His basic presuppositions are different, and make for the continuing interest of his work. His political innovations are more procedural than substantive: the structure of power and the temper of the powerful are more distinctive than the immediate objects of power.

Believing as Draper did in the possibility of a social science deduced from the impact of the environment, he ran up against the problem of who was to practice this science, how, and to what end. At bottom it was the problem of trained intelligence in a free society. He could not help testing the issue whether the two could long survive in company. In making this test he almost seceded from the nineteenth-century liberalism of which the *Intellectual Development of Europe* formed (in great part) a minor landmark.

When Draper put to himself the question what was the great operative ideal of the American republic, he had no trouble in finding the answer. In a sense it was the same ideal which marked off American experience from European.

Every one [in the United States] is penetrated with the conviction that for social advancement to pursue the right direction, and to be pressed forward at the highest speed, it must be controlled by intelligence. Hence the public prosperity is considered to depend on education. There can be no doubt that this is a very high and noble conception. It establishes an intrinsic difference between the people of Europe and the people of America.

In Europe the attempt has been made to govern communities through their morals alone. The present state of that continent, at the close of so many centuries, shows how great the failure has been. In America, on the contrary, the attempt is to govern through intelligence. It will succeed.[49]

Faith in education set the Americans apart: "the public prosperity is considered to depend on education." Draper shared this faith—but not the end which informed it.

When he talked of the need for putting trained intelligence to work in harnessing the national energies, he could not help touching by implication a kind of sensitive nerve in every modern state: the *use* of education, whether to sort the leaders out or to mix them up together with the rest, make the steps from top to bottom of society insensible and the range itself narrow.

The reader who means to place, and weigh, Draper's thought must touch the issue for himself. If, on the one hand, the goal is to organize society on "right" principles, these might be handed down from above by leaders. If, on the other, the object is the growth of the whole people in dignity and fullness of personality, in a word, setting them free, loyalty to this ideal will be held to give society a kind of rightness to begin with; but the political structure then rests also on faith in the good sense of average people over a period of time. The polity must work, as well as recognize the claims of all its members (with the initial impetus which this may give). This proviso does not alter the view of democratic society as a kind of school—not to Greece but to the Athenians themselves. The growth of the individual is posited as a desideratum, so that it is better that he should grope his way toward right thinking—as on the whole he will—than have it thrust upon him, ready-made. This rather flexible standard, if adopted, may be thought to hold whether the good to be handed down from on high is saving religion in the eighteenth century, scientific politics in the nineteenth, or economic security in the twentieth. As these examples make clear, the tradition—the great ambient tradition of the American democracy—is more persistent than doctrinaire and more yielding than rigid. But Draper had more than half a mind to be at war with the whole idea.

Given the need, very clear to him, for men with enough intelligence to use a new science of politics in the common interest, he found American society splitting apart along the seams of a new class-structure.

Do what we may, no organization, no education will ever make all men alike. By far the most numerous portion of our race must devote itself to labor, scarcely ever learning any thing except what concerns its daily toil: whatever improvement it attains to is by mere imitation. It follows its hereditary instincts, having no idea of progress, none of development. Governed by external influences and by its own appetites, it can neither combine nor generalize. Its movements altogether depend on the unrecognized influence of external agents. That vast mass, like a cloud, drifts along to its destiny in an invisible wind.[50]

Draper made the same point by improvising on his old biological analogy:

. . . how visionary are the expectations of those who hope to produce, either by legal enactments or the artificial operation of education, an equality among the constituent parts of the social organism. In the body of man all is not for intellection, all is not for nutrition or assimilation—there is a diversity of duties, which, for perfection, must be harmoniously blended. And so in society, which is a vast individual—a great living, feeling, thinking mass—if its development is to go on to the utmost perfection, there must be a similar subordination of office implying a subordination of parts. Some, and by far the larger portion, must devote themselves to duties of a wholly material nature; in this representing those particles which, in the Individual, discharge the humbler offices of organic life, and provide for the nutrition and development of the body; some, on the other hand, and these relatively but few in number, are more immediately connected with the higher functions—the operations of intellect. Of these it is the especial, the unavoidable duty to exercise a direct influence over all.[51]

As he seemed to be hinting in these passages, Draper must neutralize an act of faith constantly renewed and an ideal diffused through the whole of American society: the faith that adult white males had all of them enough sense to participate wisely in their own government; and the ideal that men and women should grow by taking the largest possible share in running society. But by and large, when he dealt explicitly with these matters, Draper subverted the faith and rejected the ideal. The management of society, regarded as the business of the best minds, could not safely be left to the whole body of citizens acting as equals. It was of no use to defend politics as a kind of exercise for the personality if the great majority were merely to trot the same tired instincts across the field without ceasing; there was no stretch to their minds, and no point in putting up with inefficiency for the sake of a learning process which did not teach.

At first glance all of this is curious in a man like Draper, genial, libertarian, proud of the American experiment (whatever precisely it was), and zealous in supporting all kinds of schools. He seems never to have been much of a party man; but in spirit, if nothing more, he was the sort of person who migrated from the Whigs to the Unionists, and shaded off into Republicanism.[52] He lived easily enough in the midst of a free society, and sent his sons to help save it. How could the mild citizen of the Republic with all its waste energies and democratic dogmas keep from jostling the prophet of the planned state with his insatiable appetite for order at the hands of a new ruling class?

For one thing, Draper had a saving inconsistency. For another, he had the strongest possible sense of the material benefits which an efficient society might confer on its members; and the whole of his vision was used up by these benefits. He did not in the least propose to indulge the intellectuals' will to power for its own sake. Instead, he would put them to work in the service of the whole people. He seems not to have recognized the problem posed by the manipulation of myths, the calculated excitation of instincts, by leaders in their own interest as opposed to that of the people at large. Indeed, he failed to interpose between the two terms of mental inertness and rational awareness the alternative of active irrationality induced from above. The liberal ideal of the disinterested pursuit of the truth no longer descended on the whole people, but the whole ideal descended on the leaders. Draper's elite would not play on irrationality; but work toward unselfish ends by rational means. Its members were to lead, but not astray—the average citizen would be done good to, better than he could do for himself. In this attitude Draper illustrated (instead of formulating) the old tradition, "Roman," if one likes, of preferring public "virtue" to liberty.[53] By this standard it was better that things should be run on right principles than by the fullest possible participation of all the people (with the danger, amounting to a certainty, of their going wrong).

Draper, confronted with this proposition in so many words, might perhaps have shied away. Yet he had just that engineer's passion for neatness and expedition in all things, including politics, which

helped to carry the Roman tradition into the nineteenth and twentieth centuries. It is the spirit common to him, to Bentham, to the
Saint-Simonians, and to the technocrats—not so much a resolution
to deprive men of liberty as to confer on them the benefits of efficiency
at any cost. By neglecting the cost, Draper avoided an open affront
to the ideals of the people with whom he lived.

In another way Draper could make peace with his neighbors because he seems to have envisioned the efficiency state inside democratic
forms—to the extent of discerning no tension between them. Thus
his profound dissent from the equalizing impulse which helped to
build the system of free schooling did not lead to a repudiation of
the schools.[54] They seem to be the means of recruiting the new ruling
class from an open society; still of use—to provide leaders and mark
them off with a clean sharp line from the led—but not the same
use, in a society pervasively dedicated to the smudging of lines. Nor
does Draper advocate taking from the ordinary citizen his political
rights. With all of Draper's reservations about the political sense of
average men, he gave his readers no reason to suppose that they
ought to make an end of universal suffrage and of civil liberties.
The few ought to command the willing support of the many in the
construction of a society on scientific principles; and Draper hinted
(but did not state) how this might come about.

How much he had read of Comte is unknown. But he solved in-
tuitively the problem posed by Saint-Simon and his rebellious pupil
Comte: how society and the expert were to make their terms. All of
the issues were sharpened into urgency by extending the scope of the
"scientist" to social questions. Saint-Simon and Comte in Europe
and Draper in the United States did their best to effect precisely
this change, and must reckon with the consequences.

If there was a science of society, it must enlist expert practitioners.
Among them they would complete the parceling out of the citizen
into different trades, arts, and professions. Politics as a kind of ex-
ercise-ground for the "whole" man embedded in every citizen must
disappear. The last impulse to trust important matters to the good
sense of the amateur would shrivel up; and politics as an arena for
asserting the equality of all the members of society without regard
to special training would disappear. "By degrees special pursuits
pass," Draper wrote, "into the hands of particular individuals. The
process goes on until three distinct social divisions are established—
a laboring class, a trading or transferring class, an intellectual class.
Political differentiation has taken place." [55]

For his part Comte readily granted that in an age of perfected
social as well as natural sciences the effect would be to take from the
inexpert—the citizen as citizen—his political role.[56] By Comte's

standards this would be in no way impair the chance of arriving at that ideal society after which he panted with, if anything, more zeal than Draper, because for inexpert thinkers to muddle their way through political controversies for the educative effect of the process was not at all *Comte's* ideal. For him dogmas like "freedom of the conscience" and the political equality of men would vanish—not by depriving people of their liberty of opinion but by inducing them to let the desire to exercise it wither away as irrational. No one asserted the right to think "as he chose" about astronomy, and this should be true also of politics (once it was raised to the full stature of a science).

Comte had, as Draper had not, a passion for logical rigor and a ruthless clarity of thought. But the American seems most of the time to have grasped in an intuitive way the secret of this new authoritarianism: leave everyone free to think as he chooses about the problems of politics, but breed an atmosphere of *expertise* which will smother the meddling impulse of the amateur, and induce him to follow the professional within democratic forms. Do this, just as you infuse a free people with the war spirit. For happily, the willing *surrender* of initiative was going forward under the impetus of the Civil War— not so much as might be desired, one seems to read between the lines, but still going forward in the very face of American sentimentalism about equality.

War, civil war, with its dread punishments, is not without its uses. In no other school than that of war can society learn subordination, in no other can it be made to appreciate order. It may be true, as has been affirmed, that men secretly love to obey those whom they feel to be their superiors intellectually. In military life they learn to practice that obedience openly.[57]

[And this is all to the good, for:] Let us not fall into the delusion of expecting what will never happen from . . . social organization; the very term itself implies, on the one hand, superiority; on the other subordination.[58]

In this spirit of dressing ranks Draper argued the case for leaving the management of the world to the best minds. He was helping to shape a new Roman tradition, bringing the last best good of all to snatch men from error: a new science for ordering society efficiently. And he need not for his purpose smash the shell of republican institutions but merely the spirit.

In one recurring mood Draper was therefore libertarian in a profoundly equivocal sense. He then appears to have valued free inquiry only if it was suspended as a solvent inside some society run on "unscientific" principles. Yet no one who reads Draper can fail to conclude that he did somehow value freedom of thought for its own sake. He could not tolerate for a moment the prospect of persecuting men

and women for their opinions; he shrank from the inquisitor with
Galileo, he burned on the pyre with Bruno, he went down under
a hail of stones with Hypatia. Draper had no stomach for making
martyrs to science, and no doubt of making converts; and between
the two kept his balance.

Apart from this, Draper did not after all raise a very imposing
conception of social science; so that the bad effects, if any, of practicing it were neutralized at the outset. Moreover, though a bold—
if rather tenuous—writer on the subject, he took only one step toward organizing American society under experts.

One effect of the Civil War had been to carry through Congress
a bill creating a National Academy of Sciences.[59] The act incorpo-
rated the body in the names of fifty "leading" scientists; and Draper
was not among them. He was at best sensitive about his contributions
to American science; and he seems to have written an angry letter
of protest to Joseph Henry, the great physicist at the head of the
Smithsonian, himself one of the incorporators. This letter has apparently dropped out of sight. Henry's reply, however, remains, and
is worth quoting for the tact with which he tries to mollify Draper
and the skill with which he does *not* quite say that Draper should
have been included.

> You have probably seen by the newspapers an account of the establish-
> ment of a National Academy of Science [sic] by an act of Congress.
> I knew nothing of the project until after the Resolutions in regard to
> it were in the hands of Mr Wilson [Senator Henry Wilson of Massachusetts]
> who carried it through both houses on the last night of the session principally
> by means of the assistance of the other members of the Mass. delegation.
> It may do good but I do not approve of the manner of its establishment
> ["or"? "of"?] this list of members. The proper plan would have been to
> choose any twenty members of whose election [?] there could be no doubt
> and then give them the power to gradually elect the remaining thirty after
> a critical consideration of the relative merits of the several candidates. The
> list contains a number of names unknown to the history of science and omits
> an equal number richly deserving a place.
> The existance [sic] of this academy is however a fact and it is the duty of
> those whose names are on the list to remedy as far as possible the injustice
> which has been done and to give the establishment a [illegible] direction.[60]

The author of the biographical memoir read before the National
Academy of Sciences on Draper's death says that an effort was made
"to remedy this apparent oversight during the meeting which was
held in New York in 1863 for organization, but for some unexplained
reason the effort failed." [61] He was not, in fact, chosen till 1877,
though he did little research in the meantime. (A series of two con-

nected memoirs, published in the interval, was of real interest; but even these were foreshadowed by his earlier work.[62])

It seems fairly clear that this affront attracted Draper to the idea of establishing a rival for the National Academy of Sciences. In any event, he served as first president of the obscure American Union Academy of Literature, Science and Art founded in 1869.[63] He and Justices Noah H. Swayne and Stephen J. Field were perhaps the most distinguished men on the list of "founders." In his inaugural address Draper praised the new academy for "that all-embracing character—the very opposite of exclusiveness—to which your attention has been directed as essential to success." [64] This remark appears to be a slap at the National Academy of Sciences.

The American Union Academy was, indeed, altogether different from the older group: quite flexible in numbers, and intended to throw light on all the problems of society, instead of such small issues as how to keep iron-bottom ships from corroding, shield the compass on ironclads from shock, or test whisky for purity.[65] Draper soared above this kind of investigation:

In the settlement of this continent, in the utilization of its resources, in making it the fitting abode of millions of men, how numerous the mistakes, how much energy must be wasted for want of information, for want of a guide.[66]

They who are engaged in the turmoil of life have not always time to weigh acts or foresee consequences; and, indeed, nature has bestowed the gift of penetration on few.[67]

Improvements which would accelerate the progress and add to the happiness of this host of human beings will be neglected, and legislation meant for their advantage will prove inadequate, or, perhaps, prejudicial.[68]

Draper proposed as one step for seeing that the academy saved the country from inefficiency the election as its president of the Secretary of the Interior.

The Department of the Interior yields to none of the Government offices in the responsibility and magnitude of the duties it has to discharge in the next thirty years. It has to prepare the continent for a nation, and a nation for the continent. It needs whatever enlightenment it can gather. [sentence] I would anchor the Academy, like a cable, fast to the Government at one end, and let the other drift as it might in the ever fluctuating current of popular opinion.[69]

In brief, the American Union Academy should make itself as near as might be the planning arm of the Secretary of the Interior, with his department conceived on a scale somewhat larger than life as of 1870. Presumably the academicians could use this advantage to press Draper's proposals for river-control, planned immigration policies, and, possibly, more information for farmers.[70]

If this would afford the means for insinuating the social scientist into the democratic structure, a less alarming start could hardly have been made; and the academy petered out almost at once. It is only by setting Draper's address in the context of his other writings that one can see how far he had been swept along toward authoritarianism. Swept along, but also held back by flagging consistency, by want of opportunities for translating his philosophy into action, and most of all by raw sensitivity to every kind of persecution.

Chapter X

WAR HISTORIAN

THE war period, aside from helping to crystallize Draper's political views, provided him with a subject. His history of the war, the first scholarly production of the kind, appeared in three volumes between 1867 and 1870.[1] This was quick work in view of his research in the sources, and in view of his personal problems at the time. In 1865, the medical school of New York University, in which Draper had been president of the medical faculty for fifteen years, burned down.[2] He lost an "extensive" library, his lecture notes, the notebooks in which he recorded his laboratory investigations, and all of his chemical, physical, and physiological apparatus which was kept at the school. Of this equipment the less valuable part had been used for teaching purposes, but his own stock of research tools also went up in smoke, and these seem to have been worth a good deal. In all he set his personal loss at $15,000. To make the matter worse the fire occurred in term time. But Draper found temporary quarters for the school, kept the instruction going, and managed not to miss a single lecture of his own. By the fall of 1869 a new building had been provided by Courtlandt Palmer, the wealthy man whose daughter married Henry Draper in 1867. Some of the elder Draper's problems, indeed the greatest single problem, were solved by this connection with the Palmers. But the shock of his own losses, the necessity for keeping up the morale of the medical school in a bad time, and, of course, the continuing demands of his work at the college must have made the latter half of the sixties one of the busiest and roughest spells in his whole career. Yet he wrote his three volumes on the war in the same period, and wrote them largely from the sources. It was a time of long workdays, of maids up at dawn, under his sister Dorothy Catharine's eye, to propel the members of the household to their tasks as expeditiously as possible,—and a time of firm self-discipline when Archbishop Thomson wrote the famous eighty letters before breakfast, and Anthony Trollope clocked his daily stint.

In writing his account of the Civil War, Draper had unusual advantages for research. Secretary of War Edwin M. Stanton gave him "access to the Documents in the War Department," and seems also to have visited Hastings to discuss the course of the war.[3] "I am the more deeply impressed with the necessity of this," Draper had written, "after what you mentioned in relation to General Thomas." [4] As a kind of return, Draper took Stanton's side in the fight with Andrew Johnson.

So the President has perpetrated his folly, and you have answered him as we all thought you would! It should strengthen you in your vexatious contest to feel, that the intelligence and patriotism of the nation is with you. He may annoy you at present, but he can never touch the past.[5]

General William T. Sherman went even further out of his way to help. In 1868 he sent large quantities of his papers to Draper by express, in a rather offhand fashion.

. . . I understand all you want is philosophy not facts, and what of reasoning, thoughts, suggestions &c originating or passing through me. [sic] will be found in my own letters.[6]

You now have my letter Books and a package of letters received by me, all containing information of the most confidential & authentic kind. No Historian heretofore has had full access to these, and I believe if you want you can get the same or similar from General Grant or [possibly "and"] [Henry W.] Halleck [general in chief, then chief of staff of the Union Armies]. [sentence] I feel that Halleck turned on me too sharp in the closing scenes of the war, but he is the best informed military mind in our army. . . . He cannot be friendly to me, and it may be to Grant since the publication of [Adam] Badeau's Book [*Military History of Ulysses S. Grant*, 3 volumes, series commenced in 1868]. . . . [sentence] I doubt . . . [Halleck's] knowledge of men, and of the motives that usually move men, but on the military and political History of those times I believe him to be better posted and better able to record his opinions than any general officer of the Army.[7]

Since Draper's history includes no citations, it is next to impossible to tell exactly what use he made of Sherman's correspondence; or whether he used any materials provided by Grant or Halleck. It would appear, from family traditions and from a flurry of letters between Draper and Sherman, that the chief reliance was Sherman, plus the files of the War Department. This debt, in so far as it exists, does not take in either case the form of direct quotations. Perhaps this was the condition attached to his using the sources so early. If, however, one could imagine Draper's history provided with quotations and footnotes, its value might be utterly transformed and its reputation enhanced.

The batch of letters which survive from the exchange between Draper and Sherman affords the only known glimpse of Draper's methods as an historian. He agreed with Sherman that no great dependence should be put on accounts of the war by newspapermen; they distorted the facts.[8] One of them, indeed, was lying in wait to

review Draper's second volume for the *New York Times,* and make
out Shiloh as "disgraceful" to Grant, "whatever glory there was in it"
for Buell. It seems reasonable to suppose that Draper made at most
very cautious use of newspapers.

In the days before notes were taken on file cards, Draper had the
problem of sorting out his materials as he went along, or else of trying in the end to shuffle entries in notebooks. Apparently he got
around this difficulty by sketching the organization of the book in
advance of his research.

My method of working is this—I have prepared a rough sketch of all
the leading affairs of the war arranged in suitable chapters[.] Then as I
gain new information on different topics I introduce it in the proper part
of the manuscript. So at present I am going carefully through your letters
[he wrote to Sherman] and modifying my manuscript according to the new
light I get—collecting [possibly "correcting"] many interpretations and [il-
legible word] novel facts.[9]

Perhaps the history of military operations suffers less from this procedure than a history of thought; but flexibility of organization is
not its chief merit.

The Victorians had never met the file card, but they knew the
hero well. If Draper were willing to hang his history on the great
generals, many of the problems of organization would disappear
and the unwieldy mass of detail sort itself out. Offhand, one might
suppose that Draper had drowned the hero in society (only to resur-
rect him in the role of scientist). But it was one thing to catch sight
of a vision of history as the tension between society and nature and
another to write the history of the Civil War without titans. As
Draper explained to one of them:

. . . successful history-writing consists in bringing into strong and solitary relief the chief men and the important facts and putting into a sub-
ordinate position or passing almost in silence those that are of less value.[10]

As the narrative of the war goes on to its culminating point there are but
two Soldiers standing forth pre-eminently[;] they are yourself [Sherman]
marching to the Sea and . . . [Grant] marching Southward.[11]

An author who is attempting to write for futurity must abstain from diminishing the importance of his chief actors by introducing them in a
crowd[;] he must avoid details as far as he can and grasp his facts in the
mass.[12]

The great bulk of the work composed on these principles dealt
with military campaigns as such. There would be no point in trying
to assess this side of the history without expert preparation of a rather
technical kind. The great strength of the book seems, however, to

lie not in the description of battles but in the account of what produced the war. Here Draper showed a surprising freedom from the
obsession with moral issues, of the kind associated with Von Holst.
Draper's explanation of the rift was at once fresh, provocative in the
best sense, and, in view of the date, notably objective. The wonder is
not that he sometimes convicted himself of bias but that most of
the time he shook off the war fever in the North.

He began by recalling his old thesis that climate was constantly
pulling the regions of the United States apart: "There is . . . a tendency to disintegration or disruption of the republic arising from
climate. Communities separated by many degrees of latitude become
in the course of time antagonistic in their feelings and thoughts." [13]
But for once he was careful to show the influence of the physical
environment acting at several removes.

> This antagonism is more dangerous when either or each of the opposing
> communities is consolidated by some common industrial bond, a condition
> not unfrequently arising in the very circumstances of the case. Thus the
> cultivation of cotton gives to the Gulf communities a united, it might be
> said, almost a single interest, increasing their predisposition to think and
> act as one man.
>
> If, again, there be any common political bond, such, for instance, as the
> institution of slavery, it, too, will act in the same way. But the growth of
> cotton and the perpetuation of slavery were both connected with the cause
> that was establishing physiological distinction in the Gulf communities,
> that is to say, with climate.
>
> Antagonisms thus re-enforced can readily find political expression; and
> when in action, will manifest unanimity and surprising power, as was shown
> by the cotton states in the civil war.[14]

Even this was thin, and merely set the conventional factors in a
new context. But Draper went on to sketch the character of two
different nationalities molded by the physical setting.

> . . . side by side, in the free states and in the slave states, partly through
> an initial social difference, partly through the climate, interests, and avoca-
> tions of life, two distinct nationalities were tending to form.
>
> In the North the population was in a state of unceasing activity; there
> was corporeal and mental restlessness. Magnificent cities in all directions
> were arising; the country was intersected with canals, railroads, telegraphs;
> wherever navigation was possible there were steamboats in the rivers. Com-
> panies for banking, manufacturing, commercial purposes, were often con-
> centrating many millions of capital. There were all kinds of associations for
> religious, charitable, educational purposes. Churches, hospitals, schools,
> abounded. The foreign commerce at length rivaled that of the most powerful
> nations of Europe.[15]

Draper argued that slavery had widened the gap between the two societies by making Southerners scornful of mechanical improvements.

> In a servile community mechanical invention will always be held in low
> esteem. In his forced daily toil, what does it signify to the slave whether
> the implement in his hand be an improved one or not? The thing that
> concerns him is the passing away of the weary hours; he has no interest in
> the fruit of his labor. And as to the master, it required no deep political
> penetration for him to perceive that the introduction of machinery must
> in the end result in the emancipation of the slave. Machinery and slavery
> are incompatible—the slave is displaced by the machine.[16]

Here Draper was grappling with a real issue—the low energy level
of the innovating spirit in the Old South. But then he veered off and
accused the planters of staying on this level out of calculation. The
charge cannot seriously be defended. There is even less to be said
for the assertion that the political leaders of the region formed a conspiracy to keep out mechanical improvements.

> Under the Constitution an increased negro force had a political value, ma-
> chinery had none. The cotton interest was therefore persuaded by those
> who were in a position to guide its movement, that its prosperity could be
> secured only through increased manual labor; and though with so many
> wonderful examples before it of the successful application of machinery
> in the most unpromising cases, it persisted in affirming that in this instance
> it was chimerical, and not worthy of attention.[17]

If Draper went wrong in imputing motives to the planters, he had
a good point in the absence of great technological changes in the
South. He made clear that he regarded this as merely one side of a
conservative temper in Southern society. He also made clear that,
though the two nationalities were different, good and evil were not
the defining characters.

> In the South, if the ostensible prosperity was less, the actual happiness
> was not inferior. Society was in a condition of repose; the planters were
> hospitable and proud. Few, except those in affluent circumstances, had been
> in foreign countries; and, unacquainted with the fictitious wants of civili-
> zation, the people were content with their own lot, in their simplicity
> imagining that there was nothing better in the world. The youth did not
> despise rural avocations, and rush to the towns in pursuit of instant
> fortune.[18]

Moreover, though the people of the North had built every kind
of business, improved transportation and communication, concentrated their capital, and created churches, schools, and clubs, "under
this splendid prosperity lay great evils concealed." [19]

The family tie was weakened. Children left their home the moment they could take care of themselves. Life became an Arab warfare. The recognized standard of social position was wealth. No other criterion could be established, for all were originally on a level, and wealth became the only distinction.[20]

The vaunted "INDIVIDUALISM" of the North and the Great Valley was drowning nearly as many ties in "the icy water of egotistical calculation" as Marx and Engels claimed.[21] If the Northerners were not "cannibals all" in Fitzhugh's phrase, they were Arab warriors among themselves.[22] But Draper had none of the economic insight of Marx or Fitzhugh; and, in this context, none of their scorn for individualism if it could only be harnessed for social ends.

The wonderful activity of the Free States of America turns on the principle we are here considering—individual discontentment. Labor is gladly encountered in the expectation that it will bring an adequate return. For this reason it is that the civilization of the North is altogether pacific, and that it looks upon war, save under very exceptional circumstances, such as the preservation of its own life, as mere folly. Its condition of progress is self-interest, enlightened, as far as can be accomplished, by a diffusion of knowledge. The individual, changing his prospect without reluctance, not only becomes reconciled to, but aids in the accomplishment of rapid social changes. The intellectual atmosphere through which things are regarded is being continually modified; opinion is perpetually improving.[23]

Leaving aside his preference, Draper summed up the causes of the war in reasonably neutral terms:

INDIVIDUALISM was the governing principle of the North, INDEPENDENCE that of the South. In the former, each man was pursuing his own welfare against all the rest; in the latter, apart from the rest. The one was connected with the competitions of compact society, the other with the isolation of plantation life.

Each year the social divergence of these two great communities was becoming more marked. It was obvious to every observant person that it would at length find political expression. Intercommunication, which so powerfully smooths the asperities of rivalry, did not keep pace with the increase of population and territorial spread.[24]

It cannot be argued that Draper made at all clear this distinction between individualism and independence. But in general he seems to have been approaching Sir Henry Maine's famous thesis of the progress from status to contract.[25] The North, as Draper portrayed it, was the society built on free movement, ruthless competition, the contracting out of a man's efforts at will, and the maximum release of energy. It built more, changed oftener, and wove more complicated relationships; but, on the other side, as Draper was careful to point

out, it produced more tensions in society. The South was the civilization more nearly based on status, a great sum of economic islands
rather than a product of the maximum interplay of effort. But "if
the ostensible prosperity was less, the actual happiness was not inferior." Draper ought no more to be confused with Maine than with
Marx or Fitzhugh; he never put his finger on the difference between
North and South in terms of contract and status. But he made the
distinction empirically in his account of the two nationalities straining to tear the Union apart.

It is fairly clear that he preferred one to the other; and sometimes
he betrayed a preference for the North a good deal less rationalized
than in his main thesis. But it can scarcely be emphasized too much
that for the most part he avoided laying down a moral issue between the contenders. He blocked out in a rough way the theory
least offensive to the Southerners of the twentieth century—that the
slavery dispute merely caught up the difference between two ways
of life. Draper did not argue that the South had institutionalized
an act of sin; but it had made its own civilization and tried by seced-
ing to clothe it with the attributes of political sovereignty. If some
residual trace of sin stuck fast to the South, the sin was not so much
slaveholding as rebellion.

> Shall he who writes the story of this hideous war hide from his reader
> its fearful lesson? shall he not remember that on this widespread continent
> climate is making us a many-diversified people? that, in the nature of things,
> we must have our misunderstandings and our quarrels with one another?
> If, in the future, there should be any one who undertakes to fire the heart
> of his people, and to set in mortal battle a community against the nation,
> let us leave him without the excuse which the war-secessionist of our time
> may perhaps not unjustly plead, that he knew not what he did.[26]

This plain statement was plainly offensive to Southerners; but it
made out an issue not so much against them alone, as might
have been done with regard to slavery, as against breakers of the
peace and bad nationalists.

Moreover, this fierce accusation ought not to outweigh the bulk
of Draper's treatment of the matters in dispute. And here he almost
proved the right of the South to make a nation of itself. In addition,
when he talked of the differences as springing in the end from climatic
conditions, he drew the sting from any moral recrimination. Indeed,
one might suppose that the chief convenience—and possibly the
chief defect—of the "climatic" view of history was to by-pass ethical
concerns altogether.

> . . . when we appreciate how much the actions of men are controlled by
> the deeds of their predecessors, and are determined by climate and other

natural circumstances, our animosities lose much of their asperity, and the return of kind feelings is hastened.

While the tempest of war is raging, such ideas can not secure attention; but when peace succeeds, the voice of philosophy is heard calming our passions, suggesting new views of the things about which we contended, whispering excuses for our antagonist, and persuading us that there is nothing we shall ever regret in fraternal forgiveness for the injuries we have received.[27]

With such resistless energy and such rapidity does the Republic march to imperial power, that social changes take place among us in a manner unexampled in the more stationary populations of Europe. There, public calamities are long remembered, and ancient estrangements are nourished for centuries. Here, perhaps in a little more than a' single generation, our agony will have been forgotten in the busy industry of a hundred millions of people, animated by new intentions, developing wealth and power on an unparalleled scale, and looking, as Americans always do look, only to the future, not to the past.[28]

The "little more than a single generation" of which Draper spoke brought North and South to the verge of fighting side by side in the war with Spain; but he got no credit for helping to bring this about. The critic who reviewed his book for the *Southern Review* found it "literally stuffed with the lying traditions, the cunningly devised fables, and the vile calumnies, with which a partizan press and a Puritanical pulpit have flooded the North." [29]

The part, however, of Draper's first volume in which he tried to explain why there was a war to write the history of is a surprising accomplishment. He was now complex, where one would think that he had already reduced history to the barest possible simplicity, a question of the weather. If he built on inadequate data, he showed how to marshal all of the right data when they appeared. Instead of making a rhetorical tour around the slavery issue, he insisted that the war was a contest between civilizations. Here his instinct was notably sound. Slavery may have been the clue through the maze of Southern history, but Draper saw that, whether this is so or not, the job of the historian is to describe the maze instead of proclaiming boldly "there is a way through." If slavery impinged on every aspect of Southern life, it did so one way and another, more and less, at different removes and with different force. It is these differentiae that have to be treated by the serious historian over against the moral polemicist. When Draper set the two ways of life opposite each other, he was recognizing the need for a sketch of what *happened* in the South and how, whatever may have caused it. This is a remarkable achievement in a man who knew for certain what the cause was.

It did him no great good with the book-buying public. Harper's
had asked him to write six volumes—"they know it would sell," but
"I do not write for money but with the higher ambition of control-
ling the thoughts of men if I can." [30] The three volumes, however,
which actually appeared made no money for Harper's, and they
had to do their work on the thoughts of a very small public.[31] But
Draper had the comfort of Sherman's verdict on the earlier part of
the history, "on the whole" "judiciously" treated so as to correct
"many popular errors, in which our histories abounded." [32] And
German and Russian translations were eventually made of the
Civil War, as of the *Civil Policy.*[33]

Chapter XI

SCIENCE AND RELIGION

DRAPER decided to go to Europe in 1870, mainly to try to get his *Civil War* published in London, but partly to see Paris and Rome for the first time. The whole trip was marred before it began by the death of his wife Antonia on July 31, 1870, after she had been a rather sturdy invalid for nearly twenty years.[1] Yet he went ahead with his plans. His unmarried daughter Antonia and his indomitable sister, the Dorothy Catharine who had daubed her face for photographs, mothered his children, and run the house on the Hudson, went along. His daughter Virginia, now Mrs. Mytton Maury and the mother of small children, stayed in America. So did his three sons. The youngest, Daniel, for a time his father's amanuensis, then an apprentice in the Iron Works in Brooklyn, was now head of the meteorological observatory in Central Park. The tradition has it that he owed the job to his Aunt Dorothy's old suitor Andrew H. Green.[2] The eldest boy, John Christopher, was a chemist, from whom the father was now in some degree estranged. According to one account, objections were raised to John Christopher's marrying a wealthy divorcée.[3] This may really have been the explanation; Edith Wharton—the only débutante who ever climbed Parnassus—set *The Age of Innocence* in New York City of the seventies. But there are conflicting reports about the matter; and perhaps the offense lay in calling his mother "that woman" immediately after her death.[4] The middle son, Henry, had married the heiress Anna Palmer—this match at least was thoroughly agreeable to the family—taken his place in the faculties of New York University alongside his father, and made himself one of the great astronomical photographers of the world. The father was ferociously proud of Henry, and he took along all kinds of errands to perform in the way of ordering scientific apparatus.[5] He also took along the intention of spying out the land to see what kind of research would make Henry famous in Europe in the least possible time.[6]

It was like probing an open wound to go back to London, which he had left arm in arm with his young bride almost forty years before. The old house which they had lived in in Camberwell brought back the memory of "sweet Mother," his children's mother, "with her long black ringlets." [7]

I could not help remarking that I am not quite so strong as I used to be in those old times. I could then *walk* without fatigue [from the center of London to Camberwell], but it tires me to *ride* that distance now. Perhaps it was that mother was there, a bright young girl to welcome me that lightened the toil.[8]

When he went to see his father's grave in the churchyard at Sheerness, it was the same church in which he and his wife had been married.

There we were married—the happiest event of my life, and indeed of hers too. I was with Mother more than 40 years before and after our marriage and I never knew her do a wrong thing or one which now I now [sic] would have otherwise than it was. How few men there are who can truly say so much as that! [9]

When he met old friends from the visit of ten years before, they asked for his wife.[10] When he went to bed,

Since I have been here there have not been many nights that I have not been with her or rather she has been with me, chattering and laughing as she used to do. When she has not been and I wake up in the morning I cannot tell you how sorrowful I feel.[11]

And when the party ran into some hitches in traveling, if his wife had been there, they would have had to turn back; and she had been with them last Christmas.[12]

If she had lived to make the trip, it would certainly have been the happiest time of his whole career in many ways. He did not, as it happened, find a publisher for the *Civil War*, but he met with the warmest possible reception from the people for whose opinions he cared the most.

He had dinner at the Athenaeum as the guest of John Tyndall, the head of the Royal Institution, with Herbert Spencer in the party.[13] "Good as the dinner was the conversation was still better" —but like all good conversation except Dr. Johnson's it seems not to have been communicable. Tyndall also had Draper to lunch at the Institution itself, and then took him down into the laboratory where Davy and Faraday had worked and went through a long series of experiments set up for his benefit.

. . . he had two assistants who performed the experiments and they were very skillful men. He simply stood by and directed. I could not help thinking how much more I should have done if I had had such advantages! [14]

He dined with the Royal Society, met the Prime Minister and the Lord Chancellor, and sat at the table with three of the best English astronomers, Warren de la Rue, whom he knew from ten years back, William Lassell, who had verified the discovery of Neptune, and Norman Lockyer, who discovered helium.

I took [Draper wrote to Henry] quite a fancy to Lockyer[.] He is such another young fellow as you and has a wife (so Mr. de la Rue told me) who takes the same interest in his pursuits that Anna does in yours. He told me that he is coming to America year after next and I am truly glad that you should have the opportunity of seeing him[.] He is the *rising English astronomer.*[15]

Professor G. G. Stokes of Cambridge, who had first expounded the theory of Fraunhofer's lines, came to call and discuss astronomical photography.[16] A. W. Williamson, the chemist of University College, asked Draper to dinner, and they talked of the "woman" question, whether women were entitled to university lectures.[17] Draper went down to Lady Augusta Stanley's to meet Père Hyacinthe, the French clergyman Charles Loyson, who had made a famous break with the Catholic church; [18] a prominent instrument-maker named Browning promised to show him a dog-eared copy of the *Physiology* which "he reads . . . whenever he has any spare time"; [19] W. H. Flower, the curator of the Hunterian museum, asked Draper to come and see it; [20] the Astronomical Society had him to dinner and he made a little speech on Henry's research (keeping to himself some things which he thought Henry could work up into a memoir); [21] he dined with the eighth Duke of Argyll and the Duchess, the current delegates of the British aristocracy for lending countenance to science (the Duke was still a "cataclysmic" in geology, but Draper makes no mention of this); [22] and in Munich on the short trip down to Rome—France at war being out of the question—Draper had a distinguished caller.

This evening we had a visit from the celebrated Dr. [Ignaz von] Döllinger who bears the reputation of being the first theologian in Europe. He has distinguished himself by his opposition to papal infallibility. I had a long and interesting conversation with him on the modifications which the Church impresses on men and its influence in the distribution of Catholics & Protestants[.] [23]

Just before Draper left for home, he had word from another enemy of the Vatican.

I have just had a very long and a very kind letter from the Prime Minister, Mr Gladstone. He expresses himself very cordially not only to me personally, but also to our Country. I do not see how one so occupied as he must be, and with so many overwhelming cares, can find time for such private attentions.[24]

But Draper only half appreciated the highest compliment of all.

I was at the American Legation today to see about our passports. Mr Moran told me that on Saturday he dined with a large circle of foreigners and a Russian gentleman of the name of Ivan Tourgueneff announced to the company that all that was known in Russia about modern America was through my writings[.] They had translated my "Physiology" "Europe" "Policy of America" and two volumes of the "Civil War" and he spoke in such terms of extravagant laudation of them that I should almost blush to repeat it[.] [25]

Apparently Draper had never heard of the Russian gentleman.

In spite of his flattering reception Draper wound up his stay of over three months by declaring that he was "right glad of it." [26] Early in April 1871, he was back in the United States in time for the third term in the college.

In this same year Edward L. Youmans, the tireless popularizer of science, sketched for Daniel Appleton, the American publisher of Darwin, Huxley, Tyndall, and Spencer, an "International Scientific Library" "to contain the best work of every important scientific thinker of the day in all countries." [27] The plan called for simultaneous publication in New York, London, Paris, Leipzig, and as many other places as possible. In the face of ridicule by the London publisher who told him, " 'Why, it can't be done! You can't get these great men to write those books and no one publisher could ever issue them all!' "—Youmans persisted and brought the trick off.

Draper was asked, apparently at some time in 1873, to contribute a *History of the Conflict between Religion and Science* to a series which already contained books by Tyndall, Bagehot, Bain, and Spencer. He dated his preface as of December 1873, and the book appeared early in 1874.

How much time he had for writing is unknown, but it looks as if he may have been rushed. By far the greater part of the *Conflict* merely pulls together into a more concise account his treatment of the same subject in the *Intellectual Development of Europe*. Some passages are quoted verbatim from the earlier work. But he would not have been asked to write as an expert unless he had already had his say on the subject; Youmans meant for his authors to repeat themselves. Moreover, Draper added three new chapters: one each stating the services to "modern civilization" of "Latin Christianity" and "Science" and another summarizing the position of the Vatican Council on infallibility. The only real charge which can be brought against him on the score of repeating himself is that he showed a faulty sense of proportion in cutting his earlier book down to size. This need not obscure the fact that the *Conflict* served the purpose intended by Youmans, and reached a much larger audience than the *Intellectual Development* could hope to do.

The historical portion of the smaller book dealt in turn with the Museum of Alexandria, considered as the birthplace of "modern" science; the origins of Christianity, and its suppression of the schools in Alexandria; the "Southern Reformation," by which Draper meant the rise of Mohammedanism and its rapid spread through much of the old Roman empire; Averroism; the Inquisition, partly regarded as the means for keeping the Averroistic doctrines of emanation and absorption out of Europe; Galileo and the emergence of "correct views" on astronomy; the "Northern Reformation," or the Lutheran revolt; and the nineteenth-century disputes about "Evolution, Creation, Development." Then Draper contrasted the work of the Catholic church and of "Science," decidedly to the advantage of the latter; and condemned the stand of the Vatican Council. He is therefore not so much a historian of science in succession to Whewell and Comte as the historian of the metaphysical presuppositions and the social climate of science.

Though all of this, except for the last three chapters, had already been treated in the *Intellectual Development*, the *Conflict* nevertheless sprang from a new context—the Syllabus of Errors of 1864, the Vatican Council of 1869–70, the French defeat, the *Kulturkampf* instituted by Bismarck in 1871, and the sustained fury of the churches toward the theory of evolution (dramatized by the Oxford meeting). In the light of these events Draper pictured a mounting crisis.

Whoever has had an opportunity of becoming acquainted with the mental condition of the intelligent classes in Europe and America, must have perceived that there is a great and rapidly-increasing departure from the public religious faith, and that, while among the more frank this divergence is not concealed, there is a far more extensive and far more dangerous secession, private and unacknowledged.[28]

In England and America, religious persons perceive with dismay that the intellectual basis of faith has been undermined by the spirit of the age. They prepare for the approaching disaster in the best manner they can.

The most serious trial through which society can pass is encountered in the exuviation of its religious restraints.[29]

The four things which most contributed to the weakening of religion were, in his opinion: the declaration of war on modern civilization by the pope, the claim of papal infallibility, the political role of the Catholic churches in Germany and France, and the literal interpretation of Genesis. If all of these might fairly be regarded as attacks from the side of religion, it was not so clear that the enemy was in each instance "science." Draper, however, consistently wrote of science as if it were synonymous with willingness to experiment in the face of authority, with hostility to any coercion of the mind.

The political and social institutions and creeds anathematized in the Syllabus of Errors stood, therefore, on an equal footing with the theory of evolution. They were all alike outgrowths of the scientific spirit, of the war on received truths. The intervention of the Church in the political life of France and Germany was a deliberate attempt to stamp out this spirit; and to make the whole of society an accretion around the grain of faith.

It would be a calumny to say, as some of his critics did, that Draper identified all the goods of life with science. Rather, he seemed to argue that every exercise of the experimental temper for some rational end is *in this aspect* scientific, and to this extent good. It was this implication which enabled him to glide from the political claims of the Church to the conflict between religion and science.

[The papacy] . . . insists on a political supremacy in accordance with its claims to a divine origin and mission, and a restoration of the mediaeval order of things, loudly declaring that it will accept no reconciliation with modern civilization.

The antagonism we thus witness between Religion and Science is the continuation of a struggle that commenced when Christianity began to attain political power. A divine revelation must necessarily be intolerant of contradiction; it must repudiate all improvements in itself, and view with disdain that arising from the progressive intellectual development of man. But our opinions on every subject are constantly liable to modification, from the irresistible advance of human knowledge.[30]

Draper ends by implying that the freedom of conscience opposed by the Church is advancing toward the truth; and so avoids the issue whether he would still prefer free inquiry if it stood still or slipped backward. In a certain temper (that of the *Civil Policy*), there is some reason for supposing that he would *not*. But the question as such hardly arose for Draper.

Granted the assumption that the scientific habit of mind asserts itself whenever some outworn tradition is dissolved by intellectual curiosity, he properly asked the question what structure of power left the most room for this curiosity. His answer is the sovereign national state.

The stumbling-block to the progress of Europe has been its dual system of government. So long as every nation had two sovereigns, a temporal at home and a spiritual one in a foreign land—there being different temporal masters in different nations, but only one foreign master for all, the pontiff at Rome—how was it possible that history should present us with any thing more than a narrative of the strifes of these rival powers? Whoever will reflect on this state of things will see how it is that those nations which have shaken off the dual form of government are those which have made the greatest advance. He will discern what is the cause of the paralysis which has befallen France. On one hand she wishes to be the leader of, Europe, on the other she clings to a dead past.[31]

Sometimes, as in writing of the *Kulturkampf*, Draper seems to have been swept along by mere nationalism for its own sake:

[Germany] . . . sees in the conflict, not an affair of religion or of conscience, but a struggle between the sovereignty of state legislation and the sovereignty of the Church. She treats the papacy not in the aspect of a religious, but of a political power, and is resolved that the declaration of the Prussian Constitution shall be maintained, that "the exercise of religious freedom must not interfere with the duties of a citizen toward the community and the state." [32]

But in the main he valued the sovereign state as the natural habitat of the scientific spirit, of free inquiry, and of cultural diversity. The Syllabus of Errors was trying to clear away this environment:

Will ["Science"] . . . submit to the dictation of a power, which, claiming divine authority, can present no adequate credentials of its office; a power that is founded in a cloud of mysteries; that sets itself above reason and common-sense; that loudly proclaims the hatred it entertains against liberty of thought and freedom in civil institutions; that professes its intention of repressing the one and destroying the other whenever it can find the opportunity; that denounces as most pernicious and insane the opinion that liberty of conscience and of worship is the right of every man. . . .[33]

Claims such as these mean a revolt against modern civilization, an intention of destroying it, no matter at what social cost. To submit to them without resistance, men must be slaves indeed! [34]

Draper went to the heart of a great issue when he investigated the political setting of the scientific outlook. He was rightly criticized for making very little of the antagonism toward science of the Protestant churches. In fact, he thought, and said, that they were wrong to burn Servetus and resist Darwin.[35] (He had in mind particularly the Evangelical Alliance which met in New York in the fall of 1873.) But the nature of the Protestant churches was to disintegrate; and, the decisive issue for Draper, they had mostly made their peace with the sovereign state as the guardian of cultural diversity.

It is only in the context of Draper's convulsive embrace of national sovereignty—valued, as Hobbes valued it, as the scourge of conflicting sovereignties but also as the fit occasion for the disuse of sovereignty—that the *Conflict between Religion and Science* can be seen as a whole.

In this setting Draper sketched a new tradition of history. On one level he created a myth of the reifications Science and Religion wrestling together for dominance. On another plane he composed a martyrology of science: the late Alexandrians, Copernicus, Kepler,

Bruno, Galileo, Servetus, the German higher critics of the Penta-
teuch, and the nineteenth-century evolutionists. As one of his critics
shrewdly remarked: "What a glorious army of martyrs this Church
of the Scientists is! It sends out a cry of 'persecution,' . . . . The
ferocious theologians are after them with a Bible in one hand and
a fiery fagot in the other." [36]

Draper drew up in fact the practical counterpart of a new calendar
of saints (including Newton, who had an unaccountably quiet life).
His book was a first draft of a new Scripture, a guide to the faithful
and a warrant of their triumph over their enemies—who were notwithstanding incredibly sly and perservering.

The Church declared that the earth is the central and most important
body in the universe; that the sun and moon and stars are tributary to it.
On these points she was worsted. She affirmed that a universal deluge had
covered the earth; that the only surviving animals were such as had been
saved in an ark. In this her error was established by geology. She taught
that there was a first man, who, some six or eight thousand years ago, was
suddenly created or called into existence in a condition of physical and
moral perfection, and from that condition he fell. But anthropology has
shown that human beings existed far back in geological time, and in a
savage state but little better than that of the brute.[37]

This trumpet-note of heretics confounded and martyrs justified is
part of a massive (but by no means consistent) inversion of the whole
religious tradition. Everything is upside-down and inside-out—the
authors of the Index on the roll of the saints and faith a bad thing,
"faith in its nature unchanging, stationary," at the other pole from
science "in its nature progressive"—but the doctrinal intransigence,
the solidarity of the believers, the pitch of assurance and exultation
remain.[38] There is besides a residual pursuit of the annihilation of
self and of sense—the communion supper attenuated into the study of
geometry:

. . . within this world of transient delusions and unrealities there is a
world of eternal truths.
    That world is not to be discovered through the vain traditions that
have brought down to us the opinions of men who lived in the morning
of civilization, nor in the dreams of mystics who thought they were inspired. It is to be discovered by the investigations of geometry and by the
practical interrogation of Nature.[39]

The dove descending breaks the air with theorems.
    In this sense Draper undermined religion by lending to science its
psychological gratifications. He offered, without saying so, an alternative for draining off the religious impulse. But he did not thrust the
alternative upon his readers by directly attacking religion itself. His

130 JOHN WILLIAM DRAPER

target was the wrong kind of theology; and the right kind did not even need to be new-founded if the Protestants were thoroughly Protestant.

> . . . it . . . [has] come to this, that Roman Christianity and Science are recognized by their respective adherents as being absolutely incompatible; they cannot exist together; one must yield to the other; mankind must make its choice—it cannot have both.
>
> While such is, perhaps, the issue as regards Catholicism, a reconciliation of the Reformation with Science is not only possible, but would easily take place, if the Protestant Churches would only live up to the maxim taught by Luther, and established by so many years of war. That maxim is, the right of private interpretation of the Scriptures. It was the foundation of intellectual liberty. But, if a personal interpretation of the book of Revelation is permissible, how can it be denied in the case of the book of Nature? In the misunderstandings that have taken place, we must ever bear in mind the infirmities of men. The generations that immediately followed the Reformation may perhaps be excused for not comprehending the full significance of their cardinal principle, and for not on all occasions carrying it into effect. When Calvin caused Servetus to be burnt, he was animated, not by the principles of the Reformation, but by those of Catholicism, from which he had not been able to emancipate himself completely. And when the clergy of influential Protestant confessions have stigmatized the investigators of Nature as infidels and atheists, the same may be said. For Catholicism to reconcile itself to Science, there are formidable, perhaps insuperable obstacles in the way. For Protestantism to achieve that great result there are not. In the one case there is a bitter, a mortal animosity to be overcome; in the other, a friendship, that misunderstandings have alienated, to be restored.[40]

On the surface this was a confession that some kind of religion could be reconciled with science; and that Draper would be glad of it. In general, this is the tenor of the *Conflict between Religion and Science* when he faced the issue directly: he was trying to save religion from itself. But the tradition frozen by his book could do the chief historical religions of the West no good, and might do great harm.

Whatever lay at the core of Christianity, it involved historically the literal interpretation of the Bible (including the creation scene in Genesis) and the acceptance of higher purpose. Draper called for the abandonment of literalism and the reinterpretation of purpose. But the churches might meet in one way or another both of these demands. They might agree to read Genesis as an allegory, and to take up Asa Gray's "creation on the installment plan" as John Dewey later called it. God had manifested His purpose through natural selection, and indeed He was a great deal subtler than anyone had known. Darwin himself professed to find insuperable difficulties in assigning purpose to a process which threw up useless, as well as useful, variations. But Draper, like Gray, was willing to call natural selection the means of asserting God's "intent." For him this was merely one side of crying down supernatural intervention.

On these terms he was ready to certify the end of the conflict between religion and science. The bargain was not acceptable to his critics, most of whom went angrily about in circles from the premise that there could be no conflict to the conclusion that there was none. But it was of no use, they were beating him over the head with his own problem. They allowed him to set the terms of the debate: whether there was, or was not, a conflict. He imposed on them—and on a whole generation of thinking people—the view that this was the decisive issue in the relations of science with religion.

If in good logic no conflict could be shown to exist, Draper and his enemies agreed in thinking that religion was safe. If the truths of religion could not be *shaken* by science, they were bound to be attended. In this way Draper took no account, and distracted the churches from taking account, of the dangers for religion in a scientific age, of the lapse of attention, the failure of interest.

Yet the accommodations which he proposed—the Garden of Eden a garden of myths and the divine purpose mistaking itself and having to apply the remedies of Malthus—would make for a wrench. The articles of faith and credence would have to be thought through again, and the communicant would have to build up out of sagacity and patience new lodgings for the religious impulse.

For many people the effort might prove too much of a strain; they might take away with them only the sense of a grave malaise on the part of clergymen. In this way, the problem before the churches was not so much to show the compatibility of science and religion as to dispel the suspicion that the whole question had got wound up in a tangle of subtleties beyond the skill of ordinary people to sort out. Without losing the argument on the level of logic, the defenders of religion might find themselves losing the attention of many people. As the debate involved so many perplexities, these people might decide in an inarticulate way to put the whole issue out of mind. The chances were that this would strike not so much at the numbers as the fervor of the religious; but in the end at both.

The upshot would be at least the dilution, and at most the loss, of interest in religion; but not many would forget that somehow the churches had been put on the defensive. The process would go forward (of which we know next to nothing) by which ideas cease to hold the attention owing to some contagion of discredit or tedium. The issue between religion and science (if any) might be swallowed up by a vague suspicion that science had got the better of it, or enough the better to make it naive to proclaim the inviolability of religion. In this sense, the logical outcome of the controversy might amount to very little alongside the fatigue of seeing it through to a conclusion. Both Draper and his critics made almost nothing of this fatigue as a threat to religion; indeed, he partly imposed on them his own idea of a quite different menace, of being shown up if they did not reform.

It was not Draper's own way to be fatigued with thinking; he had the remorseless fluency and the dialectical zest to go to the end of all arguments. And the end of "the conflict between religion and science" was for him, in a way, the renovation of religion. But the old certitudes were given back with a difference—and precisely the difference which made it impossible to cope with the lapse of attention from religion. In particular cases God is never germane.

Now, we say that the little vesicles of which this cloud [which he had introduced to make a point] was composed arose from the condensation of water-vapor preëxisting in the atmosphere, through reduction of temperature; we show how they assumed the form they present. We assign optical reasons for the brightness or blackness of the cloud; we explain, on mechanical principles, its drifting before the wind; for its disappearance we account on the principles of chemistry. It never occurs to us to invoke the interposition of the Almighty in the production and fashioning of this fugitive form. We explain all the facts connected with it by physical laws, and perhaps should reverentially hesitate to call into operation the finger of God.[41]

If, on physical principles, we account for minor meterological incidents, mists and clouds, is it not permissible for us to appeal to the same principle in the origin of world-systems and universes, which are only clouds on a space-scale somewhat larger, mists on a time-scale somewhat less transient? Can any man place the line which bounds the physical on one side, the supernatural on the other? [42]

This "reverential" hesitation to rise from weather reports to God displays with beautiful clarity the problem from which Draper helped to distract the churches. If the more men studied the universe the better they were able to discuss it exclusively in "natural" terms, they might still persist, as Draper himself did, in attributing the whole scheme to some higher purpose. But they were now back, as he seems not to have known, where the shrewder minds of the eighteenth century left off: if you agree to talk of the universe as a mechanism, anyone who chooses may believe in a great Mechanic who set it going. But He is just that Mechanic and no more—and reduces none of the contradictions of existence to order.

Men might go on protesting that they did believe as much as ever—Draper was like this himself. But he did his best to sap in practice the vitality of religion. If everything could be treated as he desired in terms of natural process, no one was constrained to stop asking the question, "At bottom *why* does this 'how' proceed?" But there were so many other questions—how big the clouds were, how black, and how wet—to which the answers would be of practical use. And these sharp, discriminated questions of meteorology were discontinuous with the ultimate question of theology. With the First Cause defined in Draper's terms, the study of secondary causes had no quarrel—and no contact. The pursuit of science, full of significance for making life visibly better, did not disprove religion (on Draper's definition); but tended to displace it as an object of interest.

. . . how inadequate is the catalogue . . . [of the services of science to mankind] I have furnished in the foregoing pages! I have said nothing of the spread of instruction by the diffusion of the arts of reading and writing, through public schools, and the consequent creation of a reading community; the modes of manufacturing public opinion by newspapers and reviews, the power of journalism, the diffusion of information public and private by the post-office and cheap mails, the individual and social advantages of newspaper advertisements. I have said nothing of the establishment of hospitals . . . ; nothing of the improved prisons, reformatories, penitentiaries, asylums, the treatment of lunatics, paupers, criminals; nothing of the construction of canals, of sanitary engineering, or of census reports; nothing of the invention of stereotyping, bleaching by chlorine, the cotton-gin, or of the marvelous contrivances with which cotton-mills are filled—contrivances which have given us cheap clothing, and therefore added to cleanliness, comfort, health; nothing of the grand advancement of medicine and surgery, or of the discoveries in physiology, the cultivation of the fine arts, the improvement of agriculture and rural economy, the introduction of chemical manures and farm-machinery. I have not referred to the manufacture of iron and its vast affiliated industries; to those of textile fabrics; to the collection of museums of natural history, antiquities, curiosities. [sentence] I have said nothing adequate about the railway system, or the electric telegraph, nor about the calculus, or lithography, the air-pump, or the voltaic battery. . . .[43]

The intellectual enlightenment that surrounds this activity has imparted unnumbered blessings to the human race. In Russia it has emancipated a vast serf-population; in America it has given freedom to four million negro slaves. In place of the sparse dole of the monastery-gate, it has organized charity and directed legislation to the poor. It has shown medicine its true function, to prevent rather than to cure disease. In statesmanship it has introduced scientific methods, displacing random and empirical legislation by a laborious ascertainment of social facts previous to the application of legal remedies.[44]

This breathless catalogue—a kind of hymn of science—is the emotional climax of the *Conflict between Religion and Science;* and it makes the issues of religion not false but irrelevant. In this way the absorption in science bred the habit, not quite perfected in Draper, of ceasing to ask certain questions and finding that they need not be asked. But he took no account of this lapse of attention, and distracted the churches from what ought to have been their chief concern. He had the triumph over his critics of defining the limits of the argument.

Draper showed by his example how much buoyant faith could be liberated by science; and he helped to spend the energies of the religious on a secondary issue. Yet there can be little question that he did so unwittingly. He did not piece together the implications of his thought into a malicious pattern.

The reviews of his book mainly took the form of vindicating him altogether, as in Youmans's *Popular Science Monthly,* or of damning him roundly, as in *Brownson's Quarterly Review* ("a conflict that has never occurred, and never can occur" between "two parts of one dialectic whole").[45] Nearly all of the religious magazines made at bottom the same point as the *Presbyterian Quarterly:* "The conflict, as we read it, is not that of religion with science, but of false representations and travestied history, with truth itself." [46] Incomparably the keenest review on either side came from the liberal theologian G. F. Wright, himself a geologist of sorts. He pointed out that the scientists had heaped ridicule on new theories almost as shamelessly as the worst popes. But what he chiefly objected to was shallow optimism about the glorious Age of Machinery which as he thought Draper was proclaiming. "Even now [science] . . . has only multiplied machinery; and the outcome still depends upon the question whether in our religion there is moral power enough left to control and keep in harness the giant we have awakened." [47] He supposed that Draper would not temper his "overweening confidence in the final success of our present material civilization" by reading some theology; but perhaps he would be willing to try Malthus, Ruskin, and Matthew Arnold.[48]

Despite this brilliant attack on the soft side of the *Conflict* and the great mass of angry denunciation more or less to the point, the book proved an enormous success. The most popular volume by an American in Youmans's series, it had gone through fifty printings by the early 1930's and was still on the Appleton list as a pocket-size classic.[49] Abroad the book was published in London and translated into French, German, Italian, Dutch, Spanish (twice), Polish, Japanese, Russian, Portuguese, and Servian.[50]

The Spanish edition of 1876 came to the attention of the Holy See and was entered in the *Index Librorum Prohibitorum,* "quocumque idiomate," as of September 4, 1876: "an honor [in the words of

his friend Professor G. F. Barker] which its author has shared with
Galileo, with Copernicus, with Kepler, with Locke, and with Mill." [51]
A cartoon was soon published in New York, showing Draper dressed
as an Arab with turban, pointed shoes, and scimitar (engraved with
the name of his book), in the presence of the Pope, who brandished
a scroll "Infallibility." [52]

> "Now, by the holy Prophet's beard, ["] the paynim Draper cries,
> And flourishes his cimeter before St. Peter's eyes;
> "Tis I who am infallible, as all the world doth know!
> By Science bright and Islam's might, tis I who tell thee so!"
> But little recks that haughty priest who sits in Peter's chair,
> To him defiance seemeth naught but empty, idle air.
> "I'll take your name, my little man, with others as notorious,
> And write it in my album called 'Index Expurgatorius.' "
> And so this dreadful "Conflict" it rageth fearfully,
> And when it ends, in flame or gore, may we be there to see.

Draper's little granddaughter Antonia Maury felt the distant
echoes of this combat, when her playmates taunted her with having
a grandfather who had written "a naughty book." [53] In Ohio another youngster was in the middle teens when the *Conflict between
Religion and Science* appeared.

> . . . one of the first books to come into my possession was "The History of
> the Conflict Between Religion and Science," by John William Draper. In-
> stinctively, I knew mother would object to my reading it.
> So when that book came into my hands by loan I carried it home under
> my coat. I took it to my room, and cautiously hid it under the straw tick of
> my bed.
> And there by candlelight, when the house was still and the others were
> asleep, I read it without my mother's knowledge, fascinated by the new
> worlds which it opened.[54]

The boy's name was George William Norris. Draper's book soon
had to yield in point of scholarship to Andrew D. White's *History
of the Warfare of Science with Theology in Christendom*. But the
Conflict continued to sell, and as a rousing piece of polemics to shake
and ventilate the orthodoxies of the previous generation.

Chapter XII

TWILIGHT OF A PATRIARCH

THE *Conflict between Religion and Science* was Draper's last major publication of new work. Between 1876 and 1878 he sold eight "popular expositions of science" to *Harper's* magazine at $20 a page; for 83¼ pages this amounted to $1,665.[1] Harper's also published a collection of his old *Scientific Memoirs* in 1878.[2] The book was favorably reviewed; and the writer for *Nature* thought that an indictment had been proved against Kirchhoff for failing to give credit to Draper for discovering experimentally what he himself had worked out analytically.[3]

In spite of the gravel Draper remained active in the last six years of his life.[4] By now he had become a legendary figure at New York University.

When I came to the University in the fall of 1879 there was one man connected with it whom I wanted to see—the master whose genius had brought to excellence the marvels of photography and to success the wonders of the electric telegraph—John William Draper.[5]

So, my curiosity was great when I arrived at the University to see him, and one of my first inquiries of the janitor . . . was to find Dr. Draper's room. He directed me to the last room on the left of the north hall, and I took my stand by the window at the end of the hall at the odd moments of the first few days in the hope that I might see Dr. Draper as he came in or went out.

One day the janitor noticed me standing there, and asked me if I was watching for someone and when I told him my quest, the generous man— we called him St. Peter—took up his great bunch of keys, opened the doors and gave me a glimpse of . . . Dr. Draper's lecture room. . . . Then he told me to look for Dr. Draper just before the Faculty meeting on the afternoon of the same day. This time I saw him as he came down the hall and had my first sight of the great scientist. I saw a short, stocky man, slightly stooping, dressed in black and wearing a silk hat with his head slightly inclined. His carriage was easy and yet it had an expression of deliberate certainty. His eyes were held on the floor, yet he saw and returned my salute, as he always did when a student paid him that mark of respect.[6]

He took as great pains as ever with his lectures. When the class arrived he was already standing at the table in front with his notes and rollbook.[7] Tapping for attention with a short pencil, he would begin to speak "in a low but distinct voice."

At times, when his subject led him to present some of his own contributions to science, and to present the discussion of others concerning them, his manner would change to one of great deliberation or to one of animation, and we perceived in this change a return to the feelings of the active and successful investigator of the 50s and 60s. Then he would relapse into the cadences of his boyhood tongue and everyone of us would leave off taking notes and listen to the grand old man at his best. His sentences flowed along easily, excepting that at times, he would pause a moment to choose a word. Then he would take up the little, short pencil, set it carefully on its end, or as carefully turn it over on its side, and the word always came when the operation was completed. He did not always tell us that the experiments which he described were his own; we came to pick them out by the change in his manner. Once in a while, after presenting his own results, he would tell us that they had been called into question, and then he would give us a detailed account as if we were a jury competent to deliberate upon the dispute and render a satisfactory verdict.[8]

He was careful to explain his apparatus and the steps of his experiments so that beginners could follow.[9] When the experiment failed, he would look up with a smile:

Young gentlemen, I started out to perform a certain experiment and expected to obtain a certain result; I have not done so yet, and so far as getting that result is concerned, the experiment is a failure. But, if, when we try an experiment, we call it a failure because we have not obtained the result we looked for, we have made a great mistake. Now in this case, let us seek to find out what has happened, in place of what we expected would happen.[10]

Sometimes he would keep a bright student after class, sit down in his rocking chair in one corner of the lecture room, "and charm his young listener until the unwelcome gong broke the spell with its harsh clanging at the end of the hour." [11]

He was intolerant of a doubt, a dogma, or an unproven assumption, and was unsparing in his criticism of anyone who relied upon any of these. He hit hard, and I seem to see him now [in one of these rocking-chair conversations], his eyes sparkling, his head erect, but his voice scarcely raised above his habitual tone, disposing of his critics who had attacked with such weapons.[12]

The best tribute to his power over students Draper did not live to see; fifty years after his death one of them, William H. Nichols, gave the University several million dollars in memory of "Draper's teachings in science and history." [13]

Outside the University, Draper was receiving honors on every hand. On May 25, 1875, the American Academy of Arts and Sciences awarded him its Rumford medals "for his Researches on Radiant Energy"; the American Chemical Society elected him its first president in 1876; the National Academy of Sciences finally made him a member in 1877; and the ministers of the Unitarian church, meeting at Springfield, Massachusetts, in October 1877, asked him to expound the theory of evolution.[14] He told them that belief in discrete creations must be tested by the standard, "Is it derogatory to the awful majesty of God?" [15] He thought so.

Perhaps the thing that pleased Draper most was to end his career as the founder of a dynasty of scientists.[16] John Christopher was teaching physiology at City College and chemistry in the Medical School of New York University; Daniel was a prominent meteorologist, who had invented self-recording apparatus; and Henry was an astronomer of international reputation. Draper did not live to see his two granddaughters Carlota and Antonia Maury carry on the line, one as a palaeontologist, the other as an "American man of science" in astronomy. But he enlisted Antonia as a laboratory assistant before his death.[17]

He liked to gather this gifted family around him on the back porch of the home at Hastings, with its long view up the Hudson.

Happiest were the days when Henry could be home. Then he sat facing his father; and when they two carried on the conversation, the rest sat silent. For it was well known that everything they said was too important for any word of it to be lost. To his father, in whose face a serene repose mingled with sustained intensity of intellectual penetration, Henry was the perfect foil, his dark eyes flashing electrically over the latest discoveries in physics or astronomy, or when relating some humorous incident, they brimmed with laughter to the point of tears. Generally they discussed new plans and appara[tus] for some special research or talked about what Lockyer and Huggins were doing in England with stellar spectra, or about the strange unknown element of helium in the sun.

And shall I ever forget the day when all went over to the observatory and Henry set up the reflecting telescope in full sunshine, and looking into the attached spectroscope, we beheld, trembling on the sun's edge, that pointed yellow ray near to the dark D lines and knew that we were looking at the strange element of the sun, unknown on earth.[18]

Draper kept up this consuming interest in new scientific work to the end, and in spite of the pain which the gravel caused him, he gave his lectures in the college as late as 1881.[19] But in the fall he had to abandon his teaching for the time at least and stay home at Hastings. He died there on January 4, 1882, at the age of 70.[20] "The death of Dr. Draper [Silliman's *Journal* said] . . . removes the most renowned investigator in molecular physics and the most encyclopedic author in the circle of American scientists." [21] The old gentleman had been settling his own accounts a week before he died; and "I don't regret," he said, "a thing I have said or written for I believe it to be true." [22]

All the tensions of his mind and heart had now relaxed: scientist and poet, liberal and authoritarian, worshipful and irreverent, buoyant and pessimistic, he gave way to men of more grasp and less range both in science and the writing of history.

With a few exceptions it is hard to steer a course between European neglect and American boosting and estimate an American scientist who did significant work before 1870. Draper was not of the first rank, but if he had spoken from a chair in one of the minor German universities, he might well have had, what he now lacks, a small place in most histories of modern science written on a reasonably generous scale. The stubborn defense till nearly the close of his career of the theory of the imponderables was a serious blunder. But over against this, he helped supply some of the evidence against the imponderables; he had a striking, perhaps an unrivaled, grasp of the value of photography in scientific investigation; he was a pioneer, even by European standards, in mapping the invisible regions of the spectrum and correlating the source of light with its spectrum; and he was one of the founders of the theory of photochemical absorption. It would be fairly easy to list half a dozen American scientists who did work of greater value before 1870—Franklin, Thompson, Henry, Beaumont, Leidy, and Asa Gray are names that come to mind, if Thompson is an American—and perhaps it would be equally *hard* to name six more.

Draper began, in fact, toward the end of his career to be recognized at home as one of the principal figures in American science. But for some reason—and it was not that he was discredited; his claims were not exploded, but forgotten—after he died his reputation as a scientist went into a sharp decline. As a writer on history and politics, however, he attracted world-wide attention almost from the start; and the *Intellectual Development of Europe* and the *Conflict between Religion and Science* continued to be read, and respected, with a slackening momentum well into the twentieth century. Fresh scholarship is by no means the strength of these books; and Draper is an example of the scholar, of whom Jeans was the type later on, who does original research but lingers in memory chiefly as a popularizer. But it is a real accomplishment, for good or bad, to play a part in changing just perceptibly the tone of the popular mind, or in barely shaking even one inchoate conviction.

In reading modern history one hears of the popularization of science by fits and starts—Voltaire and *newtonianisme pour les dames,* T. H. Huxley and E. L. Youmans, Eddington and Jeans, and the advocates of instruction in the "strategy" of science. The environment of these men (in this character) has not yet been peopled, or one episode linked persuasively to another. But a good many of what seem to be the persistent issues of popularization are illuminated by Draper's later work. And probably no American writer in this tradition was more read in the nineteenth century, in more parts of the world—at home, across Europe, and even in Asia and Latin America.

Draper's popularization of science took different forms: the spreading of scientific conclusions, the spreading of scientific method, and the spreading of one kind of scientist's temper. A great deal of his "science" would now be written off as unscientific, but this merely displaces without destroying the interest of his work.

The two theories for which Draper mainly spoke, in the belief that they were scientific, were environmentalism and Comte's law of historical stages. He seems not to have sensed the latent opposition between them, and the difference made by the idea of natural selection. But with a rather doubtful consistency he took to a large audience the word that supernatural intervention had been banished from biology and history. The more this seems in the middle of the twentieth century to be a commonplace, a transposition instead of a dissipation of problems, the more effectively Draper and people of his mind did their work. There is a persuasive body of evidence, by its nature scattered and qualitative, that the *Intellectual Development of Europe* and the *Conflict between Religion and Science* were once books which made a difference in the lives of their readers. But the great success of a popularizer is to chip away from year to year at his own reputation.

Comte's law of three stages and the environmentalism which Draper ended by associating with Darwin supplied among other things prescriptions for the writing of history; and this was the cause in which Draper mainly put them forward. As a practicing historian he had grave faults—not enough knowledge and too much bias. But he pioneered in the writing of intellectual history, for which he found the suggestive clue in the stages of Comte. He also struck off in terms of environmentalism a searching thesis about the westward movement in the United States (though the best statement of this occurs in a short address which cannot have been very widely read)—the using up of the soil, the premium put on this by a great fund of land "farther on," and the breeding of social instability. With an insight of this kind Draper showed what good might come of intruding the data of agricultural chemistry into history books. But his main accomplishment was to help lift the *relevance* of supernaturalism off the minds of average men, in the name of science; more to commend than supply the natural history of history.

In using Comte's law of three stages Draper spread about him a particular conception of what it meant to employ the scientific method, as well as scientific results, in writing history. Sometimes another conception appears to speak from the pages of the *Conflict:* simply to do one's damnedest with new ideas and weigh their tangible results. But this is distinctly recessive; and it would be fair to characterize Draper's dominant idea of science as involving predictability, infallibilism, determinism, and interchangeability of the units of investigation. *Social* science becomes by these standards, a special kind of nineteenth-century physics; and the generalized form of the scientific method is the construction of theories on the physical pattern. The prescription laid down is to rise to social science by way of physics, except that you do *not* rise but rather stay within the limits of physics. One cannot by this account bring the empirical habit of mind directly to bear on history, or even make history logically distinguishable from exact science as an exercise of this habit. How many false expectations were raised—and dashed—of bringing history within the limits of this caricature of the scientific method, no one can say; but they were part of the influence exerted by Draper. He belongs in this regard to the popularizers of science who impoverish the naturalistic tradition by missing the complexity and diversity of scientific investigation. Their mistake induces the ultimate loss of confidence in the experimental and pragmatic outlook. The more this disillusionment is welcomed or deprecated, the more importance attaches to a writer as much read as Draper. He set himself the task of defining the community of effort among scholars of an open mind, regardless of their subject—but muffed the definition. In particular, he did not profit as he should have done from one of the best things in Comte: the ordering of the sciences to take account of the reliance of new ones on old without adopting the genetic fallacy of "reducing" each logically posterior science to the disciplines on which it drew. But Draper had the merit at least of obtruding on his readers' attention a problem that must be resolved before some of the chief fissures in modern thought were healed: how to transfer the truth-warrants and the use-returns of experimental science to the analysis of society.

In some ways the least conscious side of Draper's work as a popularizer of science and of attitudes taken to be scientific consisted in spreading not so much conclusions or methods as a kind of temper. Some of the ideas which he considered scientific implied the vanity of human exertions. But he showed by his example and sometimes by his expressed views how much optimism and buoyancy, how much zest and exuberance, accrued to the scientist, almost without regard to his particular findings. Draper was to some extent the heir of the Enlightenment, the spokesman for progress, the trumpet of a beneficent utilitarianism which would usher in the age of free minds and creature comforts by grace of science. He belonged in this way to the main currents of nineteenth-century liberalism. But he thought that his own chief contribution to the golden age ahead lay in a science of society. And in considering the application of this science, he nearly seceded from liberalism. In one mood, a flagging but persistent mood, Draper thought that particular men and women, with their aimless concerns and waste energies, ought to get in tune with science—to order their lives systematically. When he faced the issue directly, he concluded from the law of historical stages that if only one took large enough numbers of individuals and averaged them together, one might wrest order from chaos. But sometimes at least he wished the world, including the behavior of individuals, to be trim and systematic throughout. The question then arose of who was to make the peace of the individual with the spirit of science, fit him within the terms of scientific law. The answer which Draper returned seems often, if not invariably, to have been: some kind of scientific elite. Here he reflected the temper of the sort of scientist who cannot bear to see things out from under tight control. This leaning toward authoritarianism ought not to be exaggerated. But it ought not to be and cannot be explained away; it was one of the ideas which he clothed with the sanctions of science and carried to his readers.

Draper deserves, then, to be remembered for his honorable record as a research scientist, for his pioneering in new kinds of history, and for his courage in popularizing unpopular ideas. But his chief merit, in spite of grave equivocations, was to bring his weight down hard on the side of free inquiry and the free play of the minds of men. To the protest that *unclean* ideas ought to be hushed up, he continues to hurl back the reply: "But our opinions on every subject are continually liable to modification, from the irresistible advance of human knowledge."

NOTES

CHAPTER I

1 According to one of the two main accounts of the genealogy of the Draper family, its founder fled from Italy in the eighteenth century, maybe as a political refugee, and changed his name to Draper after settling in England. On the other hand, the line is traced, with no change of name, to a well-to-do Roman Catholic family of Lancashire.

The account of the "Italian" line *in its entirety* seems to come exclusively from John William Draper's son and amanuensis, Daniel Draper; conversations of the author with his children and daughter-in-law, Mrs. Dorothy Draper Nye, of Hastings-on-Hudson, N.Y., and Professor and Mrs. John William Draper, of Morgantown, W. Va., 1945.

A change of name is vouched for in Elwood Hendrick, "John William Draper," *Dictionary of American Biography*, V, 438; where he says of his subject's father that the real name was "unrecorded." The only member of the Draper family whom Hendrick lists, p. 441, as having been consulted for "personal information" is "Dr. John W. Draper of New York." Evidently this is the John William Draper Maury who dropped his last name in honor of his grandfather.

The history of a Roman Catholic family, such as would fall in with the alternative account, a family ultimately of Heptonstall in the West Riding of Yorkshire, is treated by Thomas Waln-Morgan Draper, *The Drapers in America* (New York, 1892); but no claim is made in the appendix on John William Draper's family, "The Drapers of Drapersville, Va.," pp. 225–28, that there is any connection between the families. It is probable that the data here given were furnished by Daniel Draper or his sister-in-law Mrs. Henry Draper.

Mr. Charles Lennox Wright, of New York, John William Draper's great-nephew, links the family treated in the body of *The Drapers in America* with that of his great-uncle. Letter to the author, June 13, 1945. Mr. Wright told Theodore F. Jones, librarian of New York University, that he had talked with a first cousin, Dr. Daniel Gardner, who had lived in Europe till 1940, and that this cousin had heard through his father that the Drapers "were all of Lancashire from near Liverpool, Catholics. . . ." Memorandum of T. F. Jones, October, 1941. Mr. Wright's mother and Dr. Gardner's father were sister and brother, and of the same generation with Daniel Draper. If there was an accommodation of the sister's and brother's versions of the family origin, it must have taken place before their separation in 1882 (date in letter of C. L. Wright, New York, to author, May 30, 1945).

Hendrick, "Draper," p. 438, says that John William Draper's father was of an "influential Roman Catholic family." This statement is possibly to be attributed to John William Draper [Maury], a grandson of John William. Whether it may be fairly said to confirm either of the clear-cut traditions is a question.

2 The attributions of localities are suggested by Mr. Charles Lennox Wright, John William Draper's great-nephew, of New York, to author, June 13, 1945. A photograph of John Christopher Draper's gravestone, with the dates of his birth and death, is in the possession of Mrs. Dorothy Draper Nye, of Hastings-on-Hudson, N.Y., John William Draper's granddaughter. The place of birth is given

in T. W-M. Draper, *Drapers in America,* p. 227. A family tree in the possession of Mrs. D. D. Nye shows three generations preceding John William Draper; and those who contend that there was no change of the family name would, of course, grant *at least* these generations.

³ Quoted from the report of his death to the Wesleyan Conference of 1829; "Professor Draper A St. Helens Man," *St. Helens Newspaper & Advertiser* (St. Helens, Lancashire, England), February 18, 1882. On the conversion: conversations of the author with John William Draper's grandchildren and granddaughter-in-law, Mrs. Nye and Professor and Mrs. John William Draper, of Morgantown. W.Va., 1945; from Mrs. Nye's and Professor Draper's father, Daniel Draper (John William Draper's son and amanuensis). Hendrick, "Draper," p. 438, says that the revival was led by John Wesley himself, but he died when J. C. Draper was only fourteen.

⁴   "Made by converting grace salvation's heir,
                      He longed that others might the blessing share;"
[J. S. Featherstone], *A Tribute of Grateful Remembrance to the Memory of The Rev. John Christopher Draper* ([Sheerness, England, 1829]), p. 4.

⁵ The classic account of this change is given by Elie Halévy, *A History of the English People,* E. I. Watkin (and for Vol. I, D. A. Barker), trans. (London, 1926–48), I, Book III, "Religion and Culture." This cultural revolution may be detected (along with age and poor health) overtaking Jane Austen in her later novels.

⁶ Family disavowal: Nye conversations, 1945; Draper conversations, 1945; C. L. Wright, New York, to author, June 13, 1945; Hendrick, "Draper," p. 438. Miss Antonia C. Maury, John William Draper's granddaughter, of Hastings-on-Hudson, N.Y., heard her Aunt Dorothy Catharine, a sister of John William Draper, recall the visit of "two tall and elegant ladies" in her childhood, and thinks they figured in the recollection as sisters of the aunt's father. The visit seems to have been marked as notable, and this may bear out the tradition of some kind of estrangement or disavowal. Conversations of Miss Maury with the author, 1945. On J. C. Draper's early service: quoted report of his death to Conference, 1829, in "Professor Draper A St. Helens Man."

⁷ Marriage: "Professor Draper A St. Helens Man." Sarah Ripley was the daughter of William and Dorothy Ripley; baptismal certificates of her three eldest children, Nye papers, Hastings-on-Hudson, N.Y.   C. L. Wright, New York, to author, June 13, 1945, asserts that John C. Draper was converted to Wesleyanism through his love for Sarah, herself a Methodist; but as their marriage took place roughly seven years after his conversion, one would like positive proof of this nearly Biblical "seven years' servitude."

Emigration to America: George F. Barker, *Memoir of John William Draper 1811–1882* ([Washington? 1886?]), p. 352; T. W-M. Draper, *Drapers in America,* p. 225. The manuscript life, "Professor John W. Draper," unsigned, the hand probably his own or possibly his son Daniel's, A. C. Maury papers, Hastings-on-Hudson, N.Y., does not make clear *who* the relatives were who preceded him to America. If Hendrick, "Draper," p. 438, is based on conversations with John William Draper [Maury], John William Draper's grandson who dropped a last name in his honor, there is additional confirmation for the naming of the Ripleys as the emigrants to America.

⁸ J. C. Draper: undated engraving, Maury papers; quoted, report of his death to Conference, 1829, in "Professor Draper A St. Helens Man." Sarah Draper: miniature in the possession of Mrs. D. D. Nye; the coloring is of doubtful authenticity.

⁹ Halévy, *English People*, I, 361. Allowances to J. C. Draper: abstracted from Wesleyan reports, "Professor Draper A St. Helens Man."

¹⁰ The phrase is from [Featherstone], *Tribute,* p. 5. In nearly every circuit that

J. C. Draper joined, the numbers of Methodism swelled, as from 317 to 900 in one year at Namptwich; "Professor Draper A St. Helens Man." A brilliant sketch of the higher reaches of the philanthropic community is struck off in the opening chapter of George Otto Trevelyan, *The Life and Letters of Lord Macaulay* (London, 1876), I.

11 [Featherstone], *Tribute*, pp. 4–5. Hannah More died in 1833, her old friend Zachary Macaulay in 1838; *Vanity Fair* (and Lady Southdown) appeared in numbers in 1847–48, and *Bleak House* (and Mrs. Jellyby) in 1852–53.

12 See the remarkable book by M. G. Jones, *The Charity School Movement* (Cambridge, England, 1938), especially pp. 3–14.

13 Telescope: Barker, *Memoir*, p. 351; Benjamin N. Martin, "A Sketch of John W. Draper," *The Magazine of American History*, VIII, Pt. I (1882), 240. Barker, p. 351, says that the elder Draper was interested in chemistry and astronomy. The liberal curriculum of the Dissenting academies, at the most famous of which, Warrington Academy, Joseph Priestley himself taught, is well known; provision was made for the sciences.

14 Baptismal certificates, Nye papers.

15 As, £15, 7s. from the ministers' fund in 1806; £12 for expenses in attending the Conference at Bristol in 1808; £6, 17s. for domestic sickness in 1809; £10 for attending the Conference at London in 1810; and £1, 12s. 6d. for traveling expenses in 1811. Taken from Wesleyan proceedings and published in "Professor Draper A St. Helens Man."

16 Baptismal certificate, Nye papers.

17 Baptismal certificate, Nye papers. See Thomas Percival Bunting, *The Life of Jabez Bunting, D.D.* (London, 1859), I (but no more were ever published).

18 Sarah's birth: T. W-M. Draper, *Drapers in America*, p. 227. Stations noted: Wesleyan proceedings, "Professor Draper A St. Helens Man."

19 John W. Draper, *Lecture. Introductory to the Course of 1869–70* (New York [1869]), p. 11.

20 Trevelyan, *Macaulay*, World's Classics edition, I, 27–28; John Stuart Mill, *Autobiography of John Stuart Mill*, Columbia University Press ed. (New York, 1924; the first ed., 1873), p. 4.

21 See J. W. Draper, *Lecture* [1869], *passim*; the quotation from p. 11.

22 Antonia C. Maury, "Recollections of my Grandfather, John William Draper," typewritten manuscript, p. 4; Maury papers.

23 Martin, "Sketch," p. 240.

24 "Professor Draper A St. Helens Man"; and [J. W. Draper? or Daniel Draper?], "Draper," MS, p. 1.

25 [J. W. Draper? or Daniel Draper?], "Draper," MS, p. 1.

26 J. W. Draper, *Lecture* [1869], p. 11.

27 Maury conversations.

28 [J. W. Draper? or Daniel Draper?], "Draper," MS, p. 1.

29 *Loc cit.*; "Professor Draper A St. Helens Man."

30 "Professor Draper A St. Helens Man."

31 Letter of J. C. Draper, Sheerness, to Rev. F. A. Cox [of the projected University of London], September 1, 1826; copy in New York University archives, from the archives of University College, University of London. University of London, *Proprietors of Shares* ([London, 1827]), p. 6.

32 J. C. Draper, Sheerness, to Leonard Horner, June 28, 1828; NYU archives copy, from University College, University of London, archives.

33 Photograph of gravestone, Nye papers. Quotation from the report of his death to Conference, 1829; "Professor Draper A St. Helens Man."

³⁴ The date and the assertion that he was studying with a view to medicine rest on [J. W. Draper? or Daniel Draper?], "Draper," MS, p. 1, where, after mention of the date, it is said: "He came to America, and completed his medical education. . . ."

³⁵ Conversation of C. L. Wright with T. F. Jones, librarian of NYU; Jones's memorandum, October 1941, in the NYU archives.

³⁶ See the "designs" in H. Hale Bellot, *University College London 1826–1926* (London, 1929), between pp. 58, 59. The dome was one of the less disastrous victims of the Blitz.

³⁷ Draper's appearance: a distinctly youthful, but undated, miniature in the possession of Mrs. D. D. Nye. Maurice and Sylvester: the three are spoken of as "contemporaries" in Bellot, *University College*, p. 186; but it sometimes looks as if the word "roughly" ought to be slid in ahead of Bellot's references to "contemporaries." The issue of when Sylvester was expelled appears to be a little muddled; Raymond Clare Archibald, "Material Concerning James Joseph Sylvester," in M. F. Ashley Montagu, ed., *Studies . . . Offered . . . to George Sarton* (New York [1947?]), p. 211. On the refectory: Bellot, p. 179.

³⁸ See the "Plan of the Distribution of the Departments within the Building, 1828–1876," Bellot, *University College*, between pp. 172, 173.

³⁹ Sketch of Turner by J. Norman Collie, *A Century of Chemistry*, pp. 8–10, quoted by Bellot, *University College*, pp. 125–27. See also Arthur Harden, "Edward Turner," *Dictionary of National Biography*, XIX, 1262–63; and Bernard Jaffe, *Crucibles: The Story of Chemistry*, revised [2d?] ed. (New York, 1948), p. 148.

⁴⁰ He is the only teacher mentioned in [J. W. Draper? or Daniel Draper?], "Draper," MS.

⁴¹ The experience is often recounted, as *ibid.*, p. 2; the connection with Turner is stated in [the editor H. H. Snelling?], "Some Facts Connected with the Early History of Photography in America," *Photographic and Fine Art Journal* [Snelling's], n.s., VII (1854), 381.

⁴² Higgins was recommended for the chair of geology in University College, letter of J. C. Draper, Sheerness, to Leonard Horner [Warden], August 15, 1828; NYU archives copy from University College, University of London. This is not the Higgins sometimes claimed to have anticipated Dalton.

"On Volcanoes," *Magazine of Natural History*, V (1832), 164–72, 262–72, 632–37, VI (1833), 344–50; the quotation from V, 165. "Remarks on the Formation of the Dead Sea and the Surrounding District," *Magazine of Natural History*, V (1832), 532–34. "Remarks on Electrical Decompositions," *Edinburgh New Philosophical Journal*, XIV (1832–33), 314–17.

⁴³ Original of the certificate, Nye papers.

⁴⁴ All the students named "entered" for Austin's lectures between 1828 and 1830; Bellot, *University College*, p. 187, from the University Register.

⁴⁵ Draper recalls his meeting with Pattison in London in "The Life and Services of Granville S. Pattison, M.D.," *New York Herald*, January 11, 1852, p. 1. Pattison's dismissal and its upshot are recounted, Bellot, *University College*, pp. 194–212.

⁴⁶ Mrs. Barker's connection with Draper's father: Barker, *Memoir*, p. 380. The age of Miss Gardner is warmly disputed, for reasons which will shortly appear. According to C. L. Wright, New York, to author, March 5, 1946, she was born in 1820. According to traditions handed down by Daniel Draper, she was born in 1814; Nye conversations. She was certainly married in 1831, in regular form, and this weighs very heavily on the side of the earlier birth date.

⁴⁷ Barker, *Memoir*, p. 381, speaks of the mother as belonging to "the celebrated de Piva-Pereira family of Portugal." C. L. Wright, New York, to author, June 13, 1945, March 5, 1946, argues for her being the Infanta, and the morganatic wife

of Dr. Daniel Gardner; gives a circumstantial account of their connection; says
that his thesis is confirmed by his European cousin, another Dr. Daniel Gardner;
and quotes the *Hastings Gazette* (Hastings-on-Hudson, N.Y.), January 13, 1906,
as referring to "a tie that bound him [Dom Pedro II, Emperor of Brazil] very
closely to Dr. Draper and his family." The European cousin does agree in accepting this thesis; the Hastings paper does not appear in the *Union List*. As
there is a persistent family tradition (Barker, *Memoir,* pp. 380–81; C. L. Wright,
New York, to author, June 13, 1945) that Gardner was a court physician in Rio
de Janeiro, this, if true, would be a close tie of a sort; though there is, of course,
no good reason why this connection should not be plainly stated instead of hinted
at. It is clear that Gardner was a lecturer in chemistry at the college of Sao
Joaquim: ". . . the college of St. Joaquim has undergone considerable improvement: a lectureship on chemistry has been instituted, to which our countryman,
Dr. Gardner, has been nominated by His Royal Highness. . . ." John Mawe,
Travels in the Interior of Brazil (London, 1812), p. 105.

That Isabel Maria, dying single, had borne two children is called "traditional"
by Angelo Pereira, *As Senhoras Infantas Filhas d'el Rei D' João VI* (Lisbon, 1938),
p. 121. The burden of Pereira's treatment follows: (1) he names a "Hintze Ribeiro"
as reputedly the grandson of King John VI, and under the *less* likely of two
versions of this relationship, the son of Isabel Maria (p. 122, n.); (2) he refers, not
unfavorably, to a tradition that Isabel Maria made some kind of secret provision
for her "illegitimate son" in her will (pp. 128–29). But none of this establishes
the Gardner children as Isabel Maria's; and it does put forward another "claimant."
Perhaps it would be safest to return the Scotch verdict: not proved.

48 Nye, Maury, and Draper conversations. C. L. Wright, New York, to author,
June 13, 1945, argues that the marriage was a device of Dom Pedro I to get his
sister Isabel Maria's children out of Europe and thus forestall their claims to
her estate when she died. He offers no documentary evidence.

49 Marriage certificate, Nye papers.

50 Letter of J. W. Draper [London], to Henry Draper, November 23, 1870;
Draper papers, New York Public Library, Manuscript Division.

51 [J. W. Draper? or Daniel Draper?], "Draper," MS, p. 1; Barker, *Memoir,*
p. 352.

CHAPTER II

1 George F. Barker, *Memoir of John William Draper 1811–1882* ([Washington?
1886?]), p. 352; Elwood Hendrick, "John William Draper," *Dictionary of American
Biography,* V, 438.

2 See William W. Bennett, *Memorials of Methodism in Virginia, from . . . 1772,
to the year 1829* (Richmond, 1871), pp. 103, 152, 170, 344, and *passim.*

3 See Barker, *Memoir,* p. 352; Professor John W. Draper of Morgantown, West
Virginia, "A Trip to Drapersville, Va.," 1939, MS in his possession, p. 2; W. A.
Garner to Editor, *Chase City Progress* (Chase City, Virginia), July 20, 1939.

4 W. A. Garner, Roanoke, Virginia, to the author, November 17, 1945.

5 J. W. Draper [of Morgantown], "Drapersville [1939]," MS, p. 1.

6 Garner in *Chase City Progress;* from Mrs. L. M. Carter's recollection of conversations with her mother Susannah Annesley Coleman Dance.

7 J. W. Draper [of Morgantown], "Drapersville [1939]," MS, p. 1; from Mrs.
L. M. Carter.

8 W. A. Garner, Roanoke, to J. W. Draper [of Morgantown], August 28, 1941;
in Draper's possession.

9 Mainly, it would seem, with Daniel Gardner and his wife Sarah Draper Gardner

on one side. J. W. Draper [of Morgantown], "Drapersville [1939]," MS, p. 2; from Mrs. L. M. Carter.

10 *Loc cit.*

11 J. W. Draper, "Some Experimental Researches to Determine the Nature of Capillary Attraction," *Journal of the Franklin Institute*, n.s., XIV (1834), 147–65 (quotation, p. 149).

12 *Ibid.*, p. 150.

13 *Ibid.*, pp. 149–50.

14 "Idolatry and Philosophy of the Zabians," *American Journal of Science*, XXVIII (1835), 219.

15 Including "Nature of Capillary Attraction"; "Influence of Electricity on Capillary Attraction," *American Journal of Science*, XXVI (1834), 399–400; "Of the Tidal Motions of Conductors, Free to Move," *Journal of the Franklin Institute*, n.s., XVII (1836), 27–33; "Experiments Made to Determine Whether Light Exerts Any Magnetic Action," *Journal of the Franklin Institute*, n.s., XV (1835), 79–85, 155–58.

16 Hendrick, "Draper," p. 439, puts the sister's savings at $4,000. For the length of Draper's studies, see Barker, *Memoir*, p. 353.

17 Edward Potts Cheyney, *History of the University of Pennsylvania* (Philadelphia, 1940), 209, 228–29.

18 J. W. Draper, *Lecture. Introductory to the Course of 1869–70* (New York [1869]), p. 6.

19 *Loc. cit.*

20 See Edgar Fahs Smith and Helen C. Boatfield, "Robert Hare," *Dictionary of American Biography*, VIII, 263–64; and portraits in Edgar Fahs Smith, *Robert Hare* (Philadelphia, 1917).

21 See Charles W. Barr, "John Kearsley Mitchell," *Dictionary of American Biography*, XIII, 54–55; and Anna Robeson Burr, *Weir Mitchell* (New York, 1929), chapters I–III.

22 *Indecision* (Philadelphia, 1838), p. x.

23 Barker, *Memoir*, p. 353.

24 It is listed by The Society of the Alumni of the Medical Department, *Catalogue of the Alumni of the Medical Department of the University of Pennsylvania. 1765–1877* (Philadelphia, 1877), p. 49. The testimony to publication is given in [J. W. Draper? or Daniel Draper?], "Professor John W. Draper," MS in Maury papers, p. 1. Barker, *Memoir*, 353, testifies to a vain search for the thesis, not to be found at the University of Pennsylvania.

25 "Experiments on Absorption," *American Journal of Medical Sciences*, XVIII (1836), 13–32; "Experiments on Endosmosis," *Journal of the Franklin Institute*, n.s., XVII (1836), 177–82, and XVIII (1836), 27–31.

26 "Absorption," p. 31.

27 See Avery Craven, "Edmund Ruffin," *Dictionary of American Biography*, XVI, 214–16; and Avery Craven, *Edmund Ruffin Southerner* (New York, 1932), chapter III.

28 See on this general subject, Charles A. Browne, *A Source Book of Agricultural Chemistry* (Waltham, Mass., 1944), especially chapters VI and VII. The title of this book is misleading; there is a most substantial text of the author's own composition, plus extracts from the sources.

29 Communication to Editor [Ruffin himself], "Proceedings of the Mineralogical Society of Virginia," *Farmers' Register*, IV (1836–37), 316. I owe this reference, in the first instance, to Alfred J. Morrison, ed., *The College of Hampden-Sidney. Calendar of Board Minutes 1776–1876* (Richmond, 1912), pp. 114–15, n.

30 "Mineralogical Society," p. 316. In an appended note, pp. 316–17, Ruffin tries to turn the Society from its talk of gold to the possibility of coal fields.

31 *Ibid.,* p. 316. Turner's initial is mistakenly given as "B." instead of "E."

32 [J. W. Draper? or Daniel Draper?], "Draper," MS, p. 2.

33 See Wesley M. Gewehr, *The Great Awakening in Virginia, 1740–1790* (Durham, North Carolina, 1930), chapter IX, especially pp. 226–30.

34 *Introductory Lecture to a Course of Chemistry and Natural Philosophy, Delivered in Hampden Sidney College* (Richmond, 1836), pp. 10–11.

35 *Ibid.,* p. 19.

36 Morrison, *Calendar,* p. 115; Board of Trustees in session, September 27–29, 1836.

37 *Ibid.,* p. 118.

38 The dates and places of both births are recorded, Thomas Waln-Morgan Draper, *The Drapers in America* (New York, 1892), p. 227; of Henry's, George F. Barker, *Memoir of Henry Draper* ([Washington? 1888?]), p. 4.

39 The college schedule, Morrison, *Calendar,* p. 118, n.

40 *Loc. cit.;* J. W. Draper, "Lecture," "on the occasion of the award of an annual prize, given to members of the Junior and Senior Classes," *Southern Literary Messenger,* III (1837), 693–98; the memorial quoted, Morrison, *Calendar,* pp. 116–17 (the quoted phrases, p. 117).

41 "Observations on Microscopic Chemistry," *Journal of the Franklin Institute,* n.s., XVIII (1836), 378 (both quotations).

42 "Simultaneous Meteorological Observations," *Journal of the Franklin Institute,* n.s., XXI (1838), 39–40.

43 *Ibid.,* p. 39.

44 "Analysis of Solar Light," *American Journal of the Medical Sciences,* XX (1837), 268–69; "Experiments on Solar Light" [I, II, III, IV], *Journal of the Franklin Institute,* n.s., XIX (1837), 469–79, XX (1837), 38–46, 114–25, 250–53.

45 Kinds of rays, "Experiments, Solar Light [I]," p. 469; interference, "Experiments, Solar Light [II]," p. 45–46.

46 See above, p. 6. The researches on the subject are to be found in "Experiments, Solar Light [III]," pp. 116–25.

47 See Browne, *Agricultural Chemistry,* chapter VII; and H. T. Pledge, *Science Since 1500* (London, 1939), 128–30.

48 "Experiments, Solar Light [IV]," pp. 252–53.

49 The unhappy fact is that Draper backed and filled on the issue just a little, but by and large he seems to have got the point of the correlation.

50 "Experiments, Solar Light [IV]," p. 251.

51 "Experiments, Solar Light [II]," pp. 45–46; "Experiments, Solar Light [III]," p. 115.

52 J. W. Draper, "Who Made the First Photographic Portrait," *American Journal of Photography and the Allied Arts & Sciences,* n.s., I (1859–60), p. 3. See Robert Taft, *Photography and the American Scene, A Social History, 1839–1889* (New York, 1938), pp. 102–6.

53 J. W. Draper, "First Portrait," p. 3.

54 *Loc. cit.*

55 *Ibid.,* p. 4. See also Taft, *Photography,* p. 19, for the exposition of this point.

56 J. W. Draper, "First Portrait," p. 3.

57 *Ibid.,* p. 4.

58 A camera presumably used by Draper at Hampden-Sidney was preserved there; on the initiative of Howard C. Cobbs, an alumnus of the college, this camera was presented to the National Museum of the Smithsonian Institution, as the earliest "fast-acting" camera in the world. "The First Photographic Camera," *The Record of the Hampden-Sidney Alumni Association,* XIV (1940), 14; "The Draper Camera Goes to Washington," *Record . . . H-S. Alumni,* XV (1941), 10. I cannot see that there is sufficient evidence for these very dogmatic statements.

150   JOHN WILLIAM DRAPER

⁵⁹ "Remarks on the Action of Presence [Draper's term for catalysis applied to physiology]," *American Journal of the Medical Sciences,* XXI (1837–38), 128.

⁶⁰ *Loc. cit.*

⁶¹ *Loc. cit.* For "therapeutic nihilism," see Richard H. Shryock, *The Development of Modern Medicine,* 2d ed. (New York, 1947), at various places but especially p. 249.

⁶² "Further Remarks on the Action of Presence," *American Journal of the Medical Sciences,* XXIII (1839), 68.

⁶³ Chapter XV of *Middlemarch* (1871–72) is a very shrewd blend of medical and social history, of a kind where it benefited George Eliot to be the most intellectual of English novelists. See Shryock, *Modern Medicine,* chapters IX, X.

⁶⁴ See Shryock, *Modern Medicine,* chapter XIII.

⁶⁵ Benjamin N. Martin, "A Sketch of John W. Draper," *Magazine of American History,* VIII, Pt. I (1882), p. 243.

⁶⁶ [J. W. Draper? or Daniel Draper?], "Draper," MS, p. 3.

⁶⁷ D. P. Gardner, Philadelphia, to J. W. Draper, November 17 [1838]; Nye papers.

⁶⁸ Gardner to Draper, November 17 [1838]. I leave the original spelling and punctuation largely unremarked.

⁶⁹ See Theodore Francis Jones, ed., *New York University 1832:1932* (New York, 1933), pp. 46–53.

⁷⁰ New York University, Council Minutes, July 1838–June 1843, MS, p. 31; meeting of September 28, 1838. Minutes in NYU archives.

⁷¹ Jones, *NYU,* pp. 50–51.

⁷² NYU, Council Minutes, 1838–43, MS, pp. 51, 54; meetings of December 29, 1838, and January 10, 1839.

⁷³ Draper, Hampden-Sidney, to Rev. J. Matthews [*sic*], February 5, 1839, in Autograph Collection of Simon Gratz, Historical Society of Pennsylvania; and Draper, New York, to Gen. [James] Tallmadge [of the Tallmadge amendment; president of the NYU Council], May 20, 1839, in NYU archives.

⁷⁴ NYU, Council Minutes, 1838–43, MS, p. 92; meeting of September 25, 1839.

⁷⁵ Morrison, *Calendar,* p. 121.

CHAPTER III

¹ On the city at approximately this time, see: Draper, *A Valedictory Lecture* (New York, 1842); Richard B. Morris, "The Metropolis of the State," in Alexander C. Flick, ed., *The Empire State* (New York, 1937; Alexander C. Flick, ed., *History of the State of New York,* X), pp. 171–214; Frank L. Tolman, "Libraries and Lyceums," in Alexander C. Flick, ed., *Mind and Spirit* (New York, 1937; Alexander C. Flick, ed., *History of the State of New York,* IX), pp. 45–91; Harriet Martineau, *Retrospect of Western Travel* (New York, 1838), I, 35–37; Charles Dickens, *American Notes* (London, 1842), chapter VI; Philip Hone, *The Diary of Philip Hone 1828–1851,* Allan Nevins, ed. (New York, 1927), I and II, *passim,* under the appropriate years; the retrospective biographical notes in [Moses Yale Beach], *Wealth and Biography of the Wealthy Citizens of New York City,* 6th ed. (New York, 1845); I. N. Phelps Stokes, *The Iconography of Manhattan Island 1498–1909* (New York, 1915–28), V, *passim,* under the appropriate years. The cigar-girl was immortalized as Marie Rogêt by E. A. Poe, "The Mystery of Marie Rogêt," reprinted in his *Tales* (New York, 1845).

² Robert Taft, *Photography and the American Scene, A Social History, 1839–1889* (New York, 1938), p. 14.

³ Taft, *Photography,* pp. 15–17.

⁴ Taft, *Photography,* pp. 33–34. But Draper always maintained that he had

been first; see, for example, his letter dated May 3, 1858, "Who Made the First Photographic Portrait?" *American Journal of Photography and the Allied Arts & Sciences*, n.s., Í (1858–59), 2–6. His friendly competitor Morse wrote in a letter of February 10, 1855, ". . . whether he or myself took the first portrait successfully, I cannot say." Edward Lind Morse, ed., *Samuel F. B. Morse: His Letters and Journals* (Boston, 1914), II, 146, after quoting this, adds: "It was afterwards established that to Professor Draper must be accorded this honor, but I understand that it was a question of hours only between the two enthusiasts."

So the order of success in taking portraits may tentatively be set, on the basis of the scanty evidence turned up by Professor Taft's diligent researches, as: Wolcott or Draper, and then Morse. To decide between Wolcott and Draper, Taft, pp. 458–59, summarizes the positions of the three editors of American photographic journals, S. D. Humphrey of *Humphrey's Journal*, Seely of the *American Journal of Photography*, and H. H. Snelling of the *Photographic and Fine Art Journal:* Humphrey and Seely in favor of Wolcott's claim as opposed to Draper's, and Snelling neutral. But the evidence cited by Taft does not, I think, quite justify the positive statement that Seely preferred Wolcott's claim, though this seems likely.

I agree, however, that Taft is right in favoring Wolcott over Draper *on the evidence now available.* As Taft says, the two really damaging facts against Draper are these: (1) so far as we know, the earliest *specific* date ever claimed for him was December, as against October 6 or 7 for Wolcott; and (2) W. H. Goode, Draper's own chemical assistant in 1840, if not in 1839, could make no stronger statement than that Draper and Wolcott had succeeded "about the same time" and independently. Goode, "The Daguerreotype and Its Applications," *American Journal of Science*, XL (1840–41), 142.

5 See the photograph, Theodore Francis Jones, ed., *New York University 1832: 1932* (New York, 1933), facing p. 386.

6 Draper, *The Indebtedness of the City of New-York to its University* (New York, 1853), pp. 16–17.

7 See Carleton Mabee, *The American Leonardo: A Life of Samuel F. B. Morse* (New York, 1943), p. 181; and Jones, *NYU*, p. 43.

8 S. I. Prime, *Life of Samuel F. B. Morse* (New York, 1875), p. 407. The significance of this letter was first pointed out in Taft, *Photography*, p. 25.

9 *American Leonardo*, pp. 231–33, treats of Taft's conclusion.

10 "Remarks on the Daguerreotype," *American Repertory of Arts, Sciences, and Manufactures*, I (1840), p. 403. It was Professor Taft who first unearthed this article, and pointed out its significance. If Draper's statement appeared in the context of different techniques of daguerreotypy at different seasons of the year, one might argue that he gave us no reason to suppose that he *first* succeeded in December. But this is not the context.

11 For E. L. Morse's statement, see note 4 above.

12 See above, pp. 16–17; for his reading the London newspapers, Draper, "First Portrait," p. 4.

13 Draper, "Remarks on Daguerreotype," 402–3, and "First Portrait," p. 4.

14 The story which follows is based on conversations of the author with Mrs. Dorothy Draper Nye, of Hastings-on-Hudson, N.Y., in August and October 1945, and with Professor and Mrs. J. W. Draper of Morgantown, W.Va., in September 1945. Mrs. Nye and Professor Draper, grandchildren of John W. Draper, heard (with Mrs. Draper) the story from their father, Daniel Draper.

15 See the daguerreotype taken at about thirty years, John Foord, *The Life and Public Services of Andrew Haswell Green* (New York, 1913), facing p. 40.

16 See Foord, *Green, passim*, and H. W. Howard Knott, "Andrew Haswell Green," *Dictionary of American Biography*, VII, pp. 535–36.

17 Nye conversations, 1945.

18 Draper, "On the Process of Daguerreotype, and Its Application to Taking Portraits from the Life," *Philosophical Magazine*, 3d s., XVII (1840), 222; and "First Portrait," p. 4.

19 [The editor, H. H. Snelling?], "Some Facts Connected with the Early History of Photography in America," *Photographic and Fine Art Journal* [Snelling's], p. 382.

20 Draper, "Process of Daguerreotype," pp. 222–23, and "First Portrait," p. 5.

21 "Portraits in Daguerreotype," *Philosophical Magazine*, 3d s., XVI (1840), 535.

22 Challenge to Daguerre: Draper, "Process of Daguerreotype," p. 219, and Goode, former chemical assistant in New York University, "Daguerreotype and Applications," p. 140. Use of chlorine: Taft, *Photography*, pp. 28–29.

23 Draper, "Process of Daguerreotype," p. 223.

24 *Ibid.*, p. 224, and Goode, "Daguerreotype and Applications," p. 142.

25 Taft, *Photography*, pp. 32, 458 (the notes for 32).

26 See above, p. 15.

27 "Portraits in Daguerreotype," p. 535.

28 See, for example, Mabee, *American Leonardo*, p. 241. Taft's remarks: *Photography*, p. 30.

29 Taft, *Photography*, p. 30; on other grounds, I think his decision is sound.

30 In the *Evening Post;* Stokes, *Iconography of Manhattan*, V, 1762.

31 Taft, *Photography*, p. 34.

32 For the date: John Werge, *The Evolution of Photography* (London, 1890), p. 108; but Werge is inaccurate on other matters, if not on this. Morse in his letter of February 10, 1855, calls the structure "a glass building"; quoted, E. L. Morse, ed., *Letters and Journals*, II, 146. Mabee, *American Leonardo*, p. 241, seems to make a distinction by calling it merely "glass-roofed."

33 Letter of February 10, 1855, quoted, E. L. Morse, ed., *Letters and Journals*, II, 146.

34 Werge, *Evolution*, p. 108.

35 The names of some students credited to Morse alone are given, Mabee, *American Leonardo*, p. 243, n. But Elwood Hendrick, "John William Draper," *Dictionary of American Biography*, V, 440, speaks of Draper's instructing men and women one or two evenings a week for a "considerable" time. This may rest on the testimony of Draper's grandson John William Draper [Maury].

36 Draper, "Remarks on Daguerreotype," p. 402.

37 See Josef Maria Eder, *History of Photography*, Edward Epstean, trans. and ed. (New York, 1945), p. 271.

38 Draper, "First Portrait," p. 5.

39 Draper, "Remarks on Daguerreotype," pp. 402–3, and "Process of Daguerreotype," p. 220.

40 Draper, "Process of Daguerreotype," p. 220; the imports, "First Portrait," p. 5.

41 Goode, "Daguerreotype and Applications," pp. 137–38.

42 Draper, "Process of Daguerreotype," p. 223, and Goode, "Daguerreotype and Applications," p. 142.

43 Draper, "Process of Daguerreotype," p. 225.

44 Diffused light: *ibid.*, p. 223. After rain, etc.: Goode, "Daguerreotype and Applications," p. 141.

45 Goode, "Daguerreotype and Applications," p. 141.

46 Draper, "Process of Daguerreotype," p. 223.

47 *Ibid.*, p. 224.

48 *Ibid.*, pp. 224–25.

49 *Ibid.*, p. 224.

NOTES 153

50 *Loc. cit.*

51 Moles, freckles, warts, and iris: *ibid.*, p. 225.

52 Draper, "Remarks on Daguerreotype," pp. 403–4, and "Process of Daguerreotype," p. 221; and Goode, "Daguerreotype and Applications," p. 141.

53 The abandonment of Draper's process is asserted in Goode, "Daguerreotype and Applications," p. 141.

54 An easily accessible reproduction is that made from the portrait sent to Herschel; Taft, *Photography*, p. 22.

55 University of New York, July 28, 1840; the letter first published, Taft, *Photography*, pp. 29–30.

56 Quoted, Taft, *Photography*, p. 31; dated from Collingwood, Hawkhurst, Kent, October 6, 1840. See the vindication for Draper as alleged, Anonymous, "Draper's Scientific Memoirs," *Nature*, XIX (1878–79), 27: "The similarity between [Pierre Jules César] Janssen's [1824–1907, the French astronomer's] use of an uncorrected lens for solar work and this [Draper's argument against the indispensability of an achromatic lens] is apparent."

57 Now owned by Professor J. W. Draper of Morgantown; there is a reproduction, from another source, Taft, *Photography*, p. 106.

58 See Daniel Norman's two articles: "The Development of Astronomical Photography," *Osiris*, V (1938), 560–594; and "John William Draper's Contributions to Astronomy," *The Telescope*, V (1938), 11–16.

59 Draper, "Remarks on Daguerreotype," p. 402. See also, "Process of Daguerreotype," p. 222.

60 "Remarks on Daguerreotype," p. 402. But cf. "Process of Daguerreotype," p. 222, where he says apparently of this same image, ". . . the places of the dark spots might be *indistinctly* traced." Italics mine. See also note 61 below.

61 Not later than January 1864, the then secretary of the Lyceum sent Henry Draper, J. W. Draper's son, an extract from the minutes of the Lyceum on March 23, 1840. It includes the following statement: "This is the first time that anything like a distinct representation of the moon's surface has been obtained." Quoted, Henry Draper, "On the Construction of a Silvered Glass Telescope, Fifteen and a Half Inches in Aperture, and Its Use in Celestial Photography," *Smithsonian Contributions to Knowledge*, XIV (1865), #180, 33. The minutes are no longer in existence.

62 Draper, "Remarks on Daguerreotype," p. 401, and "Process of Daguerreotype," p. 222.

63 The phrase is from Draper, "Process of Daguerreotype," p. 223.

64 Draper, "First Portrait," p. 2.

65 Charles L. Bristol, "Some Reminiscences of John William Draper," in "Draper Centenary Supplement," *Colonnade* [of NYU], IV (1911), 7 (June), 18–24.

CHAPTER IV

1 Claude Edwin Heaton, *A Historical Sketch of New York University College of Medicine 1841–1941* (New York, 1941), pp. 2–4; William Frederick Norwood, *Medical Education in the United States before the Civil War* (Philadelphia, 1944), pp. 134–35.

2 Æsculapius: S. D. Gross, *Memoir of Valentine Mott* (New York, 1868), pp. 35–36; memorial address: *A Biographical Memoir on the Late John Revere* (New York, 1847), pp. 9–10.

3 Gross, *Mott*, pp. 87–88.

4 *Ibid.*, pp. 39–49; Edward Preble, "Valentine Mott," *Dictionary of American*

Biography, XIII, 290–91; Alfred C. Post, *Eulogy on the Late Valentine Mott* (New York, 1866).

[5] For his life, see Heaton, *NYU College of Medicine*, p. 7; Mott, *Revere*.

[6] Mott, *Revere*, pp. 13, 16.

[7] Norwood, *Medical Education*, p. 138, n.

[8] See above, p. 7; D'Arcy Power, "Granville Sharp Pattison," *Dictionary of National Biography*, XV, 503; Heaton, *NYU College of Medicine*, p. 7.

[9] See the list of pamphlets and counterpamphlets given by Norwood, *Medical Education*, p. 449.

[10] John W. Draper, "The Life and Services of Granville S. Pattison, M.D.," *New York Herald*, January 11, 1852, p. 1.

[11] Heaton, *NYU College of Medicine*, pp. 6–9; Norwood, *Medical Education*, p. 137; Benjamin N. Martin [professor in the academic college at NYU], "A Sketch of John W. Draper," *Magazine of American History*, VIII, Pt. 1 (1882), 243.

[12] Heaton, *NYU College of Medicine*, p. 7.

[13] Norwood, *Medical Education*, pp. 135–38. The importance of the Southern students may be gathered from a survey of the annual announcements of the medical faculty; thus, I find, for example, that of 128 graduates in 1859, 62 came from Virginia south. New York University, Medical Department, [*Announcement*] session 1859–60, p. 4.

[14] Norwood, *Medical Education*, pp. 134, 136.

[15] *Ibid.*, pp. 136–38.

[16] *New York Lancet*, I (1842), pp. 49, 57.

[17] *Ibid.*, I (1842), p. 284.

[18] *Ibid.*, II (1842), p. 28.

[19] *Ibid.*, I (1842), p. 377.

[20] *Ibid.*, II (1842), p. 187.

[21] "*Introductory Lecture to the Course of Chemistry in the Medical Department of the University of New York*. Delivered by Professor Draper. Session 1841–42," *Lancet*, I (1842), p. 25.

[22] [J. W. Draper? or Daniel Draper?], "Professor John W. Draper," Maury papers, MS, p. 4.

[23] *Loc. cit.*

[24] New York University, Medical Department, *Annual Announcement* (New York, 1842), p. 10.

[25] The standard work on American nativism in this period is Ray A. Billington, *The Protestant Crusade, 1800–1860, A Study of the Origins of American Nativism* (New York, 1938). On the leading nativist of New York University, see Carleton Mabee, *The American Leonardo: A Life of Samuel F. B. Morse* (New York, 1943), chapters XI, XII, XV.

[26] This is the *Foreign Conspiracy against the Liberties of the United States;* published serially in 1834, as a book in 1835. Mabee, *American Leonardo*, pp. 164–66.

[27] I do not mean to suggest that much store should be set by the family tradition that Draper took little interest in politics; this is derived from conversations with Mrs. Dorothy Draper Nye and Miss Antonia Maury of Hastings-on-Hudson, N.Y., and Professor and Mrs. John W. Draper of Morgantown, W.Va., in 1945, and is useful as far as it goes. But it probably means only that Draper was no great *partisan;* and it happens that Morse put forward his nativism as a cause in which Whigs and Democrats could unite.

[28] A financial crisis of the worst kind occurred in the academic department in the 1850's.

[29] The connection with Irving is attested by conversations of the author with

Mrs. Nye and Miss Maury, Draper's grandchildren, in 1945. At the present time part of the estate is a public park.

30 They are rather substantial by present standards, and face on Broadway, Hastings-on-Hudson. Maury conversations, 1945.

31 Robert Kane, *Elements of Chemistry*, John W. Draper, ed. (New York, 1842); *Text-book on Chemistry* (New York, 1846); *A Text-Book on Natural Philosophy* (New York, 1847).

32 Letter from Robert Kane, Dublin, to Draper, June 2, 1843, Nye papers.

33 There are scattered financial statements from Harper's to Draper in the Nye papers. Statements dated February 26, 1847, August 25, 1847, August 11, 1848, March 17, 1849, and March [1?], 1853, show that 9,469 copies of the chemistry text were sold. But the last of these shows that 2,819 copies had been disposed of in the preceding year. This would seem to indicate that the sales had held up remarkably well, so that the missing statements may well have accounted for, say, a minimum of five thousand copies. The statements of August 11, 1848, March 17, 1849, and March [1?], 1853, show that 2,236 copies of the natural-philosophy text were sold; so perhaps we may safely conjecture that another thousand figured in other reports from the publisher. The missing information is not available from Harper's; Dorothy Fiske for Harper and Brothers, New York, to author, April 26, 1946.

34 Draper's own children were John Christopher and Henry; Virginia, born in Virginia, December 26, 1839; Daniel, born in New York City, April 2, 1841; William, born in New York City, November 1845; and Antonia, born in New York City, November 15, 1849. Thomas Waln-Morgan Draper, *The Drapers in America* (New York, 1892), pp. 227–28.

35 Nye and Maury conversations, 1945.

36 Maury conversations, 1945.

37 Much of the linen, silver, and furniture now belong to Mrs. Dorothy Draper Nye and to Professor and Mrs. John W. Draper, respectively of Hastings-on-Hudson, N.Y., and of Morgantown, W.Va. Cause of Antonia Gardner Draper's ill-health: Maury conversations, 1945.

38 Maury conversations, 1945.

39 If we take Silliman's appointment at Yale as inaugurating an epoch, and an epoch different in kind. It need not be said that many people had held appointments in science and mathematics in the American colleges at an earlier date. The decisive question is the *proportion* of leaders with academic jobs.

40 The best historical work bearing on these relations in America is Richard H. Shryock, *American Medical Research Past and Present* (New York, 1947). As an example of the kind of work that needs to be done, see also G. N. Clark, *Science and Social Welfare in the Age of Newton* (Oxford, 1937).

41 As a sweeping generalization this is plain enough (and agreeable to the Marxists); but *close* historical analysis of test cases is uncommon almost to the point of not existing.

42 John W. Draper, *The Indebtedness of the City of New-York to its University* (New York, 1853), p. 16.

43 Letter of Draper [New York?], to Professor Elias Loomis of NYU, January 7, 1850, Yale University Library.

44 Letter from Draper [New York?], to the Council of NYU, October 14, 1858, reproduced in NYU, Council Minutes, March 4, 1853—May 27, 1864, MS, p. 134, entry of November 11, 1858. Council Minutes in NYU archives.

45 Citations in notes 42 and 44 above.

46 *Indebtedness*, p. 16.

47 On his assistant in 1840 if not in 1839, see above, ch. III, n. 4. On Henry Draper's help: George F. Barker, *Memoir of Henry Draper* ([Washington? 1888?]), p. 5.

48 On Henry Draper's first jobs (on the staff of Bellevue Hospital from 1858 till his appointment as professor of natural science in the college of NYU in 1860), see Barker, *Henry Draper,* pp. 4–5.

49 Barker, *Henry Draper,* pp. 5–7, 11; and below, p. 65. Barker does not discuss the financing of the observatory.

50 Barker, *Henry Draper,* p. 53. Anna Palmer Draper is a living memory among astoronomers; she left her money to the Harvard Observatory for the famous catalogue of the stars named in her husband's honor.

51 John W. Draper, New York, to "Children" [Henry Draper, Anna Palmer Draper, and Antonia Draper], August 12, 1874; Draper papers, New York Public Library, Manuscript Division.

52 *Indebtedness,* pp. 11–15.

53 On the early history of the three American journals, see Frank Luther Mott, *A History of American Magazines* (New York and Cambridge, Mass., 1930–[the third and most recent volume, 1938]), I (1741–1850), 556–58, 302–5, 566–68 respectively. On the merit of the best work in the *American Journal of the Medical Sciences,* before 1840, see Shryock, *Medical Research,* pp. 29–30.

54 See Shryock, *Medical Research,* pp. 112–14.

55 See letters from Draper, New York, to Joseph M. Wightman, 33 Cornhill corner of Franklin Avenue, Boston, of September 20, 1845, December 15, 1845, and undated (the cover postmarked September 20 with no year); MSS respectively in the University of Pennsylvania Library, the Historical Society of Pennsylvania, and the University of Pennsylvania Library. These are orders for apparatus, with detailed instructions and sketches.

56 Draper, New York, to Wightman, cover postmark September 20, no year given.

57 French photographic supplies: see above, p. 24. Shopping for apparatus: see, e.g., John W. Draper, London, to Henry Draper, February 16, 1871; Draper papers, New York Public Library.

58 Draper was very much inclined to dispute the priority with Moser; and the whole episode contributed to Draper's conviction, soon quite settled, that European scientists willfully neglected his claims. He traded some angry words on this subject with Robert Hunt, an English expert on photography. Draper's "roric image" experiments: "On the Process of Daguerreotype, and Its Application to Taking Portraits from the Life," *Philosophical Magazine,* 3d s., XVII (1840), 217–25, especially pp. 217–18. Draper's assertion of his claims against Moser: "On Certain Spectral Appearances, and on the Discovery of Latent Light," *Philosophical Magazine,* 3d s., XXI (1842). 348–49. Dispute with Hunt: Draper, "On Mr. Hunt's Book, Entitled 'Researches on Light,' " *Philosophical Magazine,* 3d s., XXV (1844), 49–51; Robert Hunt, "Reply to Professor Draper's Letter," *Philosophical Magazine,* 3d s., XXV (1844), 119–22.

59 Josef Maria Eder, *History of Photography,* Edward Epstean, trans. and ed. (New York, 1945), p. 260.

60 Eder, *Photography,* pp. 260, 758 (the note on 260).

61 *Ibid.,* 260–61.

62 "On Some Analogies between the Phaenomena of the Chemical Rays, and Those of Radiant Heat," *Philosophical Magazine,* 3d s., XIX (1841), 195–210; Draper says, p. 195: ". . . the chemical action produced by the rays of light, depends upon the ABSORPTION of those rays by sensitive bodies; just as an increase of temperature is produced by the absorption of those of heat."

For estimates of the importance of this principle, see: C. E. K. Mees, "The Color Sensitivity of Photographic Materials," *Journal of the Franklin Institute,* CCI (1926), 525–26; and Eder, *Photography,* pp. 166–67, 418–19.

63 "Analogies," p. 196.

[64] Eder, *Photography*, pp. 166–67.

[65] This is the point, though not exactly the emphasis, of Eder, *Photography*, pp. 166–67.

[66] This point is well brought out by Alexander Findlay, *A Hundred Years of Chemistry*, 2d ed. (London, 1948), pp. 82–83.

[67] "On the Chemical Action of Light," *Philosophical Magazine*, 4th s., I (1851), 392–93.

[68] See Sir William Dampier, *A History of Science and Its Relations with Philosophy and Religion*, 3d ed. (Cambridge, England, 1942), p. 258; and H. T. Pledge, *Science since 1500* (London, 1939), p. 146.

[69] "Analogies," p. 196; and "Description of the Tithonometer," *Philosophical Magazine*, 3d s., XXIII (1843), pp. 401–15. The claim for the discovery of photochemical induction is put forward by Findlay, *Hundred Years*, p. 83. It is obvious that the work of Gay-Lussac and Thenard with hydrogen and chlorine also bears on this phenomenon; but in the citation at the beginning of this note, Draper focuses attention on the lapse of time before chemical rays take effect.

[70] See Eder, *Photography*, pp. 151–53.

[71] Findlay, *Hundred Years*, pp. 82–83.

[72] See Eder, *Photography*, pp. 412–14; Bunsen and Roscoe's views on the inadequacy of Draper's instrument summarized, pp. 413. Without the derogatory implications, this work of Draper's is also treated in American Academy of Arts and Sciences, *Proceedings*, n.s., III (1875–76), 326 [presentation of Rumford medals to Draper]. See Findlay, *Hundred Years*, p. 83.

[73] See the exposition of these matters in Eder, *Photography*, pp. 418–19; and Findlay, *Hundred Years*, pp. 251–53, the latter of which I have relied on for the statements which immediately follow.

[74] See Dampier, *History*, pp. 221–24; Charles Singer, *A Short History of Science to the Nineteenth Century* (Oxford, 1941), pp. 297–98.

[75] "On a New Imponderable Substance, and on a Class of Chemical Rays Analogous to the Rays of Dark Heat," *Philosophical Magazine*, 3d s., XXI (1842), 453–61.

[76] "Should a compound beam [of what we should call "radiant energy"] . . . fall upon a sensitive surface, the chemical rays sink into it, . . . lose all their force, and the rays of light are left alone. Photographic results thus resulting from the reposing of the chemical rays on the sensitive surface are not however in themselves durable, . . . for the rays escape away under some new form.

"Tithonus was a beautiful youth whom Aurora fell in love with and married in heaven. The Fates had made him immortal, but unlike his bride, in the course of events he became feeble and decrepit, and losing all his strength was rocked to sleep in a cradle. The goddess, pitying his condition, metamorphosed him into a grasshopper."

"New Imponderable," pp. 454–55. Draper's nomenclature survives as "rare" in the Merriam-Webster, second edition; but "actinic," "actinism" are the terms that prevailed.

[77] See above, note 76.

[78] See John W. Draper, "On the Interference Spectrum, and the Absorption of the Tithonic Rays," *Philosophical Magazine*, 3d s., XXVI (1845), pp. 465–78; and "Remarks on the Existence and Mechanism of the Negative or Protecting Rays of the Sun," *Philosophical Magazine*, 3d s., XXX (1847), 93, where Draper gives this summary of his purpose:

"It is proper to observe, that some of the phaenomena recorded in this communication which seem to be in opposition to the principle set forth are not so in reality. All reasonings founded on the decomposition of light by the prism, and the action of the prismatic spectrum on changeable surfaces, are liable to error. . . .

the only method free from these difficulties is to employ the interference spectrum formed by a ruled surface or a grate; a method which was proposed eight years ago by Sir J. Herschel with a view of getting rid of the disturbing agencies arising from the ideal coloration of glass, and which I first carried into effect in 1844 with so much success, that the resulting Daguerreotype impressions contained Fraunhofer's lines, even with microscopic minuteness."

For remarks on this work, see George F. Barker, *Memoir of John William Draper 1811–1882* ([Washington? 1886?]), p. 367; American Academy of Arts and Sciences, *Proceedings*, p. 327; Daniel Norman, "John William Draper's Contributions to Astronomy," *The Telescope*, V (1938), 14.

79 John W. Draper, *A Treatise on the Forces which Produce the Organization of Plants* (New York, 1844), chapter V; and "Interference Spectrum," p. 468 ("I would suggest . . . that when we wish to indicate spectrum regions with precision, we should use wave-lengths").

80 Draper wrote in the interesting chapter V of *Organization of Plants:*

"There is an inherent defect in the prismatic spectrum, a defect originating in the very cause which gives rise to that spectrum itself—unequal refrangibility. Of two groups of rays compared together, one taken in the red the other in the violet region, it is clear that in the same spectrum, from the very circumstance of their greater refrangibility, those in the violet will be relatively more separated from each other than those in the red. The result of this increased separation in the more refrangible regions is to give an apparent dilution to them, while the less-refrangible are concentrated. The relative position of the colours must also vary; the fixed lines must be placed at distances greater than their true distance as the violet end is approached."

See also John W. Draper, "On the Production of Light by Heat," *Philosophical Magazine*, 3d s., XXX (1847), 350, where he treats the significance of the use of the interference spectrum in the important context of the location of the maximum of luminosity:

". . . in the interference spectrum, where the colours are arranged side by side in the order of their wave-lengths, the centre is occupied by the most luminous portion of the yellow; and from this point the light declines away on one side in the reds, and on the other in the blues, the terminations being equidistant from the centre of the yellow space."

See below, note 81.

81 For an exposition of the issue, see Agnes M. Clerke, *A Popular History of Astronomy* (Edinburgh, 1885), p. 265; note 1 to this page treating of Draper. Miss Clerke seems to show in this note that she had not read Draper's relevant memoirs published before 1872.

82 For these successive epochs: *Organization of Plants;* "On the Diffraction Spectrum.—Remarks on M. Eisenlohr's Recent Experiments," *Philosophical Magazine*, 4th s., XIII (1857), 153–56; and "Researches in Actino-Chemistry. Memoir First. On the Distribution of Heat in the Spectrum," *Philosophical Magazine*, 4th s., XLIV (1872), 104–17. In "Diffraction Spectrum," Draper writes of his earlier work, in a rather obscure chronological framework, and says, p. 155, ". . . I could do no more than satisfy myself that in the diffraction spectrum the centre of the yellow is really the hottest space, as well as the most luminous." I cannot find that this was clearly stated previously. "Distribution of Heat" shows that there is equal heating-power on either side of the center of luminosity. It is here, p. 116, that he says, ". . . the conception that there exist in an incident ray various principles disappears altogether." On the botanical occasion for some of Draper's early experiments bearing on these issues, see Julius von Sachs, *History of Botany (1530–1860)*, Henry E. F. Garnsey and Isaac Bayley Balfour, trans. (Oxford; 2d imp., 1906), pp. 556–57.

83 See Clerke, *Astronomy*, p. 265.

84 "On a New System of Inactive Tithonographic Spaces in the Solar Spectrum Analogous to the Fixed Lines of Fraunhofer," *Philosophical Magazine*, 3d s., XXII (1843), 360–64. He indicates, p. 363, that these great "lines" may simply be clusters of exceedingly fine lines.

85 See Draper's reference, "Distribution of Heat," pp. 104–5.

86 "Tithonographic Spaces," (1843), p. 363. Compare with this: "Spectral Appearances," (1842), p. 350; and "Interference Spectrum," (1845), p. 470.

87 "Tithonographic Spaces," especially p. 363.

88 "Spectral Appearances," pp. 349–50.

89 Eder, *Photography*, pp. 263–64.

90 *Ibid.*, p. 263.

91 *Ibid.*, p. 264.

92 "On the Production of Light by Heat," *Philosophical Magazine*, 3d s., XXX (1847), 345–60. For estimates of this work, see: Anonymous, "Draper's Scientific Memoirs," *Nature*, XIX (1878–79), 26–27; American Academy of Arts and Sciences, *Proceedings*, pp. 326–27; Norman, "Contributions to Astronomy," p. 13. Norman points out that Kirchhoff, reaching the same conclusions theoretically rather than experimentally, referred to Draper's work in a footnote (*Poggendorff's Annalen*, CIX (1860), 275).

In this celebrated memoir Draper threw off a suggestion for incandescent lighting by the connection of electrical currents with platinum; and this is often said to have foreshadowed Edison's lamp. What Draper says, pp. 359–60, is this:

". . . it has been a desideratum to obtain an artificial light of standard brilliancy. The preceding experiments furnish an easy means of supplying that want, and give us what might be termed a 'unit-lamp.' A surface of platinum of standard dimensions, raised to a standard temperature by a voltaic current, will always emit a constant light. A strip of that metal, one inch long and 1/20th of an inch wide, connected with a lever by which its expansion might be measured, would yield at 2000° a light suitable for most purposes. . . . An ingenious artist would have very little difficulty, by taking advantage of the movements of the lever, in making a self-acting apparatus, in which the platinum should be maintained at a uniform temperature, notwithstanding any change taking place in the voltaic current."

It will be remarked that this passage shows no interest in, let alone a solution of, the difficulties in making a practical device for lighting homes and offices. I find no evidence for the persistent tradition that Draper had the chance to forestall Edison's patent. See the assertion, Arthur B. Lamb, "The Contribution of John W. Draper to Photography," *Colonnade* [of NYU], IV (1911), 7 (June), 8. Edison's incandescent-lighting patent is file #214,636, U.S. Department of Commerce, Patent Office, Search Room; the only hitch was the fear of conflict with an English patent.

93 See Pledge, *Science*, pp. 145–46.

94 "On the Nature of Flame, and on the Condition of the Sun's Surface," *Philosophical Magazine*, 4th s., XV (1858), 93. This is a letter, dated December 10, 1857.

95 He argues, p. 93, that the sun cannot be incandescent, because it has dark lines in its spectrum!

96 Compare H. Kayser, *Handbuch der Spectroscopie* (Leipzig, 1900–1912), I, 39: "Wenn so die Arbeiten Drapers eine ganze Reihe wichtiger Fortschritte bringen, so sind doch die Anschauungen, welche er entwickelt, fast durchweg recht verkehrte."

97 Norman, "Contributions to Astronomy," p. 12, calls Draper a pioneer in this field. See Draper's articles: "Analogies between Chemical Rays and Radiant Heat," (1841), p. 202; "On the Tithonotype, or Art of Multiplying Daguerreotypes,"

Philosophical Magazine, 3d s., XXII (1843), 365–68; "On the Decomposition of Carbonic Acid Gas and the Alkaline Carbonates, by the Light of the Sun; and on the Tithonotype," *Philosophical Magazine,* 3d s., XXIII (1843), 175–76.

98 *Indebtedness,* p. 11.

99 S. F. B. Morse, "Experiments Made with One Hundred Pairs of Grove's Battery, Passing through One Hundred and Sixty Miles of Insulated Wire," with the annex by Draper, "On the Law of the Conducting Power of Wires," *American Journal of Science,* XLV (1843), 390–94. See the comment by Draper, *Indebtedness,* pp. 12–13; and Mabee, *American Leonardo,* pp. 266–67.

100 "Conducting Power of Wires," p. 393.

101 *Indebtedness,* p. 13.

102 Henry Draper, "On the Construction of a Silvered Glass Telescope, Fifteen and a Half Inches in Aperture, and Its Use in Celestial Photography," *Smithsonian Contributions to Knowledge,* XIV (1865), #180, 47–48. See also: John W. Draper, "On the Application of Photography to Printing," *Harper's Monthly,* XIII (1856), 433–41. I do not think that the claim made in this connection by Draper is the same as that which is rejected, letter of G. Reissman, librarian, Research Library, Eastman Kodak Company, to P. B. McDonald [Professor in the College of Engineering of NYU], December 20, 1922: "We doubt if Draper's claim of having made the first photomicrographs of metal sections is correct." Letter in NYU archives.

103 Some articles of a high quality were published on scientific subjects in 1857 and 1872.

104 See the photograph preserved in the archives of NYU, from an album of the class of 1857.

105 The portraits are reproduced by Robert Taft, *Photography and the American Scene, A Social History, 1839–1889* (New York, 1938), pp. 18, 125 respectively.

CHAPTER V

1 The main body of the Methodists, to which John C. Draper belonged, was not, of course, Calvinistic.

2 See the elegy on John Christopher Draper, above, p. 3.

3 See above, pp. 6–7.

4 See the formulation of this contradiction in Elie Halévy, *The Growth of Philosophic Radicalism,* Mary Morris, trans. (London, 1928), p. 498:

"The first principle [of the Benthamites; the artificial identification of people's interests by jurisprudents] sums up the modern conception of science as active and as permitting man, just in so far as he is acquainted with nature, to act upon it methodically so as to transform it according to his desires. The second principle sums up the old conception of science as contemplative, and as assigning to itself the single rôle of discovering the harmonious simplicity of the laws which nature obeys when undisturbed by man."

The translation is not as sharp as might be desired.

5 It need hardly be said that generalizations about the a priori reasoning and want of historical sense of Bentham himself can readily be overstated.

6 One need not condemn the Positivists for their reliance on the all-sufficiency of the scientific method for arriving at knowledge. But when this reliance took, as it not uncommonly did, the form of an intransigent conviction, a jealous act of faith, it was the kind of thing which they had attacked in others. In so far as the Positivists *deduced* the character of the remainder of knowledge as yet undisclosed, a deductive temper that bangs the head of each of its deductions against the world-as-received is indispensable. But there was a tendency among people

of the Positivistic temper to stop short in this banging of the head of theory, when it came to their own theory of knowledge. The trouble with this theory lies in the rather insistent use of words like "direct" and "immediate" as applied to observation. Their use was largely engendered by fear of "metaphysics." But they involve a grave error, and this error was borne along mostly unchallenged as part of the one conception of the Positivists which in a general state of funk they tended to exempt from sharp criticism in the light of experience. And any exemption of this kind is intellectually fatal.

[7] See *A Treatise on the Forces which Produce the Organization of Plants* (New York, 1844), p. 2; *Human Physiology, Statical and Dynamical; or, The Conditions and Course of the Life of Man* (New York, 1856), pp. 24–26.

[8] *Science and the Modern World* (New York, 1925), p. 110.

[9] *The Influence òf Physical Agents on Life* (New York, 1850), p. 6.

[10] Whitehead, *Science*, p. 111.

[11] *Plants*, p. 2.

[12] *Ibid.*, p. 1.

[13] "There is that unity of plan in all the works of Nature which causes us at once to understand that in these various mechanisms the same physical principles are resorted to; that the flow of the sap and the circulation of the blood are due to the same powers."
Ibid., p. 22.

[14] See *Plants*, p. 39, and *Physiology*, pp. 129–46.

[15] Chambers' book was published anonymously in 1844; Lyell's appeared from 1830 to 1833. A sketch of Darwin's and Wallace's forerunners may be found in: Charles Darwin, *On the Origin of Species by Natural Selection*, introductory chapter in the fourth edition; Sir William Dampier, *A History of Science and Its Relations with Philosophy and Religion*, 3d ed. (Cambridge, England, 1942), pp. 292–95; H. T. Pledge, *Science since 1500* (London, 1939), pp. 154–57; Emanuel Rádl, *The History of Biological Theories*, 2d ed., E. J. Hatfield, trans. and adapt. (London, 1930), pp. 1–11; and Charles Singer, *A Short History of Science to the Nineteenth Century* (Oxford, 1941), pp. 371–79.

[16] *Plants*, p. 3.

[17] The phrase is Sir Ernest Barker's.

[18] *Plants*, p. 8.

[19] Ward's position is characterized in Richard Hofstadter, *Social Darwinism in American Thought, 1860–1915* (Philadelphia, 1944), pp. 52–67.

[20] *Introductory Lecture, to the Course of Chemistry . . . on the Relations and Nature of Water* (New York, 1845), p. 15.

[21] They appeared respectively in 1853, 1853, and 1851.

[22] *Physiology*, p. 13.

[23] *Loc. cit.*

[24] *Ibid.*, p. 253.

[25] That a hash was made of the work of Johann Friedrich Meckel (1781–1833) and that of Karl Ernst von Baer (1792–1876), to the unmerited disadvantage of the latter, is the point of Rádl, *Biological Theories*, 134–35. Draper's quotation from *Physiology*, p. 379.

[26] *Physiology*, p. 15; see also pp. 542–43. Lambert Adolphe Jacques Quetelet (1796–1874) passed from his work as director of the royal observatory of Belgium to statistical investigations of the body and mind of man; and so uncorked the bottle on "the average man."

[27] See for example the most recent conspicuous example: Erwin Schrödinger, *What Is Life?* (Cambridge, England, 1945).

[28] See Walter B. Cannon, *The Wisdom of the Body* (New York, 1932). A sci-

162 JOHN WILLIAM DRAPER

entist's book springing from Cannon's work is E. S. Russell, *The Directiveness of Organic Activities* (Cambridge, England, 1945).

[29] *Physiology*, pp. 111–12.

[30] *Physiology*, pp. 190–212, treats of this subject.

[31] The conspicuous figures in this tradition include the biologist Lloyd Morgan and the philosophers Samuel Alexander and Alfred North Whitehead.

[32] See *An Appeal to the People of the State of New-York, to Legalise the Dissection of the Dead* (New York, 1853), p. 16.

[33] See John W. Draper, *The Indebtedness of the City of New-York to Its University* (New York, 1853), pp. 11–15. On his own work with daguerreotypy, and the opening up of jobs for respectable women, see pp. 14–15. For the political implications drawn from better communications and transportation, see Merle Curti, *The Roots of American Loyalty* (New York, 1946), pp. 115–17.

[34] *Water*, p. 14.

[35] Maybe Draper had got to know Mrs. Jellyby, author of the proverb that housekeeping begins abroad, and the Reverend Chadband, who suspended theology in a great globule of oiliness. Even if Draper never read *Bleak House,* published in monthly parts in 1852–53, he had some hard words for their kind:

"I stand here in the midst of a community familiar with Missionary projects— a community which pours out its wealth for the spiritual welfare of heathen tribes all over the globe. I ask that community what answer it will render when it is called to an account for the extinction of the Indian tribes of this Continent? For want of a physician who could vaccinate, the small-pox has swept off whole nations, not leaving a solitary survivor. Do you suppose that the interest you have taken in Syria, or India, or Burmah, will excuse you for this awful desolation at your own door?"

Dissection, p. 16.

[36] "Look at the statistics of mortality and the investigations of Sanatory [*sic*] Commissions: poverty, wretchedness, the want of fresh air, impure water, bad food, the filth of cities, the effluvia of crowded places, contagions, miasms [*sic*],— these are the agents that decimate our race. . . . The science of the good physician is already expanding; it looks to a higher duty than in former times—to prevent disease, rather than to cure it; to deal with communities rather than with the individual."

Physical Agents, p. 6.

[37] See Richard H. Shryock, *The Development of Modern Medicine*, 2d ed. (New York, 1947), chapter XII.

[38] "Preface" to 2d ed., *Physiology*, p. vi (the word "edition" being used to mean printing).

[39] Clergymen, he said, needed to study science. ". . . the scientific priest . . . will arrest at once the man of thought, make him an unconscious and involuntary missionary, and through him control a whole nation."

"Let the native bent, the native talent, the native instinct of our young men, find its means of development unshackled, and you will have what you have not now,—men in the pulpit who can check the tendency of the age to materialism."

Indebtedness, pp. 24–25.

[40] The phrase is Whitehead's; *Science*, p. 110.

CHAPTER VI

* It would hardly do to plunge the reader unprepared into the interests which mark the latter half of Draper's career; and to account for the change one must draw conclusions from the whole body of his work including that yet to come.

But I have purposely omitted citations (unless some special reason seemed to dictate), so as not to tell the rest of the story twice. In this regard, then, the remainder of the book is a species of documentation for much of this chapter.

1 Allan Nevins, *Abram S. Hewitt with Some Account of Peter Cooper* (New York, 1935), p. 179. Nevins says that the speech "later made part of his famous book, *The History of the Conflict Between Religion and Science.*" But it was first worked into *A History of the Intellectual Development of Europe* (1862).

2 I quote from the manuscript of the address, now in the possession of Mrs. Dorothy Draper Nye, Draper's granddaughter, of Hastings-on-Hudson, N.Y.

3 The Johns Hopkins University was opened in 1876; and this is the great landmark in the process of "naturalization." But, of course, graduate studies had begun to take hold elsewhere.

4 Theodore Francis Jones, ed., *New York University 1832:1932* (New York, 1933), pp. 80–84. The statements immediately following rest on Jones's account.

5 Draper's most important memoirs date from the end of the forties; see chapter IV. The Teutonic tradition of scholarship first got a firm foothold between, say, 1876 and 1880.

6 See Jones, *NYU*, 59:

"It was unfortunate that men like [Tayler] Lewis and Draper, and a few years later, Elias Loomis, had no opportunity to give advanced instruction to graduate students. But, even if the resources of the University had permitted, it is doubtful whether the United States in 1840 would have supplied such students. In any case, Lewis, Draper, Loomis, and their colleagues spent their efforts on drilling unruly schoolboys in the University College, and wasted their time in the faculty meetings on interminable discussions on discipline."

7 Draper's original appointment was in "Chemistry and Botany"; Jones, *NYU*, p. 50. I find no evidence that he taught botany specifically, though he did research on plant physiology. He never had an actual appointment in physics, but the pathetically inadequate faculty of NYU as well as his own interests obliged him to deal with much of what would now be considered the material of a course in physics. His appointment in physiology at the medical school came in 1850. Of Draper's instruction in geology, Jones, *NYU*, p. 97, writes: "Dr. John W. Draper had for many years [prior to 1871] given a certain amount of instruction in Geology."

8 See above, chapter IV, note 58.

9 How Draper got acquainted with Comte is unknown, but the acquaintance is unmistakable. In many ways Draper would appear to be the most influential of American Positivists and Positivizers. Failure to mention him at all vitiates the two books of Richmond Laurin Hawkins, *Auguste Comte and the United States* (Cambridge, Mass., 1936) and *Positivism in the United States (1853–1861)* (Cambridge, Mass., 1938). It is, however, true that the only one of Draper's major works betraying the influence of Positivism to be published within the period of which Hawkins treats is the *Physiology* (1856).

10 See R. G. Collingwood, *The Idea of History*, T. M. Knox, ed. (Oxford, 1946), pp. 126–204, from which I have benefited, without going the whole way with the author's thesis.

11 See the definitive account by Lucien Lévy-Bruhl, *La Philosophie d'Auguste Comte*, 3d ed. (Paris, 1913), chapter II, "La loi des trois états," pp. 39–54, where the author quotes, p. 410, from Comte's *Plan des travaux scientifiques nécessaires pour réorganiser la société* of 1822:

"Par la nature même de l'esprit humain, chaque branche de nos connaissances est nécessairement assujettie dans sa marche à passer successivement par trois états théoriques différents: l'état théologique ou fictif, l'état métaphysique ou abstrait, enfin l'état scientifique ou positif."

164 JOHN WILLIAM DRAPER

The application of these "stages" to history is the subject of chapter IV, "La philosophie de l'histoire," pp. 320–47, where Lévy-Bruhl says, p. 320:

"Si la dynamique sociale est une science, et si la loi des trois états, découverte par Comte, en est la loi fondamentale, cette loi (et celles qui en dérivent), doivent expliquer les phases successives de l'humanité, depuis les premières ébauches de la civilisation jusqu'à la situation présente des populations les plus avancées. Elles doivent 'introduire l'unité et la continuité dans cet immense spectacle, où l'on voit d'ordinaire tant de confusion et d'incohérence.'" [Quoted from Cours de philosophie positive, VI, 457.]

[12] Cooper Union address, Nye MS; and above, p. 56.

[13] See the remarks of Benedetto Croce, History as the Story of Liberty, Sylvia Sprigge, trans. (New York, 1941), pp. 187–95.

[14] This is the point of Draper's address at the Oxford meeting of the British Association for the Advancement of Science; see below, chapter VII.

[15] Mainly, that society had a life-history in the most literal sense and even a case-history.

[16] See the superb "Introduction" to Jonathan Edwards, Images or Shadows of Divine Things, Perry Miller, ed. (New Haven, 1948).

[17] Edward L. Youmans, The Correlation and Conservation of Forces (New York, 1864), dedication to Draper, p. iii. The book was published in 1865.

[18] John Dewey, The Influence of Darwinism on Philosophy (New York, 1910), p. 14.

[19] It was Gray who early insisted that Darwinism merely threw light on the ingenious means by which God worked the same ends as had always been attributed to Him.

[20] See below, pp. 81–82.

CHAPTER VII

[1] Robert Kane, Dublin, to John W. Draper, June 2, 1843; Nye papers.

[2] "On the Decomposition of Carbonic Acid Gas and the Alkaline Carbonates, by the Light of the Sun; and on the Tithonotype," British Association for the Advancement of Science, Report, 1843, Pt. 2, pp. 33–34.

[3] See George F. Barker, Memoir of Henry Draper ([Washington? 1888?]), p. 4.

[4] See Henry Draper, "On the Construction of a Silvered Glass Telescope, Fifteen and a Half Inches in Aperture, and Its Use in Celestial Photography," Smithsonian Contributions to Knowledge, XIV (1865), #180, p. 1.

[5] John W. Draper, New York, to A. D. Bache, May 1, 1860; Huntington Library, San Marino, California.

[6] Draper to Bache, May 1, 1860, gives the name of the ship.

[7] Roast beef: conversations of Draper's granddaughter, Miss Antonia Maury, with the author. Silver: conversations of Draper's grandson, Professor John W. Draper, of Morgantown, W.Va., with the author.

[8] Henry Draper, "Telescope," pp. 2–3.

[9] T. H. Huxley; Leonard Huxley, Life and Letters of Thomas Henry Huxley (London, 1900), I, 180; quoted from The Athenaeum of July 14, 1860. See T. H. Huxley to Francis Darwin, June 27, 1891, quoted in Huxley, Huxley, I, 187: ". . . I was quite aware that if he [Samuel Wilberforce] played his cards properly, we should have little chance, with such an audience, of making an efficient defence."

[10] Richard Owen; Huxley, Huxley, I, 180; from The Athenaeum.

[11] Owen; Huxley, Huxley, I, 180; from The Athenaeum.

[12] Huxley; Huxley, Huxley, I, 181; from The Athenaeum.

13 The quoted words are apparently a paraphrase from Darwin himself, and occur in Geoffrey West, *Charles Darwin* (New Haven, 1938), p. 261.

14 Huxley to Francis Darwin, June 27, 1891, quoted in Huxley, *Huxley*, I, 187–88.

15 J. D. Hooker, Oxford, to Charles R. Darwin, July 2, 1860; quoted in Leonard Huxley, *Life and Letters of Sir Joseph Dalton Hooker* (London, 1918), I, 525–27.

16 J. R. Green to W. Boyd Dawkins, July 3, 1860; J. R. Green, *Letters of John Richard Green*, Leslie Stephen, ed. (New York, 1901), p. 44.

17 Huxley, *Huxley*, I, 181.

18 *Loc. cit.*

19 *Loc. cit.*

20 Conversation of the author with Miss Maury. She possesses a letter from her mother describing the meeting, written from England at the time; but she declines to let it be read. She says that it does not remark on Draper's own part in the proceedings.

21 Huxley, *Huxley*, I, 182.

22 *Loc. cit.*

23 Location of the platform: *Loc. cit.* Biographical information about those present comes from the sketches in the *Dictionary of National Biography*, unless otherwise attributed.

24 See below, p. 70.

25 See George Richmond's portrait, 1855; Huxley, *Hooker*, I, frontispiece.

26 See George Richmond's drawing, 1867; Horace G. Hutchinson, *Life of Sir John Lubbock Lord Avebury* (London, 1914), I, frontispiece.

27 The seating is discussed in Huxley, *Huxley*, I, 182, and Huxley, *Hooker*, I, 523.

28 See the striking photograph of Huxley by Maull and Polyblank, 1857; Huxley, *Huxley*, I, facing p. 149.

29 There is a mammoth three-volume biography, A. R. Ashwell, *Life of Samuel Wilberforce* (London, 1880–82).

30 Wilberforce's and Huxley's resemblance: Huxley, *Huxley*, I, 184, n. 2.

31 "Section D.—Zoology and Botany, including Physiology. Saturday," *The Athenaeum*, 1860, 2 (July–December), #1707 (July 14), 64.

32 I rely on photographs taken in the 1850's and descriptions of his appearance in his later years; I do not know of any photograph exactly from this time.

33 J. R. Green ("his hour and a half of nasal Yankeeism"); Green, *Green*, p. 44. "One who was present" ("the American accents of Dr. Draper's opening address when he asked 'Air we a fortuitous concourse of atoms?' "); quoted in Huxley, *Huxley*, I, 181. J. D. Hooker:

"A paper of a Yankee donkey called Draper . . . was being read, and it did not mend my temper, for of all the flatulent stuff and all the self-sufficient stuffers, these were the greatest; it was all a pie of Herbert Spencer and Buckle without the seasoning of either."

Huxley, *Hooker*, I, 525–26.

34 Conversations of the author with Miss Maury; Charles L. Bristol, "Some Reminiscences of John William Draper," *Colonnade* [of NYU], IV (1911), 7 (June), 20.

35 Huxley, *Huxley*, I, 182 ("Dr. Draper droned").

36 British Association for the Advancement of Science, *Report*, 1860, p. 115.

37 *Loc cit.*

38 *Ibid.*, pp. 115–16.

39 *Ibid.*, p. 116.

40 *Loc. cit.*

41 Huxley, *Hooker,* I, 523.

42 Huxley, *Huxley,* I, 182.

43 Greswell's remarks are summarized (and attached to the name "Cresswell") in "Section D," *The Athenaeum,* p. 65. Otherwise, recollections of "Professor Farrar" quoted in Huxley, *Huxley,* I, 182. See also, quotation from "Fremantle," Huxley, *Huxley,* I, 187:

"Mr. Gresley [*sic*], an old Oxford don, pointed out that in human nature at least orderly development was not the necessary rule: Homer was the greatest of poets, but he lived 3000 years ago, and has not produced his like."

44 Huxley, *Huxley,* I, 182.

45 *Loc. cit.*

46 Farrar; Huxley, *Huxley,* I, 183.

47 Summarized in "Section D," *The Athenaeum,* p. 65.

48 The order of speakers appears to be disputed; the statement that Beale spoke at this point comes from the quotation from Farrar; Huxley, *Huxley,* I, 183.

49 Quoted in Huxley, *Hooker,* I, 523. See also "Reminiscences of a Grandmother," *Macmillan's Magazine,* allegedly October 1898; quoted in Huxley, *Huxley,* I, 183.

50 "Section D," *The Athenaeum,* p. 65; Huxley, *Hooker,* I, 523.

51 Green, *Green,* p. 45.

52 Remark to Brodie: Huxley to Francis Darwin, June 27, 1891; quoted in Huxley, *Huxley,* I, 188.

53 Huxley, *Huxley,* I, 181.

54 "Reminiscences of a Grandmother," quoted in Huxley, *Huxley,* I, 184.

55 The earliest attempt to sift out what exactly it was that Huxley said is in Francis Darwin, *The Life and Letters of Charles Darwin* (London, 1887), II, 322.

56 Fainting: Hooker to Darwin; Huxley, *Hooker,* I, 526.

57 West, *Darwin,* pp. 260–61.

58 Huxley, *Hooker,* I, 526; "Section D," *The Athenaeum,* p. 65.

59 Huxley, *Huxley,* I, 189, from the author of "Reminiscences of a Grandmother."

60 Huxley, *Huxley,* I, 188–89.

61 W. M. Higgins and J. W. Draper, "On Volcanoes"; Charles Daubeny, Oxford, to John W. Draper, August 27, 1863, in Nye papers.

62 Huxley, *Huxley,* I, 188, from the "Grandmother."

CHAPTER VIII

1 *History of the Intellectual Development of Europe* (New York, copyrighted 1862, published 1863), pp. iii–iv.

2 In 1859.

3 See chapter V above.

4 His daughter Virginia was the pianist—"Virginia, your La Somnambula in [*sic*] woven all through my Intellectual Development of Europe." Antonia C. Maury, "Recollections of My Grandfather, John William Draper," MS in the Maury papers.

5 Trübner & Co., London, to John W. Draper, June 6, 1863; Draper, New York, to William Darling, June 18, 1863. Both in the Nye papers.

6 Augustus Churchill, London, to Draper, December 23, 1863; Nye papers.

7 Herbert Spencer, London, to Draper, July 15, 1863; Nye papers.

8 John Tyndall, London, to Draper, July 15, 1863; Nye papers.

9 Churchill to Draper, December 23, 1863.

10 Churchill to Draper, December 23, 1863; Bell & Daldy, London, to John W. Draper, November 17, 1863, in Nye papers.

11 An inference from Churchill to Draper, December 23, 1863.

12 Bell & Daldy to Draper, November 17, 1863.

13 The point is that we possess a manuscript copy of the *Intellectual Development*, with excisions, which appears to be the one (or a copy of it) from which Harper's set the book. But we do not have the date for the manuscript; we are therefore not entitled to assert that before the cuts were made it was the manuscript of *ca.* 1858. Since we know that changes of *some* sort were made before publication, and since the cutting down of a manuscript may alter its proportions, it would be dangerous to treat the book as having been produced before its copyright in 1862. No doubt much of it did exist long before, but we have no way of telling how much and what. The manuscript is in the Nye papers.

14 See the estimate of John Spencer Bassett, "Later Historians," in W. P. Trent, John Erskine, S. P. Sherman, Carl Van Doren, eds., *The Cambridge History of American Literature* (New York, 1921), III, 181: "He had little history to begin with and his statements, taken from uncritical secondary works, were full of errors."

15 See, for example, *Intellectual Development*, pp. 5, 97, 494.

16 See the blistering attack upon them; *ibid.*, pp. 100–101.

17 *Ibid.*, pp. 13–14.

18 See the statement by James Henry Robinson, *The New History* (New York, 1912), pp. 103–4:

"This work has for years enjoyed a reputation far exceeding its merits. From a modern standpoint the book is deficient in almost every respect, except its effective style and the assurance of its author. Dr. Draper has not seen fit at any point to give the reader the slightest clue to the sources of his information, but it is clear to the critical reader that his impressions were derived from such miscellaneous works as were available in the early sixties, and that his conclusions do not at any point rest upon a conscientious study of first-hand material. His object, he frankly tells us, was to prove two laws, which no one nowadays would believe to be laws at all."

19 *Intellectual Development*, p. 16.

20 *Ibid.*, pp. 16–17.

21 See Arthur O. Lovejoy, *The Great Chain of Being* (Cambridge, Mass., 1936), pp. 10–14.

22 *Intellectual Development*, p. 74.

23 *Ibid.*, p. 557.

24 *Ibid.*, p. 506.

25 *Ibid.*, p. 89.

26 *Ibid.*, p. 104.

27 *Ibid.*, p. 16.

28 *Loc. cit.*

29 *Ibid.*, p. 17.

30 *Ibid.*, p. 511.

31 *Ibid.*, p. 521.

32 See Lovejoy, *Great Chain*, chapter IV, "The Principle of Plenitude and the New Cosmography."

33 *Intellectual Development*, p. 531.

34 *Ibid.*, p. 537.

35 See John Dewey, *The Influence of Darwinism on Philosophy* (New York, 1910).

36 *Intellectual Development*, pp. 543–44.

[37] The *Esquisse* was written by Condorcet just before his death in 1794, and first published in 1795.

[38] *Mélanges*, p. 510; cited in Harold J. Laski, *Studies in the Problem of Sovereignty* (New Haven, 1917), pp. 221. The translation is mine.

[39] *Intellectual Development*, p. 486.

[40] *Loc. cit.*

[41] *Ibid.*, p. 492.

[42] *Loc. cit.*

[43] *Ibid.*, pp. 492–93.

[44] *Ibid.*, p. 175.

[45] Daumier was born in 1808 and died in 1879; Anatole France was born in 1844.

[46] *Intellectual Development*, p. 408.

[47] *Ibid.*, p. 609.

[48] *Ibid.*, p. 412.

[49] *Ibid.*, p. 175.

[50] *Ibid.*, p. 613.

[51] *Ibid.*, p. 510.

[52] *Loc. cit.*

[53] Edward B. Freeland, "Buckle, Draper, and the Law of Human Development," *Continental Monthly*, VI (1864), I (July), 59.

[54] Freeland, "Buckle, Draper," p. 59.

[55] After he had written the *Intellectual Development*, Draper began, as will appear in chapter IX, expressly to separate the classes in society which were interested in free inquiry from the ones which were not. But even this distinction merely contracted the area of rationality, to which he opposed not so much irrationality as inertness of the reason. If this constituted a heresy inside liberalism, it was not an act of apostasy; and it lay ahead.

[56] See above, pp. 79–82.

[57] There is a brisk discussion of the subject by Jean Gottmann, "Doctrines Géographiques en Politique," in Boris Mirkine-Guetzévitch, ed., *Les Doctrines Politiques Modernes* (New York, 1947), pp. 17–40.

[58] *Intellectual Development*, pp. 21–22.

[59] For an interesting discussion of this analogizing from the Marxist point of view, see G. V. Plekhanov, *In Defence of Materialism*, Andrew Rothstein, trans. (London, 1947)—originally published in 1894.

[60] I suppress the word "inane" so as to have the benefit of an historical statement without the sting. Benedetto Croce, *History as the Story of Liberty*, Sylvia Sprigge, trans. (New York, 1941), pp. 191–92.

[61] *Intellectual Development*, p. iii.

[62] *Ibid.*, p. 2.

[63] *Ibid.*, p. 8.

[64] *Ibid.*, p. 11.

[65] See Arthur O. Lovejoy, "Prolegomena" and "Appendix" in Arthur O. Lovejoy and George Boas, *Primitivism and Related Ideas in Antiquity* (Arthur O. Lovejoy, Gilbert Chinard, George Boas, Ronald S. Crane, eds., *A Documentary History of Primitivism and Related Ideas*, I) (Baltimore, 1935).

[66] *Intellectual Development*, p. 463.

[67] John W. Draper, New York, to Robert Chambers, July 19, 1864; Nye papers.

[68] Anonymous, "The Intellectual Development of Europe," *Westminster Review*, LXXXIII (1865), CLXIII (January), 43–65.

[69] Anonymous, "The Science of History," *Anthropological Review*, III (1865), 8 (February), 29.

[70] Anonymous, "The Intellectual Development of Europe," *Saturday Review*, XVII (1864), 450 (June 11), 727.

71 *Ibid.*, p. 726.
72 *Ibid.*, p. 727.
73 Undated clipping in the Nye papers.
74 Anonymous, "A History of the Intellectual Development of Europe," *Atlantic Monthly*, XIII (1864), LXXIX (May), pp. 642–47.
75 *Ibid.*, pp. 646–47.
76 *Ibid.*, p. 646.
77 Anonymous, "Draper's Philosophy of European History," *New York Times*, August 18, 1863.
78 Undated clippings in the Nye papers.
79 Clipping in the Nye papers.
80 These included the *Boston Review* (Catholic), the *Church Journal* of New York (Protestant Episcopal), a *Presbyter* possibly that of Cincinnati, the *Methodist* of New York, the *Independent* (Congregational), and the *Church Review* of New York (Protestant Episcopal). Undated clippings in the Nye papers.
81 [Orestes A. Brownson], "Professor Draper's Books," *Catholic World*, VII (1868), 38 (May), 164–65, 170.
82 In the *Church Review*, undated clipping in the Nye papers.
83 A mixture compiled from clippings in the Nye papers.
84 See the statement by John Theodore Merz, *A History of European Thought in the Nineteenth Century* (Edinburgh, 1896–1914), I, 25:
". . . it is—in my opinion—mainly the writings of Carlyle, Buckle, Draper, Lecky, Leslie Stephen, and, considering its size, perhaps more than all, Mark Pattison's 'Essay,' which have fixed in our minds the meaning of the word Thought as the most suitable and comprehensive term to denote the whole of the inner or hidden life and Activity of a period or nation."
85 A no doubt partial list compiled from the catalogues of the Widener, New York Public, and Congressional Libraries.
86 There is a copy dated from this year in the Widener; Harper's professes to have no record of the printing history.
87 Joseph Leidy, Philadelphia, to John W. Draper, September 15, 1863; Moritz Altman, Vienna, to Draper, February 25, 1878, original and translation; George Bancroft, New York, to Draper, October 1, 1865. All in the Nye papers.
88 Statement by Virchow to E. L. Youmans, quoted by Editor [E. L. Youmans], "The Conflict of Religion and Science," *Popular Science Monthly*, VI (1874–75), XXXIII (January 1875), 363.
89 M.A. De Wolfe Howe, *James Ford Rhodes: American Historian* (New York, 1929), p. 21.
90 Professor Waldo Palmer of Simmons College; conversation with the author.
91 Max Lerner, *Ideas Are Weapons* (New York, 1939), p. 260.

CHAPTER IX

1 See the *American Journal of Photography and the Allied Arts and Sciences*, n.s., IV (1861–62), 9 (October 1, 1861), 213–14; and Robert Taft, *Photography and the American Scene, A Social History, 1839–1889* (New York, 1938), pp. 224–25.
2 Sanitary Commission, 498 Broadway, New York, to John W. Draper, October 19, 1862; in Nye papers.
3 Obituary notices, unascribed and undated, in the possession of Miss Antonia C. Maury. There are some letters about his work in the possession of Mrs. Dorothy Draper Nye (his daughter).
4 George F. Barker, *Memoir of Henry Draper* ([Washington? 1888?]), p. 54; and letters in the Nye papers.

5 Letters in the Nye papers; on astronomical photographs, Henry Draper, Harpers Ferry, Virginia, to "Dear Parents, Aunt & Sisters," August 8, 1862, and August 15, 1862.

6 Barker, *Memoir of Henry Draper,* p. 54.

7 Henry Draper, "On the Construction of a Silvered Glass Telescope, Fifteen and a Half Inches in Aperture, and Its Use in Celestial Photography," *Smithsonian Contributions to Knowledge,* XIV (1865), #180, 41–42.

8 J. H. Dickson, Philadelphia, to John W. Draper, July 26, 1863; in Nye papers.

9 See, for example, the recollections of Charles L. Bristol, "Some Reminiscences of John William Draper," *Colonnade* [of NYU], IV (1911), 7 (June), 19; and R. E. McIntyre, "In Memoriam [John William Draper]," New York University, *University Quarterly,* V (1882), 2 (February), 52.

10 Albert E. Henschel, "Centenary of John William Draper," *Colonnade* [of NYU], IV (1911), 7 (June), 27.

11 Henschel, "Centenary," p. 27.

12 Conversations of the author with Draper's grandson, Professor John W. Draper of Morgantown, W.Va.; through Professor Draper's father, Daniel Draper.

13 Theodore Francis Jones, ed., *New York University 1832:1932* (New York, 1933), pp. 66–67.

14 *Ibid.,* pp. 84–85.

15 *Loc. cit.*

16 *Ibid.,* p. 85.

17 The Farraguts figure in some letters in the Nye papers.

18 John W. Draper, New York, to unknown addressee, May 8, 1863; Nye papers.

19 Robert Chambers, St. Andrews, Scotland, to Draper, June 23, 1864; Nye papers.

20 Copy of letter from Draper, New York, to Robert Chambers, July 19, 1864; Nye papers.

21 On the occasion for the address to the American Union Academy, see below, pp. 110–111.

22 John W. Draper, *Thoughts on the Future Civil Policy of America* (New York, 1865), p. 159.

23 *Ibid.,* p. 158.

24 See the penetrating discussion by M. G. Jones, *The Charity School Movement* (Cambridge, England, 1938), pp. 3–14. For Draper's own background in Evangelicalism, see chapter I, above.

25 John W. Draper, *The Historical Influence of the Medical Profession* (New York, 1863), p. 28.

26 See above, chapter II, for Draper's life in Virginia. For Liebig's reference to Virginia, see Charles A. Browne, *A Source Book of Agricultural Chemistry* (Waltham, Mass., 1944), p. 268.

27 *Medical Profession,* pp. 28–29.

28 *Ibid.,* p. 29. On this matter of the American "desert," see Walter P. Webb, *The Great Plains* (Boston, 1931), pp. 152–60.

29 *Medical Profession,* p. 29.

30 See *Civil Policy,* pp. 56–57:
". . . in no part of America has that exact concordance [between the 'strands' of population and 'the climate zones in which they dwell'] as yet had time or opportunity to be truly established, though in the Southern States an approach has been made to it."

31 *Ibid.,* pp. 84–85.

32 *Ibid.,* p. 85.

33 *Loc. cit.*

34 *Loc. cit.*

35 *Ibid.,* p. 86.

36 *Medical Profession,* p. 30.

37 *Ibid.,* p. 29.

38 *Ibid.,* p. 30.

39 It is a "motto of which profound statesmanship can never approve"; *ibid.,* p. 30.

40 *Civil Policy,* pp. 265–66.

41 *Ibid.,* p. 267.

42 *Ibid.,* p. 168.

43 John W. Draper, *Address Delivered to the American Union Academy of Literature, Science, and Art* (Washington, 1870), p. 6.

44 *Ibid.,* p. 7.

45 *Ibid.,* p. 9.

46 A statesman can affect population in two ways. Means exist for thwarting the natural consequence of sexual intercourse:
". . . its consequences may be indirectly interfered with or rendered nugatory. It seems to me, however, that practice in this direction must always imply immorality, and that an enlightened man will rely exclusively on the other mode."
Civil Policy, p. 155.

47 *Ibid.,* pp. 155–56.

48 I mention these men as leading philosophers of American nationalism. The two best treatments of the subject are: Merle Curti, *The Roots of American Loyalty* (New York, 1946); and Herbert W. Schneider, *A History of American Philosophy* (New York, 1946), part III, "Nationalism and Democracy."

49 *Civil Policy,* pp. 267–68.

50 *Ibid.,* pp. 250–51.

51 *Ibid.,* pp. 260–61.

52 His grandchildren, Mrs. Dorothy Draper Nye and Miss Antonia C. Maury of Hastings-on-Hudson, N.Y., and Professor John W. Draper of Morgantown, W.Va., all have the distinct impression that he had very little, if anything, to do with party politics. Conversations with the author. But I think he is closer to the Whig-Republican tradition than anything else.

53 See W. H. Auden's introduction to Henry James, *The American Scene* (New York, 1946).

54 For example, he urges the people of the West to assimilate the anticipated flood of Oriental immigrants by schooling:
"The Pacific States will do well to look to their public schools, laying broad and munificent foundations for their educational system, giving no encouragement to the use of any foreign tongue, and fusing into their mass, as thoroughly and rapidly as may be, their inevitable hybrid population."
Civil Policy, p. 172.

55 *Ibid.,* p. 254.

56 See Lucien Lévy-Bruhl, *La Philosophie d'Auguste Comte,* 3d ed. (Paris, 1913), particularly pp. 343–45.

57 *Civil Policy,* pp. 251–52.

58 *Ibid.,* p. 250.

59 See Ralph S. Bates, *Scientific Societies in the United States* (New York, 1945), pp. 78–84.

60 Joseph Henry, Washington, to Draper, March 10, 1863; Nye papers.

61 George F. Barker, *Memoir of John William Draper 1811–1882* ([Washington? 1886?]), p. 380.

62 See chapter IV, above.

63 See The American Union Academy of Literature, Science and Art, *Constitution and By-Laws* (Washington, 1869).

64 *American Union Academy,* p. 11.

65 These were the rather prosaic kinds of investigations undertaken by the

National Academy of Sciences in its early years at the behest of the government;
Bates, *Scientific Societies*, pp. 81–84.

66 *American Union Academy*, p. 6.

67 *Loc cit.*

68 *Loc. cit.*

69 *Ibid.*, p. 16.

70 Just exactly what these immigration policies would be is not clear to me;
but anyhow they ought to be thought out on a scientific basis.

CHAPTER X

1 John W. Draper, *History of the American Civil War*, 3 v. (New York, 1867,
1868, 1870).

2 All statements on this fire from George F. Barker, *Memoir of John William
Draper 1811–1882* ([Washington? 1886?]), pp. 355–56.

3 Letter from John W. Draper, New York, to Edwin Stanton, August 7, 1867;
Stanton papers, v. 33 (June 10–August 9, 1867), #56690–56691, in the Library of
Congress.

4 Draper to Stanton, August 7, 1867; what the disclosure about General Thomas
—presumably George Henry Thomas (1816–70) rather than Lorenzo Thomas
(1804–75)—may have been does not appear.

5 Draper to Stanton, August 7, 1867.

6 William T. Sherman, St. Louis, to John W. Draper, September 12, 1868; Nye
papers.

7 Sherman to Draper, September 19, 1868; Nye papers.

8 Draper to Sherman, September 16, 1868; Nye papers.

9 Draper to Sherman, September 23, 1868; Nye papers.

10 Draper to Sherman, September 18, 1868; Nye papers.

11 Draper to Sherman, September 18, 1868.

12 Draper to Sherman, September 18, 1868.

13 Draper, *Civil War*, I, 95.

14 *Loc. cit.*

15 *Ibid.*, I, 207–8.

16 *Ibid.*, I, 304.

17 *Ibid.*, I, 304–5.

18 *Ibid.*, I, 208.

19 *Loc. cit.*

20 *Loc. cit.*

21 So Draper spells "individualism"; and he points out, *Civil War*, I, 412, that
the men of the Mississippi Valley have been a great reliance of the Union. The
quotation from the *Communist Manifesto* does not, of course, occur in Draper.

22 *Cannibals All! or, Slaves without Masters* (1857) by the Southern apologist
George Fitzhugh (1806–81) attacked the industrial economy in the North as producing its own slaves and providing them with less security than the Southern
system.

23 *Civil War*, I, 348.

24 *Ibid.*, I, 210.

25 Maine's *Ancient Law* was published in 1861.

26 *Civil War*, I, 567; cited in Paul H. Buck, *The Road to Reunion* (Boston,
1937), p. 56.

27 *Civil War*, I, iii–iv.

28 *Ibid.*, I, iv.

29 A. T. Bledsoe in *Southern Review*, III (1868), 4–5; cited in Buck, *Road to
Reunion*, p. 57.

³⁰ Draper to Sherman, September 16, 1868.

³¹ See J. Henry Harper, *The House of Harper* (New York, 1912), p. 244: "Dr. John W. Draper's *Future Civil Policy of America* and *History of the American Civil War* . . . were not . . . lucrative properties."

³² Sherman, St. Louis, to Draper, June [?] 23, 1868; Nye papers.

³³ The German titles are: *Gedanken über die zukünftige Politik Amerikas*, A. Bartels, trans. (Leipzig, 1886); and *Geschichte des amerikanischen Bürgerkrieges*, A. Bartels, trans. (Leipzig, 1877). Both were published by the house of O. Wigand, as was the *Intellectual Development—Geschichte der geistigen Entwickelung Europas* (Leipzig, 1865).

CHAPTER XI

¹ The date from conversations with her granddaughter, Mrs. Dorothy Draper Nye.

² Conversations with Mrs. Nye.

³ Conversations of the author with Professor John W. Draper, of Morgantown, W. Va., Draper's grandson.

⁴ Conversations with the elder Draper's granddaughter, Miss Antonia C. Maury.

⁵ See for example the letter from John W. Draper, [London] to Henry Draper, December 13, 1870; Draper papers, New York Public Library, Manuscript Division.

⁶ See John W. Draper, [London] to "Henry, Daniel & Jinny" Draper, December 19, 1870; Draper papers.

⁷ John W. Draper, [London] to Henry Draper, November 24, 1870; Draper papers.

⁸ *Ibid.*

⁹ John W. Draper, [London] to Henry Draper, December 10, 1870; Draper papers.

¹⁰ John W. Draper, [London] to Henry Draper, December 1, 1870; Draper papers.

¹¹ John W. Draper, [London] to Virginia Draper Maury, December 19, 1870; Draper papers.

¹² John W. Draper, Munich, to Daniel, Virginia, and Henry Draper, December 25, 1870; Nye papers.

¹³ John W. Draper to Henry Draper, December 1, 1870.

¹⁴ *Ibid.*

¹⁵ *Ibid.*

¹⁶ *Ibid.*

¹⁷ John W. Draper to Henry Draper, December 10, 1870.

¹⁸ John W. Draper to Virginia Draper Maury, December 19, 1870.

¹⁹ John W. Draper to Henry Draper, December 10, 1870.

²⁰ *Ibid.*

²¹ *Ibid.*

²² John W. Draper, London, to Courtlandt Palmer [Mrs. Henry Draper's father], February 16, 1871; Draper papers.

²³ John W. Draper to Daniel, Virginia, and Henry Draper, December 25, 1870.

²⁴ John W. Draper to Courtlandt Palmer, February 16, 1871.

²⁵ John W. Draper to Virginia Draper Maury, December 19, 1870.

²⁶ John W. Draper, London, to Henry Draper, February 16, 1871; Draper papers.

²⁷ See D. Appleton-Century Company, *The House of Appleton-Century* (New York, 1936), pp. 13–15.

²⁸ John W. Draper, *History of the Conflict between Religion and Science* (New York, 1874), p. v.

²⁹ *Ibid.*, p. 328.

30 *Ibid.*, p. vi.

31 *Ibid.*, p. 342.

32 *Ibid.*, p. 341.

33 *Ibid.*, pp. 365–66.

34 *Ibid.*, p. 367.

35 See *ibid.*, pp. xi, 217–18, 352–54.

36 Anonymous, "*History of the Conflict between Religion and Science*," Methodist *Quarterly Review*, 57 (or 27) (1875), 1 (January), 162.

37 *Conflict*, pp. 218–19.

38 *Ibid.*, p. vii.

39 *Ibid.*, p. 33.

40 *Ibid.*, pp. 363–64.

41 *Ibid.*, pp. 242–43.

42 *Ibid.*, p. 243.

43 *Ibid.*, pp. 321–22.

44 *Ibid.*, pp. 323.

45 See the frequent remarks in the *Popular Science Monthly* in 1875, 1876, and 1877; [Orestes A. Brownson?] "*History of the Conflict between Religion and Science*," *Brownson's Quarterly Review*, last series, III (1875), II (April), 153.

46 Anonymous, "Draper's Religion and Science," *Presbyterian Quarterly and Princeton Review*, n.s., IV (1875), 13 (January), 165.

47 G[eorge]. F. W[right]., "History of the Conflict between Religion and Science," *Bibliotheca Sacra*, XXXIII (1876), CXXXI (July), 585.

48 *Ibid.*, p. 585.

49 For the number of printings, Appleton-Century, *Appleton-Century*, p. 15.

50 I have compiled this list, probably incomplete, from the catalogues of the Widener, New York Public, and Congressional libraries; and George F. Barker, *Memoir of John William Draper 1811–1882* ([Washington? 1886?]), p. 375.

51 See the *Index Librorum Prohibitorum*, "ad annum 1876" (Rome, 1877), p. 97; Barker, *John William Draper*, pp. 375–76.

52 "The Conflict between Religion and Science," framed cartoon with verse, in possession of Miss Antonia C. Maury. No attribution; possibly Bonner's *Ledger*. A good rhyme is a good rhyme, but the Index Expurgatorius is not the same thing as the Index Librorum Prohibitorum.

53 Conversation with the author.

54 George W. Norris, *Fighting Liberal* (New York, 1945), pp. 12–13.

CHAPTER XII

1 Statement from Harper's to Draper, February 1, 1878; Nye papers.

2 *Scientific Memoirs Being Experimental Contributions to a Knowledge of Radiant Energy* (New York, 1878).

3 Anonymous, "Draper's Scientific Memoirs," *Nature*, XIX (1878–79), #472 (November 14, 1878), 26–27.

4 See his letters speaking of this illness: New York, to Wolcott Gibbs, January 26, 1876 (expressing his regret that he will not be able to accept the Rumford medals in person); and Hastings-on-Hudson, to George Bancroft, June 10, 1876 (refusing an invitation to visit Bancroft and meet the Emperor of Brazil at the latter's request). The Emperor went to see Draper at Hastings; undated, unattributed newspaper clipping in the Nye papers. Both letters are also in the Nye papers.

5 Charles L. Bristol, "Some Reminiscences of John William Draper," *Colonnade* [of NYU], IV (1911), 7 (June), 18.

6 *Ibid.*, p. 19.

7 *Ibid.*, pp. 19–20.

8 *Ibid.*, p. 20.

9 *Ibid.*, p. 21.

10 *Ibid.*, p. 22.

11 *Ibid.*, p. 23.

12 *Ibid.*, p. 24.

13 Philip B. McDonald, "The College of Engineering," in Theodore Francis Jones, ed., *New York University 1832:1932* (New York, 1933), p. 309.

14 See respectively: American Academy of Arts and Sciences, *Proceedings*, n.s., III (May 1875–May 1876), 324–29; John W. Draper, *Science in America*, "Inaugural Address of Dr. John W. Draper, as President of the American Chemical Society" (New York, 1876); George F. Barker, *Memoir of John William Draper 1811–1882* ([Washington? 1886?]), p. 380; and the address to the Unitarians, John W. Draper, *Evolution: Its Origin, Progress, and Consequences* (New York, 1877).

15 *Evolution*, p. 18.

16 See the anonymous articles, which the Drapers almost certainly helped to produce, "The Draper Family," and untitled, New York *Daily Graphic*, respectively December 21, 1874, and December 13, 1877.

17 Conversations of the author with Miss Maury.

18 Antonia C. Maury, "Recollections of My Grandfather, John William Draper," MS in the Maury papers.

19 R. E. McIntyre, "In Memoriam [John William Draper]," New York University, *University Quarterly*, V (1882), 2 (February), 51.

20 Barker, *John William Draper*, p. 382.

21 B[enjamin]. S[illiman]., "John William Draper," *American Journal of Science*, 3d s., XXIII (1882), 134 (February), 163.

22 Albert E. Henschel, "Centenary of John William Draper," *Colonnade* [of NYU], IV (1911), 7 (June), 29.

A BIBLIOGRAPHICAL ESSAY

N.B.: John William Draper is abbreviated as JWD.

I. MATERIALS FOR THE BIOGRAPHY OF JWD

The problems connected with the *genealogy and family history* of the Drapers and of Mrs. JWD are discussed, with an evaluation of the sources, in the footnotes of Chapter I.

Among the *biographical narratives*, the manuscript life, in either JWD's or his son Daniel's hand, in the possession of Miss Antonia C. Maury, is short but of unequaled authority. The two articles on the Draper family in the New York *Daily Graphic* for December 21, 1874, and December 13, 1877, seem to have been written or inspired by the family itself. The anonymous sketch in the *Popular Science Monthly* for January 1874 is said to have been written on the basis of information provided by the subject. G. F. Barker's *Memoir* for the National Academy of Sciences is the best large-scale sketch. In the main, it describes rather than evaluates JWD's scientific work. Knowing JWD personally, Barker probably got his information fairly close to the sources. B. N. Martin's "Sketch," by a colleague at NYU, is thin.

William Jerome Harrison's bare and annalistic sketch in the *Dictionary of National Biography* treats almost exclusively of the scientist. Elwood Hendrick's in the *Dictionary of American Biography* conveys a good many false impressions. While disseminating an extravagant estimate of JWD, Hendrick obscures his real achievements.

The *materials for a biographical narrative,* not yet drawn together, swell to a respectable flood for certain episodes and altogether dry up for others.

For JWD's early youth and first schooling, the most important source is his introductory *Lecture* of 1869, in which he reminisces pleasantly. On the University of London, there are the four letters of his father copied for the archives of NYU from the originals in the University College Library; and H. H. Bellot's *University College* with its occasional references to JWD. On his marriage, the only substantial pieces of evidence are the letter in the Nye papers transmitting the marriage license and the three letters in the Draper papers giving his recollections of the marriage as of 1870.

On the family life of the Drapers in Virginia, the best accounts are the orderly statement at a very late date of some rather sketchy local recollections, Professor John W. Draper's manuscript "Trip to Drapersville" of 1939; and the disjointed reminiscences collected by W. A. Garner. Both Draper and Garner lean on Mrs. L. M. Carter, whose mother attended the school conducted by the Misses Draper. Garner also heard of the Drapers from his own father, a boy at the time of their arrival.

For JWD's career at Hampden-Sidney, Alfred J. Morrison's edition of the *Calendar of Board Minutes* of the college is useful but only as full as need be for a bare record. The articles in the *Record* of the Alumni Association, from 1934 forward, dealing with "the Draper camera" show little judgment in evaluating the worth of evidence. I think very little had better be made of the claims presented for this camera. It may, however, have been used by JWD for some purpose. In general, the discussion of his work in photography is reserved till later in this essay.

On the move to New York, the Nye papers contain a revealing letter; and a few other letters survive in the NYU archives. Seven volumes of the Minutes of the University Council, in the archives, contain significant materials on JWD's academic career, quite formally presented. T. F. Jones's *New York University*, attributing great influence to JWD in university matters, is indispensable. For the medical school, C. E. Heaton's *New York University College of Medicine* is short, graceful, and not especially important. The volumes of J. S. Houston's *New York Lancet*, with their vituperative comment on JWD's colleagues, paint a lively picture for which due allowance can easily be made by the intelligent reader. The *Announcements* of the medical faculty, issued annually, contain some valuable information not to be had elsewhere. W. F. Norwood's *Medical Education* provides a brisk sketch of the medical school in the context of the standards and accomplishments of its rivals.

On the home life of the Draper family after they moved to New York, there are traditions handed down to the three surviving grandchildren of JWD: Mrs. Dorothy Draper Nye and Miss Antonia C. Maury of Hastings-on-Hudson, N.Y., and Professor J. W. Draper of Morgantown, W.Va. Professor Draper's wife heard perhaps more of these than he did. Only Miss Maury remembers (from her childhood and early adolescence) the old home when her grandfather and even her grandmother were still alive.

The materials for the history of the Oxford meeting of the British Association for the Advancement of Science are abundant—and rather confusing. The best accounts from a single point of view are Hooker's letter in Leonard Huxley's *Hooker*, the letter of J. R. Green in his *Letters*, and, though rid of any drama, the account in the *Athenaeum* for July 14, 1860. There are rather awkward attempts at a consensus of recollections in Francis Darwin's *Darwin* and Leonard Huxley's *Huxley*. In details, these and other descriptions are sometimes at odds. The Report of the BAAS for 1860 does not deal with the famous attack and counterattack; it digests JWD's paper, however.

A few letters in the Nye papers show JWD's attitude toward the Civil War and his anxiety over the reception of the *Intellectual Development*. Other letters there trace the war service of his sons. The letters between JWD and General W. T. Sherman, preserved in the same place, form one of the better runs of the extant correspondence.

For JWD's last years the Draper papers contain an interesting series from abroad in 1870. The two most vivid personal recollections from these years are those of his granddaughter Antonia C. Maury in her manuscript "Recollections" and of his student Charles L. Bristol in his "Reminiscences" in the NYU *Colonnade* for June, 1911.

The *correspondence* of JWD was mostly destroyed at his death, in accordance with his command. Not much seems to have survived in the hands of recipients. Incomparably the most important collections are those of Mrs. Dorothy Draper Nye (in excess of one-hundred pieces) and a small sheaf, unusually rich in interest, in the Draper papers of the New York Public Library (the letters from abroad mentioned above, plus a few others). The great bulk of the Nye letters date from 1860 forward. The scattered finds in other collections are on the whole of slight importance.

JWD's *writings* survive mainly in the form of printed books. But an undated manuscript of the *Intellectual Development* is in the Nye papers. They also include: a short, undated manuscript biography of Benjamin Franklin, of the most derivative kind and of the least conceivable interest; the manuscript of the Cooper Union inaugural; and some manuscript pieces in another hand, presumably collected for the *Civil War.*

For the published writings, there is a good bibliography of the more important at the end of Barker's *Memoir.* The body of the present biography serves as a form of annotation on the publications of JWD, and it would be superfluous to add comments here. Certain parts of his books were printed in *Harper's* magazine; these "articles" are not listed below.

Evaluations of JWD's scientific work are reasonably numerous, but with the distinct exception of Alexander Findlay's *Hundred Years of Chemistry,* they mostly fail to set him firmly in the context of nineteenth- and twentieth-century science. The most important of these (aside from Findlay, which is much the best but does not treat of physics) are: (1) the statement in the *Proceedings* of the American Academy, justifying the award of the Rumford medals; (2) the review in the *American Journal of Science* in 1878 of JWD's *Scientific Memoirs;* (3) Barker's description of experiments and conclusions in his *Memoir;* (4) Agnes Clerke's footnote in her *Popular History of Astronomy;* (5) Florian Cajori's *History of Physics;* and (6) Daniel Norman's two articles. Barker is especially poor on the scientific environment of JWD's work. On this score Norman is good, but he takes a little too much on faith from family traditions. Aside from Norman, Miss Clerke and Cajori are the most helpful.

On the special question of pioneering in photography, the value of JWD's claims in various publications is assessed in the text. For Morse's claims his *Letters and Journals* are of trifling value. The clear, judicious account in Carleton Mabee's *American Leonardo* leans on what appears to be the definitive work on American photography, Robert Taft's *Photography and the American Scene.* Taft makes a few assumptions in connection with JWD that seem to me unwarranted (they are specified in the text), but the critical history of the subject dates from his revelation of new source materials and his intelligent estimate of what the materials are worth. J. M. Eder's *History of Photography,* as translated, expanded, and edited by Edward Epstean, is of far wider scope than its title might indicate—a history of investigations into the records left by light rays (including spectroscopy, for example, as well as photography in the conversational sense). Even with Epstean's rather awkward intrusion of materials on American contributions, the bias of the book is in favor of Central European investigators; and there is almost no sense of continuity from chapter to chapter.

Estimates of the historical and political books naturally fall into two classes: contemporary reviews, of which an effort at selective annotation occurs in the text; and retrospective appraisals from the twentieth century. The most important of the latter is Donald Emerson's "Hildreth, Draper, and 'Scientific History.' " This is by far the best analysis of Draper available; but Hildreth became the subject of Emerson's doctoral thesis, and it is hard to escape the conclusion that the treatment of Draper is a kind of pendant to the discussion of a very different historian. The discussion of JWD's emphasis on the historical influence of the physical environment in Franklin Thomas' *Environmental Basis of Society* is not particularly accurate; and it is decidedly too favorable. The brisk dismissals given JWD by James Harvey Robinson in *The New History* and by John Spencer Bassett on "Later Historians" and Morris R. Cohen on "Later Philosophy" in the *Cambridge History of American Literature* are fair enough granted their point of view—that of men asked to settle the question: "Ought Draper's books *now* to be read as history or philosophy?"

II. THE CONTEXT OF JWD'S BIOGRAPHY

No attempt is made here to evaluate all of the best books on the currents of opinion playing about JWD. Only the bare minimum especially useful to me is included.

For the eighteenth-century traditions of which JWD was the heir, Paul Hazard's *Pensée Européenne au XVIIIe siècle* is an attractive and important book.

On the Evangelical temper Elie Halévy's *English People in 1815* is the landmark; it is one of the books that leave some great tract of history transformed. His *Growth of Philosophic Radicalism* is scarcely less important for the history of Utilitarianism.

Perhaps the most judicious brief analysis of the Saint-Simonians is that of Charles Rist in Gide and Rist's *History of Economic Doctrines;* it would be superfluous to praise this extraordinary book. Lucien Lévy-Bruhl's *Philosophie d'Auguste Comte* has saved a great many people the arduous task of reading Saint-Simon's most famous and most rebellious disciple. A brilliant exposition of Positivism, the book is a little vitiated by the demonstration that all of Comte's critics are always wrong; but if Lévy-Bruhl was an apologist, he was most skillful at his work. The two books of Richmond L. Hawkins on Positivism in the United States are valuable; but they are also pedestrian, and JWD is rather an important disciple to have ignored.

For general political currents, George H. Sabine's *History of Political Theory* altogether transcends the category of textbooks. The later volume(s) of Hans Kohn's *Idea of Nationalism* may be expected to provide a systematic history on the grand scale of the idea, as distinct from the practice, of nationalism in the nineteenth and twentieth centuries. In the meantime Alfred Cobban's concise *National Self-Determination* throws more light on nationalism in general than might be expected from the title. For these issues in the United States, the two most important works are Merle Curti's *Roots of American Loyalty* and (in its relevant, and quite extensive, portions) Herbert W. Schneider's *History of American Philosophy*.

The history of historiography has found a large, unilluminating manual in James Westfall Thompson's *History of Historical Writing;* unlike some previous efforts it is more than a collection of names. All American and all living historians are excluded on principle. Thompson has in no way displaced the well-known work of G. P. Gooch on *History and Historians of the Nineteenth Century*. In attempting to assimilate philosophy to history, Benedetto Croce in *History as the Story of Liberty* and R. G. Collingwood in the posthumous *Idea of History* explore the history of historical writing. Collingwood's book is more thorough and systematic; but the insights come thick and fast in Croce, even for the reader who is basically in disagreement. On the introduction of geographical factors into political and historical discussions, Jean Gottmann's "Doctrines Géographiques en Politique" is brief but intelligent.

The three best compact histories of science in English are H. T. Pledge's *Science since 1500* (the best, but rather formidably "dense"), Charles Singer's *Short History*, and Sir William Dampier's longer one. Dampier is, if not exactly strong, extremely *full*, on the philosophical ramifications of science. Florian Cajori's history of physics, though passing out of date, is still useful. J. M. Eder's *History of Photography* is, of course, a *Handbuch* of great importance for many of the questions concerning the history of physics and chemistry that are raised by JWD's work. The two most useful brief histories of chemistry are J. R. Partington's *Short History* and Alexander Findlay's *Hundred Years*. Charles A. Browne's *Source Book of Agricultural Chemistry* is an excellent *history* of the subject into which substantial citations are introduced. For biology, Emanuel Rádl's *History of Biological Theories* is more technical; Erik Nordenskiöld's *History of Biology* is more biographical (and sometimes verges on the superficial).

Of the slowly growing body of books which integrate the history of science with the history of society at large, the two works of Richard H. Shryock on the *Development of Modern Medicine* and *American Medical Research* are the ones of most relevance for JWD's career (and among the very best works of their kind).

On the interrelations of science, religion, and philosophy, Alfred North Whitehead's *Science and the Modern World* has already set the tone for a whole generation. The volume of essays edited by Yervant H. Krikorian, *Naturalism and the Human Spirit*, is making its way as a kind of interim report on the great movement; but it got rather a cool reception from reviewers not unsympathetic with its purpose. For the opposing tradition, A. D. Ritchie's *Civilization, Science and Religion* is an able statement; it is an effort on historical lines to give science its due and still have something left over for religion.

Of the general histories of American thought, Charles and Mary Beard's *American Spirit*, Merle Curti's *Growth of American Thought*, and Herbert

W. Schneider's *History of American Philosophy* attempt with more or less success to set the issues between religion and science in an American context. Richard Hofstadter deals with a segment of the debate in his *Social Darwinism,* an excellent book which discusses a multitude of questions in very brief compass.

A BIBLIOGRAPHICAL LIST

Certain possible references have been omitted as shedding little or no light or as deriving wholly from other sources. The list of secondary works is not exhaustive; certain titles of either slight or peripheral interest, cited in the footnotes, are not repeated here.

I. PRIMARY SOURCES

A. *Letters*

Boston Public Library, Rare Book Division; two letters from JWD, September 10, 1842, and February 5, 1848.

Mrs. Henry Draper papers, New York Public Library; eight letters from JWD in 1870–71 and four others of later date.

Adam Gurowski papers, Library of Congress; JWD to Adam Gurowski, January 2, 1861.

Huntington Library; three letters from JWD, May 1, 1860, May 16, 1872[?], May 18, 1875.

Miss Antonia C. Maury papers, in her possession, Hastings-on-Hudson, N.Y.; at least four letters, one by JWD, the others bearing on his biography, and a telegram from W. T. Sherman to JWD.

Miss Maury withheld from inspection by the author her mother's letter describing the Oxford meeting of the BAAS.

New York University archives. Apart from the University College letters cited below, the NYU library at University Heights contains one letter from JWD, May 20, 1839. In the seven volumes running from July 1838 to October 4, 1886, of the NYU Council Minutes, numerous communications from JWD are reproduced.

Mrs. Dorothy Draper Nye papers, in her possession, Hastings-on-Hudson, N.Y.; more than one hundred letters or copies of letters from and to JWD, beginning in 1831 but mainly from 1862 to 1878.

Historical Society of Pennsylvania, autograph collections; four letters from JWD, February 5, 1839, December 15, 1845, June 28, 1847, March 11, 1861.

University of Pennsylvania Library; five letters from JWD, September 20, 1845, June 28, 1867, July 14, 1876, January 28, 1881, and September 20, no year.

Edwin M. Stanton papers, Library of Congress, v. 33 (June 10–August 9, 1867), 56690–56691; JWD to Stanton, August 7, 1867.

Robert Taft, *Photography and the American Scene, A Social History, 1839– 1889* (New York, 1938), 29–31; JWD to Sir J. F. W. Herschel, July 28, 1840 and Herschel to JWD, October 6, 1840.

University College, University of London, archives; four letters from JWD's father, 1826–1828, and one from JWD, undated. Copies in NYU archives.

Yale University Library; eight letters from JWD, August 26, 1842, May 24, 1844, May 11, 1845 [or 1846?], August 21, 1846, January 7, 1850, November 12, 1851 [?], July 16, 1860, and undated.

B. *Oral traditions*

The seven living persons who transmit oral traditions from firsthand observers of JWD's career are: (1) his three surviving grandchildren, Mrs. Dorothy Draper Nye and Miss Antonia C. Maury of Hastings-on-Hudson, N.Y., and Professor J. W. Draper of Morgantown, W.Va.; (2) two granddaughters-in-law, Mrs. J. W. Draper of Morgantown and Mrs. John William Draper [Maury] of Hastings-on-Hudson; and (3) two grandnephews, C. L. Wright of Bayside, Long Island, N.Y., and Dr. Daniel Gardner, now of New York City after living most of his life in Europe. The firsthand traditions which they transmit derive from the following sources: (1) Mrs. Nye and Professor and Mrs. Draper of Morgantown, mainly from their father and father-in-law, Daniel, JWD's son and amanuensis; (2) Miss Maury, from her own recollections of her grandparents and their home, from her mother, aunt, and uncles, JWD's children, from her brother, John William Draper [Maury], and, finally, from her great-aunt Dorothy Catharine, JWD's sister; (3) Mrs. John William Draper [Maury], mainly from her husband, Miss Maury's brother; and (4) C. L. Wright and Dr. Daniel Gardner, from their mother and father respectively, these parents being doubly JWD's niece and nephew. It will be seen that only Miss Maury transmits without intermediary a primary tradition. Mrs. Nye and Mrs. Draper of Morgantown, however, have good memories for what they heard from Daniel Draper. He was decidedly deaf in later years, and his daughter-in-law had better success in talking with him than his son did; the old gentleman lived with them. The traditions transmitted by Wright and Dr. Gardner bear on a most restricted area of JWD's biography. As Mrs. Draper [Maury] refused to be interviewed, the importance of the tradition she received from her husband and its state of preservation in her memory cannot be judged.

C. *Primary sources for biographical narrative* (excluding correspondence, oral traditions, and scientific and historical writings).

American Photographical Society of New York City, notices of its meetings under different headings, in *American Journal of Photography and the Allied Arts & Sciences*, n.s., I (1858–59), 334, 377–81; II (1859–60), 149–53, 218–22, 251–54, 286–88; III (1860–61), 219–21, 282; IV (1861–62), 213–14, 331–33, 427–29; VI (1863–64), 349–52.

Through the whole period JWD was president of the society, and these reports quote brief remarks made by him in its meetings.

Bristol, Charles L., "Some Reminiscences of John William Draper," NYU *Colonnade*, IV (1911), 7 (June), 18–24.

Darwin, Francis, *The Life and Letters of Charles Darwin*. 3 v. London, 1887.

An attempt to pull together accounts of the Oxford meeting of the BAAS in 1860.

[Draper, John William? or Daniel Draper?], "Professor John W. Draper," handwritten manuscript in the possession of Miss Antonia C. Maury, Hastings-on-Hudson, N.Y.

[Draper, John William? or E. L. Youmans?], "Sketch of Dr. J. W. Draper," *Popular Science Monthly*, IV (1873–74), 361–67.

Richard Anthony Proctor, editor of *Knowledge* of London, allowing for editorial revision by Youmans, says that "in substance" the information here communicated was got from JWD himself.

Draper, John William, of Morgantown, W.Va. [JWD's grandson], "A Trip to Drapersville, Va." Typewritten manuscript in his possession. 1939.

Primary only in so far as it transmits the tradition received by Mrs. L. M. Carter from her mother, a student of JWD's sisters during their Virginia residence.

"The Draper Family," New York *Daily Graphic*, December 21, 1874.

["The Draper Family"], New York *Daily Graphic*, December 13, 1877.

The attribution of these two articles from the *Graphic* to some member of the immediate family, probably JWD himself, seems almost certain; but it is a conjecture.

Garner, W. A., to Editor, *Chase City Progress* (Chase City, Va.), July 20, 1939.

Garner, W. A., Roanoke, Va., to J. W. Draper of Morgantown, 1941. In the files of the recipient.

Garner transmits a primary tradition from his father, and at still another remove the tradition handed down to Mrs. L. M. Carter by her mother.

Goode, W. H., "The Daguerreotype and Its Applications," *American Journal of Science*, XL (1840–41), 137–144.

Goode had been JWD's laboratory assistant before transferring to the Yale Medical College, from which this article was transmitted; its significance is pointed out in the text.

Green, John Richard, *Letters of John Richard Green*. Leslie Stephen, ed. New York, 1901.

A letter describes the scene at the Oxford meeting of the BAAS; the reference to JWD is given in the text.

Huxley, Leonard, *Life and Letters of Sir Joseph Dalton Hooker*. 2 v. London, 1918.

A contemporary letter of Hooker's on the Oxford meeting; the reference to JWD given in the text.

———, *Life and Letters of Thomas Henry Huxley*. 2 v. London, 1900.

An effort to put together the firsthand accounts of the Oxford meeting.

University of London, *Proprietors of Shares*. [London, 1827.]

JWD's father's holding is listed.

Maury, Antonia C., "Recollections of My Grandfather, John William Draper," typewritten manuscript in her possession.

McIntyre, R. E., "The Funeral of Prof. Draper," New York University, *University Quarterly*, V (1882), 2 (February), 55–56.

Morrison, Alfred J., ed., *The College of Hampden-Sidney. Calendar of Board Minutes 1776–1876*. Richmond, 1912.

New York University, Council, Minutes, volumes dated July 1838–June 1843, December 1843–December 1848, January 1849–January 1853, March 4, 1853–May 27, 1864, March 2, 1864–December 6, 1876, January 12, 1877–October 4, 1886. University archives.

———, Faculty of the College, Faculty Minutes, 1838–56. University archives.

Of negligible importance for JWD.

———, Medical Department, *Annual Announcement* [under various slightly different titles], 1841–42, 1855, 1858, 1859–61, 1863, 1869.

There does not appear to be a complete, or even nearly complete, file of this useful publication.

"Proceedings of the Mineralogical Society of Virginia," *Farmers' Register*, IV (1836–37), 315–17.

On the plans for a mineralogical society under JWD's direction.

"Section D. [of the British Association for the Advancement of Science]— Zoology and Botany, including Physiology. Saturday," *The Athenaeum*, 1860, Pt. 2, pp. 64–65.

The major contemporary, printed account of the tilt between Wilberforce and Huxley.

Society of the Alumni of the Medical Department, *Catalogue of the Alumni of the Medical Department of the University of Pennsylvania. 1765–1877*. Philadelphia, 1877.

JWD's name and thesis are listed.

D. *Scientific memoirs* (in order of publication)

After the first citation from each, the *American Journal of Science*, the *Journal of the Franklin Institute*, the *Philosophical Magazine*, and the *American Journal of the Medical Sciences* are abbreviated, respectively, as *AJSci*, *JFrIn*, *PhilMag*, *AJMedSci*.

Higgins, W. M., and J. W. Draper, "On Volcanoes," *Magazine of Natural History*, V (1832), 164–72, 262–72, 632–37; VI (1833), 344–50.

———, "Remarks on the Formation of the Dead Sea and the Surrounding District," *Magazine of Natural History*, V (1832), 532–34.

———, "Remarks on Electrical Decompositions," *Edinburgh New Philosophical Journal*, XIV (1832–33), 314–17.

"Influence of Electricity on Capillary Attraction," *American Journal of Science*, XXVI (1834), 399–400.

"Some Experimental Researches to Determine the Nature of Capillary Attraction," *Journal of the Franklin Institute*, n.s., XIV (1834), 147–65.

"An Account of Some Experiments Made to Determine the Most Eligible Construction of Galvanic Batteries of Four Elements," *JFrIn*, n.s., XIV (1834), 289–95.

"Chemical Analysis of the Native Chloride of Carbon," *JFrIn*, n.s., XIV (1834), 295–98.

"Experiments Made to Determine Whether Light Exerts Any Magnetic Action," *JFrIn*, n.s., XV (1835), 79–85, 155–58.

"Idolatry and Philosophy of the Zabians," *AJSci*, XXVIII (1835), 201–20.

"On the Chemical Analysis of Coins and Medals," *AJSci*, XXIX (1836), 157–60.

"Of the Tidal Motions of Conductors, Free to Move," *JFrIn*, n.s., XVII (1836), 27–33.

"Experiments on Absorption," *American Journal of the Medical Sciences*, XVIII (1836), 13–32.

"Experiments on Endosmosis," *JFrIn*, n.s., XVII (1836), 177–82; XVIII (1836), 27–31.

"Observations on Microscopic Chemistry," *JFrIn*, n.s., XVIII (1836), 378–84.

"Experiments on Solar Light," *AJMedSci*, XX (1837), 268–69; *JFrIn*, n.s., XIX (1837), 469–79, XX (1837), 38–46, 114–25, 250–53.

"Remarks on the Action of Presence," *AJMedSci*, XXI (1837–38), 122–30.

"Simultaneous Meteorological Observations," *JFrIn*, n.s., XXI (1838), 39–40.

"On the Physical Action of Capillary Systems.—Identification of the Force Producing Motion with the Chemical Force," *AJMedSci*, XXI (1837–38), 289–302.

"On Some Mechanical Functions of Areolar Tissues," *AJMedSci*, XXII (1838), 23–44, 302–23.

"Remarks on the Constitution of the Atmosphere; Addressed to Dr. Dalton, F.R.S.," *Philosophical Magazine*, 3d s., XIII (1838), 241–52.

"Further Remarks on the Action of Presence," *AJMedSci*, XXIII (1839), 68–81.

"On the Use of a Secondary Wire as a Measure of the Relative Tension of Electric Currents," *PhilMag*, 3d s., XV (1839), 266–79, 339–49.

"An Account of Some Experiments Made in the South of Virginia, on the Light of the Sun," *PhilMag*, 3d s., XVI (1840), 81–84.

"On the Electro-motive Power of Heat," *PhilMag*, 3d s., XVI (1840), 451–61.

"Portraits in Daguerreotype," *PhilMag*, 3d s., XVI (1840), 535.

"Remarks on the Daguerreotype," *American Repertory of Arts, Sciences, and Manufactures*, I (1840), 401–4.

"On the Process of Daguerreotype, and Its Application to Taking Portraits from the Life," *PhilMag.* 3d s., XVII (1840), 217–25.

"On Some Analogies between the Phaenomena of the Chemical Rays, and Those of Radiant Heat," *PhilMag*, 3d s., XIX (1841), 195–210.

"On Certain Spectral Appearances, and on the Discovery of Latent Light," *PhilMag*, 3d s., XXI (1842), 348–50.

"On a New Imponderable Substance, and on a Class of Chemical Rays Analogous to the Rays of Dark Heat," *PhilMag*, 3d s., XXI (1842), 453–61.

"On the Rapid Detithonizing Power of Certain Gases and Vapours, and on an Instantaneous Means of Producing Spectral Appearances," *PhilMag,* 3d s., XXII (1843), 161–65.

"On a New System of Inactive Tithonographic Spaces in the Solar Spectrum Analogous to the Fixed Lines of Fraunhofer," *PhilMag,* 3d s., XXII (1843), 360–64.

"On the Tithonotype, or Art of Multiplying Daguerreotypes," *PhilMag,* 3d s., XXII (1843), 365–68.

"On the Decomposition of Carbonic Acid and the Alkaline Carbonates by the Light of the Sun," American Philosophical Society, *Proceedings,* III, 27 (Philadelphia meeting, May 25–30, 1843), 111–14.

"On the Decomposition of Carbonic Acid Gas and the Alkaline Carbonates, by the Light of the Sun; and on the Tithonotype," *PhilMag,* 3d s., XXIII (1843), 161–76.

"On the Law of the Conducting Power of Wires," *AJSci,* XLV (1843), 392–94.

"On a Change Produced by Exposure to the Beams of the Sun, in the Properties of an Elementary Substance," British Association for the Advancement of Science, *Report,* 1843, Pt. 2, p. 9.

"Description of the Tithonometer, an Instrument for Measuring the Chemical Force of the Indigo-tithonic Rays," *PhilMag,* 3d s., XXIII (1843), 401–15.

"On Mr. Hunt's Book, Entitled 'Researches on Light,'" *PhilMag,* 3d s., XXV (1844), 49–51.

"On Tithonized Chlorine," *PhilMag,* 3d s., XXV (1844), 1–10.

"Further Considerations on the Existence of a Fourth Imponderable," *PhilMag,* 3d s., XXV (1844), 103–16.

"Note on the Decomposition of Carbonic Acid by the Leaves of Plants under the Influence of Yellow Light," *PhilMag,* 3d s., XXV (1844), 169–73.

"Is Capillary Action an Electrical Phaenomenon?" *PhilMag,* 3d s., XXVI (1845), 185–89.

"On the Interference Spectrum, and the Absorption of the Tithonic Rays," *PhilMag,* 3d s., XXVI (1845), 465–78.

"On the Allotropism of Chlorine as Connected with the Theory of Substitutions," *AJSci,* XLIX (1845), 346–68.

"Account of a Remarkable Difference between the Rays of Incandescent Lime and Those Emitted by an Electric Spark," *PhilMag,* 3d s., XXVII (1845), 435–37.

"On the Cause of the Circulation of the Blood," *PhilMag,* 3d s., XXVIII (1846), 178–89.

"Remarks on the Existence and Mechanism of the Negative or Protecting Rays of the Sun," *PhilMag,* 3d s., XXX (1847), 87–93.

"Singular Property of Gun-Cotton Mixture," *PhilMag,* 3d s., XXX (1847), 299.

"On the Production of Light by Heat," *PhilMag,* 3d s., XXX (1847), 345–60.

"On the Production of Light by Chemical Action," *PhilMag,* 3d s., XXXII (1848), 100–114.

"On the Existence and Effects of Allotropism in the Constituent Elements of Living Beings," *PhilMag*, 3d s., XXXIV (1849), 241–46.

"On the Phosphorescence of Bodies," *PhilMag*, 4th s., I (1851), 81–100.

"On the Chemical Action of Light," *PhilMag*, 4th s., I (1851), 368–93.

"On Respiration," *AJMedSci*, n.s., XXIII (1852), 314–20.

"On a New Method for the Determination of Urea," *PhilMag*, 4th s., VI (1853), 290–92.

"On the Diffraction Spectrum—Remarks on M. Eisenlohr's Recent Experiments," *PhilMag*, 4th s., XIII (1857), 153–56.

"On the Measurement of the Chemical Action of Light," *PhilMag*, 4th s., XIV (1857), 161–64.

"On the Influence of Light upon Chlorine, and Some Remarks on Alchemy," *PhilMag*, 4th s., XIV (1857), 321–23.

"On the Nature of Flame, and on the Condition of the Sun's Surface," *PhilMag*, 4th s., XV (1858), 90–93.

"On the Motions of Camphor toward the Light," *PhilMag*, 4th s., XXV (1863), 38–39.

"On the Motions of Camphor toward the Light, and on Variations in the Fixed Lines of the Solar Spectrum," *PhilMag*, 4th s., XXV (1863), 342–44.

"Researches in Actino-Chemistry. Memoir first. On the Distribution of Heat in the Spectrum," *PhilMag*, 4th s., XLIV (1872), 104–17.

"Researches in Actino-Chemistry. Memoir second. On the Distribution of Chemical Force in the Spectrum," *PhilMag*, 4th s., XLIV (1872), 422–43.

"On the Fixed Lines in the Ultra-red Invisible Region of the Spectrum," *PhilMag*, 5th s., III (1877), 86–89.

"On a New Form of Spectrometer, and on the Distribution of the Intensity of Light in the Spectrum," *PhilMag*, 5th s., VIII (1879), 75–80.

"On a New Standard of Light," *PhilMag*, 5th s., IX (1880), 76.

"On the Phosphorograph of a Solar Spectrum, and on the Lines in Its Infra-red Regions," American Academy of Arts and Sciences, *Proceedings*, XVI (1880), 223–35.

E. *Other articles; speeches and lectures* (in chronological order, and excluding autobiographical sketches)

Introductory Lecture to a Course of Chemistry and Natural Philosophy, Delivered in Hampden Sidney College. Richmond, 1836.

"Lecture," *Southern Literary Messenger*, III (1837), 693–98.

Introductory Lecture to the Course of Chemistry. New York, 1841.

The Concluding Lecture on the Theory and Phenomena of Heat. New York, [1841].

A Valedictory Lecture. New York, 1842.

Introductory Lecture . . . on the Relations of Atmospheric Air to Animals and Plants. New York, 1844.

Introductory Lecture . . . on the Relations and Nature of Water. New York, 1845.

An Introductory Lecture on the History of Chemistry. New York, 1846.

An Introductory Lecture on Phosphorus. New York, 1847.

An Introductory Lecture on Oxygen Gas. New York, 1848.

The Influence of Physical Agents on Life. New York, 1850.

"The Life and Services of Granville S. Pattison, M.D.," *New York Herald,* January 11, 1852.

An Introductory Lecture . . . Entitled An Appeal to the People of the State of New-York, to Legalise the Dissection of the Dead. New York, 1853.

> Appended to a petition of the NYU medical faculty addressed to the legislature of New York.

The Indebtedness of the City of New-York to Its University. New York, 1853.

"On the Application of Photography to Printing," *Harper's Magazine,* XIII (1856), 433–41.

"Who Made the First Photographic Portrait?" *American Journal of Photography and the Allied Arts & Sciences,* n.s., I (1858–59), 2–6.

[Address at the Inaugural of the Cooper Institute, July 1, 1859.] Manuscript in Nye papers.

"President Draper's Address before the Photographical Society," *American Journal of Photography,* n.s., II (1859–60), 275–80.

"On the Intellectual Development of Europe, Considered with Reference to the Views of Mr. Darwin and Others, that the Progression of Organisms Is Determined by Law," British Association for the Advancement of Science, *Report* for 1860. London, 1861.

"Address to the American Photographical Society," *American Journal of Photography,* n.s., III (1860–61), 289–93.

"President Draper's Address before the Photographical Society," *American Journal of Photography,* n.s., IV (1861–62), 433–41.

The Historical Influence of the Medical Profession. New York, 1863.

"The Annual Address before the American Photographical Society," *American Journal of Photography,* n.s., VI (1863–64), 385–92.

Lecture. Introductory to the Course of 1869–70. New York, [1869].

Address Delivered to the American Union Academy of Literature, Science, and Art, at Its First Annual Meeting, January 31, 1870. Washington, 1870.

"English and American Science," *Popular Science Monthly,* II (1872–1873), 734–36.

> "Address at the Tyndall Banquet," on John Tyndall's Departure for England after an American lecture tour.

"Letter from Dr. John W. Draper," *American Chemist,* V (1874), 39–40.

> A tribute to Joseph Priestley, with a few recollections of JWD's own life.

Science in America. New York, 1876.

> Address as president of the American Chemical Society.

Evolution: Its Origin, Progress, and Consequences. New York, 1877.

> "The ministers of the Unitarian Church have recently held a meeting of their Institute at Springfield, Massachusetts. They had requested Dr. John W. Draper to deliver before them a lecture on the subject of Evolution. This accordingly was done on Thursday, October 11th.

Some passages omitted in the lecture for want of time are here introduced."

"Popular Exposition of Some Scientific Experiments. Part I.—About Red-Hot Bodies," *Harper's Magazine,* LIV (1876–77), 565–75.

"Popular Exposition of Some Scientific Experiments. Part II.—About Flame and the Combustion of Substances," *Harper's Magazine,* LIV (1876–77), 740–50.

"Popular Exposition of Some Scientific Experiments. Part III.—Things that are Invisible.—The Nature of Sight.—Visual Deceptions," *Harper's Magazine,* LIV (1876–77), 898–906.

"Popular Exposition of Some Scientific Experiments. Part IV.—Things that are Invisible," *Harper's Magazine,* LV (1877), 102–11.

"Popular Exposition of Some Scientific Experiments. Part V.—The Diffraction Spectrum," *Harper's Magazine,* LV (1877), 417–28.

"Popular Exposition of Some Scientific Experiments. Part VI.—Concerning Thermometers," *Harper's Magazine,* LV (1877), 577–89.

"Popular Exposition of Some Scientific Experiments. Part VII.—Burning Glasses and Mirrors; Their Heating and Chemical Effects," *Harper's Magazine,* LV (1877), 745–57.

"Popular Exposition of Some Scientific Experiments. Part VIII.—On the Cause of the Flow of the Sap in Plants and the Circulation of the Blood in Animals," *Harper's Magazine,* LVI (1877–1878), 244–55.

"Political Effect of the Decline of Faith in Continental Europe," *Princeton Review,* LV (1879), 78–96.

"The Practical Interrogation of Nature," *Harper's Magazine,* LVIII (1878–79), 722–28.

[Sketch of a Life of Benjamin Franklin.] Undated manuscript in Nye papers.

F. *First editions of books in English* (in order of publication)

Robert Kane, *Elements of Chemistry.* John William Draper, ed. New York, 1842.

A Treatise on the Forces which Produce the Organization of Plants. New York, 1844.

Text-book on Chemistry. New York, 1846.

A Text-Book on Natural Philosophy. New York, 1847.

Human Physiology, Statical and Dynamical; or, The Conditions and Course of the Life of Man. New York, 1856.

A History of the Intellectual Development of Europe. New York, 1862; first issued 1863.

Thoughts on the Future Civil Policy of America. New York, 1865.

A Text-book on Physiology. New York, 1866.

History of the American Civil War. 3 v. New York, 1867, 1868, 1870.

History of the Conflict between Religion and Science. New York, 1874.

Scientific Memoirs Being Experimental Contributions to a Knowledge of Radiant Energy. New York, 1878.

II. SECONDARY MATERIALS

A. Oral traditions

In transmitting, with whatever accuracy, certain primary traditions, the descendants of JWD whose names are listed under the same heading under "Primary sources" may unconsciously have admixed what are really secondary materials. Apart from this possibility, a considerable part of their information is avowedly secondary.

B. *Biographical sketches, fragments of sketches, and materials bearing on JWD's biography* (excluding reviews and scientific and literary estimates)

American Union Academy of Literature, Science and Art, *Constitution and By-Laws*. Washington, 1869.

Appleton-Century Company, *The House of Appleton-Century*. New York, 1936.

Barker, George F., *Memoir of Henry Draper*. [Washington? 1888?]

———, *Memoir of John William Draper 1811–1882*. [Washington? 1886?]

Bellot, H. Hale, *University College London 1826–1926*. London, 1929.

Cannon, Annie J., "Mrs. Henry Draper," *Science*, n.s., XLI (1915), 380–82.

Cheyney, Edward Potts, *History of the University of Pennsylvania*. Philadelphia, 1940.

Coan, Titus M., "John William Draper," *Harper's Weekly*, XXVI (1882), #1312 (February 11), 85–86.

"The Conflict between Religion and Science," framed cartoon with verse, in possession of Miss Antonia C. Maury. No attribution.

Draper, Henry, "On the Construction of a Silvered Glass Telescope, Fifteen and a Half Inches in Aperture, and Its Use in Celestial Photography," *Smithsonian Contributions to Knowledge*, XIV (1865), #180.

Draper, Thomas Waln-Morgan, *The Drapers in America*. New York, 1892.

[Featherstone, J. S.], *A Tribute of Grateful Remembrance to the Memory of The Rev. John Christopher Draper*. [Sheerness, England, 1829.]

Harden, Arthur, "Edward Turner," *Dictionary of National Biography*, XIX, 1262–63.

Harrison, William Jerome, "John William Draper," *Dictionary of National Biography*, VI, 3–4.

Heaton, Claude Edwin, *A Historical Sketch of New York University College of Medicine 1841–1941*. New York, 1941.

Hendrick, Elwood, "John William Draper," *Dictionary of American Biography*, V, 438–41.

Henschel, Albert E., "Centenary of John William Draper," NYU *Colonnade*, IV (1911), 7 (June), 26–30.

"John William Draper," *Nature*, XXV (1881–82), 274–75.

Jones, Theodore Francis, ed., *New York University 1832:1932*. New York, 1933.

Mabee, Carleton, *The American Leonardo, A Life of Samuel F. B. Morse*. New York, 1943.

McIntyre, R. E., "In Memoriam [JWD]," New York University, *University Quarterly*, V (1882), 2 (February), 51–54.

Martin, Benjamin N., "A Sketch of John W. Draper," *Magazine of American History*, VIII (1882), Pt. I, 240–53.

[Michels, John?], "John William Draper, M.D., LL.D.," *Science*, III (1882), 82 (March 4), 27–28.

New York Lancet. 3 v. published, 1842–43.

Norwood, William Frederick, *Medical Education in the United States before the Civil War*. Philadelphia, 1944.

Obituary notices in the possession of Miss Antonia C. Maury.

Obituary notices in the possession of Mrs. Dorothy Draper Nye.

"President Draper," *American Journal of Photography and the Allied Arts & Sciences*, n.s., III (1860–61), 237–39.

[Proctor, Richard Anthony], "Dr. J. W. Draper," *Knowledge* [London], I (1881–82), 263–65.

"Professor Draper A St. Helens Man," *St. Helens Newspaper & Advertiser* (St. Helens, England), February 18, 1882.

Excerpts from "Report of the Photographic Section of the Amer. Institute," *Anthony's Photographic Bulletin*, XIII (1882), 86–88.

A portrait of JWD by Sarony faces p. 65.

S[illiman]., B[enjamin]., "John William Draper, M.D., LL.D.," *American Journal of Science*, 3d s., XXIII (1882), 163–66.

Stevenson, John J., "A Tribute to John W. Draper," NYU *Colonnade*, IV (1911), 7 (June), 3–5.

Inaccurate.

West, Geoffrey, *Charles Darwin*. New Haven, 1938.

A good account of the Oxford meeting of the BAAS.

C. *Book reviews* (arranged under titles of books, and excluding notices of *Scientific Memoirs*)

Combined and miscellaneous reviews

[Brownson, Orestes A.], "Professor Draper's Books," *Catholic World*, VII (1868), 155–74.

Freeland, Edward B., "Buckle, Draper, and the Law of Human Development," *Continental Monthly*, IV (1863), 529–45, 610–24; V (1864), 161–80; VI (1864), 55–65.

Nye clippings. Two envelopes of mixed clippings, largely unattributed; in the possession of Mrs. Dorothy Draper Nye.

"Positivism," *American Quarterly Church Review and Ecclesiastical Register*, XVI (1864), 35–56.

History of the Conflict between Religion and Science (anonymous notices without distinctive titles alphabetized by the *journal*)

The Athenaeum, 1875, #2462 (January 2), 21–22.

Atlantic Monthly, XXXV (1875), 501–2.

Bauzá, Francisco, "La Relijion y la Ciencia (Juicio crítico sobre el libro de Draper)," *Estudios literarios*, 113–87. Montevideo, 1885.

[Brownson, Orestes A.?], *Brownson's Quarterly Review*, last series, III (1875), 153–73.

Canadian Monthly and National Review, VII (1875), 99–102.

[Fiske, John], "Draper's Science and Religion," *The Nation*, XXI (1875), 343–45.

Hill, Thomas, "The Struggles of Science," *Unitarian Review and Religious Magazine*, III (1875), 339–56.

Methodist Quarterly Review, LVII (1875), 159–63.

[O'Leary, C. M.], "Draper's Conflict between Religion and Science," *Catholic World*, XXI (1875), 178–200.

Popular Science Monthly, VI (1875), 371–72.

Presbyterian Quarterly and Princeton Review, n.s., IV (1875), 158–65.

Quarterly Review of the Evangelical Lutheran Church, n.s., V (1875), 143–51.

Salmeron, Nicolas, "Prólogo," in Juan Guillermo Draper, *Historia de los Conflictos entre la Religion y la Ciencia*. Augusto T. Arcimis, trans. Madrid, 1876.

Scribner's Monthly, IX (1875), 635–37.

Southern Review, XVIII (1875), 122–53.

W[right]., G[eorge]. F., *Bibliotheca Sacra*, XXXIII (1876), 584–85.

[Youmans, E. L.], "The 'Conflict' and the 'Warfare,' " *Popular Science Monthly*, IX (1876), 757–58.

[———], "The Conflict of Ages," *Popular Science Monthly*, VIII (1875–76), 493–94.

[———], "The Conflict of Religion and Science," *Popular Science Monthly*, VI (1874–75), 361–64.

[———], "Draper and His Critics," *Popular Science Monthly*, VII (1875), 230–33.

A History of the Intellectual Development of Europe (anonymous notices without distinctive titles alphabetized by the *journal*)

Atlantic Monthly, XIII (1864), 642–47.

Boston Review, III (1863), 523–27.

"Draper's Intellectual Development of Europe," New York Daily *Tribune*, September 19, 1863.

"Draper's Philosophy of European History," *New York Times*, August 18, 1863.

Saturday Review, XVII (1864), 726–27.

"The Science of History," *Anthropological Review*, III (1865), 8 (February), 29–47.

The Spectator, 37 (1864), #1,882 (July 23), 856.

Westminster Review, LXXXIII (1865), 43–65.

Human Physiology

Bedford, Gunning S., "Draper's Physiology," *Methodist Quarterly Review*, XXXIX (1857), 419–28.

S., W., "Human Physiology," *Canadian Journal of Industry, Science, and Art*, n.s., III (1858), 247–54.

Thoughts on the Future Civil Policy of America (anonymous notices without distinctive titles alphabetized by the *journal*)

    Crescent Monthly, April 1866, 43–52. Cutting in the Boston Public Library.

    "The Difficulties in Our Way," New York *Evening Post*, August 21, 1865.

    Methodist Quarterly Review, XLVII (1865), 621–24.

    New York Times, September 5, 1865.

    [Norton, C. E.], "Draper's Civil Policy of America," *The Nation*, I (1865), 407–9.

    S[terne]., S., "Draper's Civil Policy of America," *Social Science Review*, I (1865), 371–87.

D. *Scientific estimates; literary and historical estimates other than book reviews*

American Academy of Arts and Sciences, *Proceedings*, n.s., III (1875–76), 324–29.

Bassett, John Spencer, "Later Historians," in W. P. Trent, John Erskine, S. P. Sherman, Carl Van Doren, eds., *The Cambridge History of American Literature*, III, 171–200. New York, 1921.

Beard, Charles A., and Mary R. Beard, *The American Spirit* (*The Rise of American Civilization*, IV). New York, 1942.

Cajori, Florian, *A History of Physics in Its Elementary Branches*. 2d ed. New York, 1929.

Clerke, Agnes M., *A Popular History of Astronomy*. Edinburgh, 1885.

Cohen, Morris R., "Later Philosophy," in *Cambridge History of American Literature*, III, 226–65.

Curti, Merle, *The Growth of American Thought*. New York, 1943.

"The Draper Camera Goes to Washington," Hampden-Sidney Alumni Association, *Record*, XV (1941), 5 (January), 10.

"Draper's Scientific Memoirs," *Nature*, XIX (1878–79), 27–28.

Eder, Josef Maria, *History of Photography*. Edward Epstean, trans. and ed. New York, 1945.

Eggleston, J. D., "Dr. Draper and His Camera," Hampden-Sidney Alumni Association, *Record*, IX (1934), 1 (October), 5–6.

Emerson, Donald E., "Hildreth, Draper, and 'Scientific History,' " in Eric F. Goldman, ed., *Historiography and Urbanization*, 139–70. Baltimore, 1941.

Findlay, Alexander, *A Hundred Years of Chemistry*. 2d ed. London, 1948.

Gardner, Daniel, "Dr. John William Draper and His Co-workers." Manuscript address in the New York University Library at University Heights.

    I owe the use of this manuscript to the courtesy of the author and of Dr. T. F. Jones, librarian of NYU.

Kayser, H., *Handbuch der Spectroscopie*. 6 v. Leipzig, 1900–12.

Larrabee, Harold A., "Naturalism in America," in Yervant H. Krikorian, ed., *Naturalism and the Human Spirit*, 319–53. New York, 1944.

Mees, C. E. K., "The Color Sensitivity of Photographic Materials," *Journal of the Franklin Institute,* CCI (1926), 525–51.

Melloni, M., "Researches on the Radiations of Incandescent Bodies, and on the Elementary Colors of the Solar Spectrum," *American Journal of Science,* 2d s., V (1848), 1–14.

Morse, Edward Lind, ed., *Samuel F. B. Morse, His Letters and Journals.* 2 v. Boston, 1914.

Norman, Daniel, "The Development of Astronomical Photography," *Osiris,* V (1938), 560–94.

———, "John William Draper's Contributions to Astronomy," *The Telescope,* V (1938), 1 (January–February), 11–16.

Persons, Stow, *Free Religion.* New Haven, 1947.

Robinson, James Harvey, *The New History.* New York, 1912.

Schneider, Herbert W., *A History of American Philosophy.* New York, 1946.

"Scientific Memoirs," *American Journal of Science,* 3d s., XVI (1878), 390–91.

Silliman, Benjamin, "American Contributions to Chemistry," *American Chemist,* V (1874), sketch of JWD's work, 97–98.

"Some Facts Connected with the Early History of Photography in America," *Photographic and Fine Art Journal* [Snelling's], n.s., VII (1854), 381–82.

Taft, Robert, *Photography and the American Scene, A Social History, 1839–1889.* New York, 1938.

Thomas, Franklin, *The Environmental Basis of Society.* New York, 1925.

Werge, John, *The Evolution of Photography.* London, 1890.

Youmans, Edward L., ed., *The Correlation and Conservation of Forces: A Series of Expositions.* New York, 1864.

A brief tribute to JWD is included.

E. *Background* (excluding titles listed under "D")

Browne, Charles A., *A Source Book of Agricultural Chemistry.* Waltham, Mass., 1944.

Cobban, Alfred, *National Self-Determination.* London, 1945.

Collingwood, R. G., *The Idea of History.* T. M. Knox, ed. Oxford, 1946.

Croce, Benedetto, *History as the Story of Liberty.* Sylvia Sprigge, trans. New York, 1941.

Curti, Merle, *The Roots of American Loyalty.* New York, 1946.

Dampier, Sir William Cecil, *A History of Science and Its Relations with Philosophy and Religion.* 3d ed. Cambridge, England, 1942.

Gide, Charles, and Charles Rist, *A History of Economic Doctrines.* R. Richards and Ernest F. Row, trans. 2d English ed. London, 1948.

Gooch, G. P., *History and Historians of the Nineteenth Century.* London, 1913.

Gottmann, Jean, "Doctrines Géographiques en Politique," in B. Mirkine-Guetzévitch, ed., *Les Doctrines Politiques Modernes.* New York, 1947.

Halévy, Elie, *The Growth of Philosophic Radicalism.* Mary Morris, trans. London, 1928.

————, *A History of the English People in 1815* (*A History of the English People*, I). E. I. Watkin and D. A. Barker, trans. London, 1926.
Hawkins, Richmond Laurin, *Auguste Comte and the United States 1816–1853.* Cambridge, Mass., 1936.
————, *Positivism in the United States (1853–1861).* Cambridge, Mass., 1938.
Hazard, Paul, *La Pensée Européenne au XVIIIème siècle.* 2 v. with 1 v. of notes. Paris, 1946.
Hofstadter, Richard, *Social Darwinism in American Thought, 1860–1915.* Philadelphia, 1944.
Kohn, Hans, *The Idea of Nationalism.* New York, 1944.
Krikorian, Yervant H., ed., *Naturalism and the Human Spirit.* New York, 1944.
Lévy-Bruhl, Lucien, *La Philosophie d'Auguste Comte.* 3d ed. Paris, 1913.
Mead, George H., *Movements of Thought in the Nineteenth Century.* Merritt H. Moore, ed. Chicago, 1936.
Merz, John Theodore, *A History of European Thought in the Nineteenth Century.* 4 v. Edinburgh, 1896–1914.
Nordenskiöld, Erik, *The History of Biology.* Leonard Bucknall Eyre, trans. New York, 1928.
Partington, J. R., *A Short History of Chemistry.* 2d ed. London, 1948.
Pledge, H. T., *Science since 1500.* London, 1939.
Rádl, Emanuel, *The History of Biological Theories.* E. J. Hatfield, trans. and ed. London, 1930.
Ritchie, A. D., *Civilization, Science and Religion.* Harmondsworth, England, 1945.
Sabine, George H., *A History of Political Theory.* New York, 1937.
Shryock, Richard H., *American Medical Research.* New York, 1947.
————, *The Development of Modern Medicine.* 2d ed. New York, 1947.
Singer, Charles, *A Short History of Science to the Nineteenth Century.* Oxford, 1941.
Thompson, James Westfall, "with the collaboration of" Bernard J. Holm, *A History of Historical Writing.* 2 v. New York, 1942.
Whitehead, Alfred North, *Science and the Modern World.* New York, 1925.

INDEX

199

New York University, JWD's appointment, 18f.; 23; support of JWD's research, 32f.; 52; professional schools,
56ff.; 75; effect of Civil War on, 96;
fire at Medical School, 113; 136f., 138,
154
Nichols, William H., 13ʳ
Niebuhr, Barthold Georg, 76
Niepce, Nicéphore, 16
Norris, George W., 135
North, distinguished from South before Civil War, 116ff.
North American Review, 90f.

Oriental immigrants, !71
Origin of Species, by Charles Darwin,
74, 86
Owen, Richard, 66
Owen, Robert, 99
Oxford meeting of the BAAS, 1860,
66ff.

Palmer, Courtlandt, 113
Paradise Lost, by John Milton, 80
Paris, University of, 29
Pattison, Granville S., 7, 28f.
Pedro I, of Brazil, 147
Pedro II, of Brazil, 174
Pennsylvania, University of, medical
school, 10f.
Ph.D., at NYU, 57
Philosophical Magazine, 34, 57f., 65
Photochemical induction, 37, 157
Photochemical law of equivalence, 37
Photochemistry, law of photochemical
absorption, 35ff.
Photography, origins, 16f.; importation
of methods to United States, 20f.; first
portrait, 21; JWD and Morse com-
peting to achieve portraits, 21f.;
JWD and Morse's portrait studio,
23ff.; necessity for non-achromatic
lenses disputed, 23ff.; JWD first to
mention enlarging, 23; JWD's desire
for portable camera, 23; JWD's developing process, 25; beginning of
astronomical photography, 26; grasp
of its potentialities by JWD, 35; first
photograph of diffraction spectrum,
38; of Fraunhofer lines in visible and
invisible regions, 38f.; significance of
"Herschel effect" for, 39
Photometry, 37
Photomicrographs, 41, 160

Photosynthesis, 15f.
Politics, science of, 104ff.
Popular Science Monthly, 134
Popularization of science, 139ff.
Portraiture, *see* Photography
Positivism, deductivism, 43, 160f.; and
vitalism, 44f.; influence on historiog-
raphy, 58f.; 69; law of three stages,
76f.; 77; subordination of Darwinism
to, 86f.; authoritarian tendencies,
108ff.; 141
Presbyterian Quarterly, 134
Principia, by Sir Isaac Newton, 80
Principles of Geology, by Sir Charles
Presbyterian Witness, 91
Lyell, 47
Prosch, G. W., 23
Protestantism, basis of freedom of
thought, 83f.; and hostility to sci-
ence, 128, 130

Quetelet, Lambert Adolphe Jacques,
50, 53, 161

Ratel, and Choiselat, 35
Ratzel, Friedrich, 87
"Recapitulation," in embryology, 50
Rees's Encyclopedia, 4f.
Reformation, 83, 130
Religion, and science in XVIIIth cent.,
3; deductivism, 42f.; and determin-
ism, 44ff.; major strand in *Intellec-
tual Development*, 78ff.; and science,
ch. XI, *passim*
Resonance theory of Fraunhofer lines,
36f.
Revere, John, 28
Rhodes, James Ford, 94
Ritchie, William, 41
Roman Catholicism, 30f., 76, 86; and ch.
VIII and ch. XI, *passim*
"Roman" tradition, 107f.
"Roric image," 35
Roscoe, Sir Henry, and Bunsen, 37
Royal Astronomical Society, of Lon-
don, 124
Royal Institution, 123
Royal Society, of London, 123
Ruffin, Edmund, 12, 99
Rumford medals, of American Acad-
emy of Arts and Sciences, 138, 174

St. Helens, Lancashire, 4
Saint-Simon, *see* Saint-Simonianism